PENGUIN BOOKS

STAYING ON TOP WHEN YOUR WORLD TURNS UPSIDE DOWN

Kathryn D. Cramer, Ph.D., has a corporate psychology practice. Before starting Health Psychology Consultants, she founded the Stress Center at St. Louis University in Missouri.

D0105997

STAYING ON TOP WHEN YOUR WORLD TURNS UPSIDE DOWN

▲

How to Triumph Over Trauma and Adversity

▲

Kathryn D. Cramer, Ph.D.

PENGUIN BOOKS

PENGUIN BOOKS
Published by the Penguin Group
Viking Penguin, a division of Penguin Books USA Inc.,
375 Hudson Street, New York, New York 10014, U.S.A.
Penguin Books Ltd, 27 Wrights Lane, London W8 5TZ, England
Penguin Books Australia Ltd, Ringwood, Victoria, Australia
Penguin Books Canada Ltd, 2801 John Street,
Markham, Ontario, Canada L3R 1B4
Penguin Books (N.Z.) Ltd, 182–190 Wairau Road,
Auckland 10, New Zealand

Penguin Books Ltd, Registered Offices:
Harmondsworth, Middlesex, England

First published in the United States of America by
Viking Penguin, a division of Penguin Books USA Inc., 1990
Published in Penguin Books 1991

1   3   5   7   9   10   8   6   4   2

Pages 333–334 constitute an extension of this copyright page.

LIBRARY OF CONGRESS CATALOGING IN PUBLICATION DATA
Cramer, Kathryn D.
Staying on top when your world turns upside down: how to triumph
over trauma and adversity/Kathryn D. Cramer.
p.   cm.
Includes bibliographical references.
ISBN 0 14 01.2772 0
1. Adjustment (Psychology)   2. Stress (Psychology)   3. Life change
events—Psychological aspects.   I. Title.
[BF335.C65   1991]
155.9—dc20   90–20658

Printed in the United States of America

▲

Author's Note

The case histories in *Staying on Top When Your World Turns Upside Down* are drawn from the actual experiences of people struggling to survive traumatic change. However, each story is a compilation of several cases and I have purposely changed the details to protect the privacy of the individuals involved.

K.D.C.

▲

This book is dedicated to my brother Jim, who still
makes me laugh, and cry, and grow.

Without you, Jim, this work would never have been possible.
Thank you for what you have taught me. I miss you.

▲

Acknowledgments

The writing of this book has been a long project, and I have many people to thank for their contributions.

In 1976 I met Hans Selye, the world-renowned father of stress research. Over the next several years I studied with Dr. Selye, sometimes at his International Institute of Stress in Montreal, and sometimes in the United States, when he came to our Stress Center at St. Louis University. Dr. Selye gave me access to his library and his wisdom. His encouragement has been a major catalyst for this book and a driving force in my career.

During the early stages of developing this book, my colleagues at St. Louis University offered valuable encouragement and discussion. My special thanks to David Munz, Richard Stensrud, and Father Frank Severin. The feedback I received from these people was most valuable in shaping the initial concepts of this book.

Acknowledgments

When the first draft of the manuscript was complete, Denise Marcil, my literary agent, readily agreed to join the efforts. She believed in me and my message, and through her wizardry found the best editor and publisher for this book. Denise has uncommon character and competence, and continues to steer me in the right direction. I am always uplifted by her energy and spirit.

During the final phase of drafting this book, Susan Moldow, my editor at Viking Penguin, has been able to see through my often burdensome style. She has demonstrated a remarkable capacity to recast my thoughts into simpler sentences to help me connect more personally with my readers. Susan carefully read and reread each chapter, giving unceasingly of her time, literary talent, and emotional support. I am lucky to have had Roberta Maltese as my copy editor. She is a magician in bringing a spark to otherwise lifeless prose. Dr. Stevan Hobfoll, stress scholar and director of the Applied Psychology Center at Kent State University, generously offered to review the final draft of this work on the shortest of notice. His suggestions were most valuable to the final editing, and his enthusiastic support helped me over the last writing hurdles.

I owe much to researchers John Chipnal and Jane Ferry, who tirelessly collected and analyzed data, and verified source material to ensure that the information and questionnaires contained in this work are accurate and reliable. I recognize Carol Shepley for her editorial suggestions, and I am greatly indebted to Bonnie Lauer, who typed and retyped the multiple revisions of the manuscript. She was ever willing to tackle the tedious demands of the word processor.

I extend my heartfelt thanks to Jane Seagraves, who managed the administrative details of producing this book, along with running my business. Jane has been my coach and my trusted confidante and has helped me survive the most challenging of moments. My appreciation goes also to Barbara Grogan, Nancy Hughs, Gail McMillin, and Jim Walsh for their longstanding friendships and enthusiasm for this effort.

The intellectual stimulation and emotional nourishment I

Acknowledgments

have received from my closest friends and colleagues, Julie Bertrand Eschbacher and Donna Spencer, have been incalculable throughout the good and bad times of this project. And there is no way that I can adequately acknowledge the influence of my first family on my career and my writing. I thank my mother for her abiding confidence in me and her quiet dignity and courage. I thank my father for his willingness to challenge my thinking with his sharp intellect and for his determination to excel. Both my parents taught me my most valuable lessons through their spirit of generosity and survival. I thank my brother Dan and his wife, Jan, for always being there when the chips were up and when they were down.

Last, and most specially, my love and gratitude go to Grady Jim Robinson. He has made an incredible combination of contributions to my life and my work. He has been the finest of editors, the best of friends, the most loyal of business partners, while all along being my loving husband. I thank him for his patience, his prodding, his astute advice, and his unfailing ability to make me laugh.

Kathryn D. Cramer
St. Louis, Missouri
December 1, 1989

▲

Contents

Contents

PART III

▲

How to Use
This Book

As you read this book you will come to understand trauma from the point of view of its stress impact, and you will learn a system for self-directed healing. I have written this book in three parts.

In *Part I* (Chapters One through Four) you will discover how and why your health is jeopardized by traumatic stress. Through scientific evidence and case histories you will see how it is possible to be either devastated or strengthened by trauma. You will find out what types of resources are vital for restoring yourself to health and happiness, and you will learn important skills that will prepare you for reinventing your life.

In *Part II* (Chapters Five through Twelve) you will learn a four-stage system for coping with trauma. Each stage is addressed in two chapters, one of which is primarily descriptive, and the other, prescriptive. In Part II you work through your own recovery program step by step. You learn how to keep a record of your thoughts, feelings, and dreams in a journal so that you can chart your progress.

In *Part III* (Chapters Thirteen and Fourteen) you will review what behavior and attitudes to avoid when you are faced with traumatic upheaval. And as a final part of your work you will find out how to set up a mental conditioning program to help deal more effectively with the stress of daily hassles and future traumas.

The fundamental message of this entire book is summed up by the phrase

Rough weather makes good timber.

This adage, popular among the mountain people in southern Appalachia, grew out of the observation that trees on the top of a mountain stand unprotected from the elements. Relentless storms, winds, and seasons pound those trees, and only the strongest survive. Those trees that do survive provide the finest quality timber and are used for the most durable and sturdy construction.

The lesson of the mountaintop timber is the lesson of this book. I wrote *Staying on Top When Your World Turns Upside Down* so that you could strengthen yourself to survive the force of traumatic adversity, like the trees at the top of the mountain. Many people live devastated, in quiet desperation, because they are unable to recover from something that happened to them. All of us, at one time or another, question whether we can stand up to life's harsh realities.

I have developed a system you can use to cope with any traumatic life event—divorce, death, financial setback, job loss, major illness—any catastrophe that brings you tough times. This coping process will help you to survive trauma by developing inner strength and resilience. It will help you to feel good about your life again.

You know that traumas in life are as inevitable as storms on a mountaintop. But you don't have to let them disfigure your life. In fact, you can actually use crisis and disappointment to bring fulfillment and greater joy to living.

To do that, however, you must resolve to complete this book's four-stage system for recovery and growth. If you learn and practice the skills that apply to each stage, you will be able to master your adversity. You will be able to

STAY ON TOP

WHEN YOUR WORLD

TURNS UPSIDE DOWN.

▲

Then shall the maidens rejoice in
the dance,
and the young men and the old
shall be merry.
I will turn their mourning into joy,
I will comfort them, and give
them gladness for sorrow

—JEREMIAH 31:13

PART

I

▲

1

▲

Life Can Break Your Heart

HOW I CAME TO WRITE THIS BOOK

If my brother Jim had not died when he was twenty-two of an easy-to-survive illness called mononucleosis, I am sure that I would not have written this book. I know that I would not have founded a Stress Center at St. Louis University in Missouri. I certainly would not have dedicated my career in psychology to teaching people how to use their stress to grow stronger and healthier and make their lives more meaningful.

If it had not been for Jim's death, my approach to life would be very different—far less alert, far less eager, far more ordinary. I have learned how to turn the profound hurt that still wells up in my heart from missing my brother into a tool to hone myself into the person I want to be. Any major change in life can be traumatic enough to inspire the kind of growth that I am talking about. Suffering brings wisdom.

Many of the insights you will find in these pages about how to use trauma as a tool for personal growth came directly out of my struggle following Jim's untimely death. That event forced me to discover for myself how to deal with a devastating personal crisis. In the beginning stages I found that even my training as a psychologist didn't enable me to stop my own spirit from dying. I was overwhelmed with despair and grief, shocked that anything like it was happening to me—to my family. My heart was broken.

The loss of someone you love is always traumatic. However, there are circumstances that lessen or increase the pain in each individual case. The death of a loving elderly grandmother who has lived out her life is sad but understood and accepted by those left behind. But when a death is unexpected, as when a healthy young person dies, the survivors suffer deeply.

MY STORY OF TRAUMA

As I recount my feelings, and thoughts and behaviors that were triggered by the trauma of my brother's death, see if you don't recognize much of what you are going through in the aftermath of your own stressful upheaval.

The year that Jim died he was a college senior. I was just finishing my doctorate in psychology. We were attending the same university and I used to scan the busy quadrangle for him. Jim was a strapping, corn-fed tennis jock—complete with sun-streaked blond hair and electrically charged blue eyes that lit up most often at the sight of co-eds, football play-offs, and ice-cold Budweisers. He was full of energy. I enjoyed bumping into him because we knew how to banter and tease each other into a better mood.

Jim was always in a hurry. Maybe he moved with more eagerness than grace from one plateau to the next because he

4

was the *baby* in our family—playing catch-up with his older brother and me. Or maybe he was born with lightning pace because of a competitive, achievement-driven, Type A personality. Or perhaps he somehow knew that his time on earth was to be short. Who knows? Whatever it was that fueled his high-performance engine, it kept my brother far ahead of his pack, and his accomplishments and dreams ahead of his years.

I remember, too, that Jim thrived on the fantastic. He developed his artistic talent early, by blending his ability to sketch with his love for fantasy. He invented and drew his very own brands of he-man heroes. These cartoons found their way onto every pad of paper in our house.

Jim created many fantastic visions of what he could become— a star athlete, a successful executive like his father, a captivating lady's man. These visions were real to him and he protected them carefully. But when Jim pursued his images of what was possible, his wishful thinking sometimes ran into the stone wall of reality.

About a month before Jim's bout with mononucleosis, he showed up in my university office during one of his troublesome pursuits. He was panic-stricken that a lovely, spirited woman, who, he envisioned, just might be the "love of his life," did not buy into the scenario he had invented for them. Her detachment made Jim afraid that his romantic hopes would be crushed.

His anxiety was contagious that day, and I found myself swept up in it. I tried every way I could imagine to slow him down, and to comfort him with some simple version of "Que Será Será," but he clung desperately to his passion and his hope that he could ignite hers.

I'll never forget how he stared at me that day and proceeded with one of his most persuasive pleas for help. With tears in his eyes, my brother swore to me that he could never be happy again without *this* romance. He was so convincing that I canceled my next appointment so we could start immediately to resolve his dilemma.

And so, as we had done with so many of his other dreams,

Jim and I brainstormed strategies. He would call her and suggest a tennis game, a picnic, a study session. No strings attached—no promises. Jim was sure that this more casual approach would work. He was filled with excitement and new hope for his love-come-true.

As soon as we were finished, he gave me a hug, let out a deep sigh, and yelled "Thank you" as he raced headlong down five flights of stairs to the street below. As I watched him run, I mentally cheered him on. He was charged up, ready, and clearly a man on a mission. He was off to win affection from the girl of his dreams. His chase actually exhilarated me, too. I loved being on his team. That night, Jim called me to say he thought his new approach was working.

That was the last brother-sister talk we had before he went to the hospital.

Five weeks later this energetic young man, primed with anticipation, was dead. My mother was the first to notice that Jim was getting sick. She insisted that he go to a doctor. The physician he saw initially misdiagnosed his illness and sent him home. By the time the correct diagnosis was made, Jim's system was so depleted that he was too weak to fight off the disease. Within days he could barely hold his head up at the dinner table. Next, he was admitted to one of those posh community hospitals with university medical school connections, to be treated for mononucleosis.

No one at the hospital really took his situation seriously. Here was a strapping twenty-two-year-old with mononucleosis on the fifth floor with the gallbladder removals and the kidney stones. The physicians and nurses were not attentive at first because they believed he would surely recover from such a routine illness of young men and women. But Jim seemed to know that he was getting sicker and sicker.

Everyone's confusion and concern mounted as his strength ebbed. Jim underwent transfusions and countless blood tests. The baffled doctors even sought advice from colleagues in Europe, but nothing seemed to make him better.

Early one morning, my father called me to say that Jim had been admitted to intensive care. Because I was familiar with hospital routines, when I arrived I wound my way through the back corridors to avoid the roadblocks that the staff always threw up to keep family from the area. I burst into Jim's room just as the doctors were placing tubes down his throat. At that moment, his eyes caught mine—he was terrified. I knew in that instant there was nothing I could do. My heart pounded in my ears as we hung on to each other with our eyes. It was as if I could see clear through him. I am sure that our connection somehow made all of the invasive medical heroics more tolerable for Jim.

With Jim in intensive care, my horror grew. On the fifth day, I was standing in the waiting room, staring out the window at the huge complex of buildings with its perfectly manicured lawns, thinking, "I don't believe this. I can't believe this. This kid is dying. This is a joke. It must be a joke. This can't happen today. He doesn't deserve this, I don't deserve this loss. Don't things always turn out for the best?"

I took a deep breath to calm my fears and stop my defeatist thoughts. That enabled me mentally to return to my steadfast determination that Jim would live. I swore off my fear and rejected the possibility that nothing could be done to save him. From then on, I constantly reviewed Jim's chart, trying to piece together all that was known about his illness. I evaluated the credentials of those who had been consulted and attempted to generate new questions that might lead to a solution. I clung to the hope that I could break through the agonizing confusion with some fragment of a clue to solve the tragic puzzle.

I was kneeling with my family in a cold, candlelit chapel, the mantle of pain so heavy our bodies were bent in submission, when the voice of a nurse roused us. "Hurry, come with me." I knew, yet I couldn't comprehend. At twenty-two, my brother Jim was dead. Just as suddenly as his life had stopped, mine would never be the same again.

It was as if I were living out a bad dream in which none of

the old rules held. I was a helpless stranger, hopelessly lost but trying to find my way home again. My faith in a benevolent universe was shaken.

In the weeks that followed Jim's funeral, I began to struggle through the aftermath of my loss. At first I tried to handle my pain by staying busy. I assumed my new job with a consulting firm; moved into a new home; and finished my doctoral dissertation within four months. Within eight weeks of Jim's death, I was beset by strange symptoms I didn't understand. My train of thought would be disrupted by repeated flashbacks to pleasant times of childhood, or to the traumatic, wrenching days around Jim's death. If I had to meet an obligation—teaching a class, meeting a colleague for lunch, even getting to work on time—my heart would start racing, and I would break out in a cold sweat. To control these mini–panic attacks, I developed a personal first-aid kit—a cup of water or a soft drink—which I carried with me everywhere.

In fact, in those first few months I would actually think I saw Jim; I would look up and could swear he was just across the quadrangle rushing to class. I'd stare into the university Commons, where he liked to play pool, and see him laughing at a shot. Those mirages were horrible. I didn't realize that the lifelike hallucinations were clear signals of my trauma, and that I was struggling with a death I had not fully admitted.

My anger spilled out in odd ways. I'd feel rage watching the evening news, watching shoppers at the drugstore, people going about their business with no thought of my pain. How dare they? My world had been turned upside down, and they didn't seem to notice or care. Standing in line at the checkout counter of my grocery store, I would swear that people were in a conspiracy to make me wait as long as possible.

I lost weight rapidly, but never felt hungry.

I had a peculiar drive to get as much work done as possible.

I had a wide picture window in my new living room. But I kept the drapes closed. I hadn't let the light in for weeks.

At times I felt betrayed and bewildered at why the best

medical solutions and practice hadn't kept my brother alive. I had many more questions than answers about my own existence and life in general. I fought to find some meaning, some value from the loss of my brother. Could any good come from such a catastrophe?

What meaning could I possibly take from this travesty of events? Was I so naive, or so flawed, or so dense that I couldn't fathom Jim's death? Was all my training in psychology useless in helping me to cope? What about my spiritual philosophies— why didn't they support and guide me? If a just God does exist, why was this senseless death allowed to happen?

At other times I felt an eerie closeness to people and events. Having lunch with my best friend from high school and college, or telephoning the person who had been my close confidant since kindergarten, took on new importance, more vibrancy. I realized how much being connected to those people meant to me.

Once a trauma is over we need people we can count on. People who will stay with us past the initial crisis and help us heal. Sometimes talking things out was the only way I could get enough relief from my tension to be able to sleep at night. The fabric of my family life also became much tighter. I found a wonderful anchor in the relationship with my brother Dan. I noticed that my parents touched each other more. They held hands, but their eyes had changed. I had seen that same look in the eyes of my clients without ever understanding so deeply what it meant. It is a wounded, vacant look, a look of wondering and searching, punctuated by blank dullness when the pain is too much to bear. I dared not increase my parents' burden by asking them to take care of me. I had nowhere to turn.

I was scared. I needed help. I went to three physicians, none of whom found any physical basis for my weight loss, indigestion, and panic attacks. Two of them prescribed sedatives and the third shrugged his shoulders and tried to assure me that the symptoms would pass. I turned to the church, but its only consolation was that if I had faith I would survive intact. I also sought out a clinical psychologist; that counseling yielded support but very little direction.

I found all this searching for assistance still left me unwell and with no program for action. As the weeks and months passed, I fell prey to many moments of pure resentment over having to walk this path at all. In fact, I put up strong resistance to doing so.

For some time I used a variety of avoidance maneuvers so I wouldn't have to face my apprehensions about going forward with a life that seemed so pointless. For instance, I threw myself into my professional work in an attempt to anesthetize myself and forget how depressed I felt. I overextended myself—accepting too many responsibilities or overscheduling my time. Then, when things began to overwhelm me, I would lose my temper and blame others. The blaming allowed me to discharge a smattering of my hidden, smoldering anger. I was unwilling to feel my pain and to grow from it.

I tried to protect my family in their moments of pain, as a diversion from tackling my own. Whenever I could help someone else through a period of depression or anxiety, the heat would be off me. Life for me during that time of resistance held very little promise. Even my everyday chores had become a burden. I was focusing on how to *survive* another day rather than how to *thrive* on one.

As I began to grope for ways to patch myself up, I was struck by the fact that I was not alone in my confusion. People with problems similar to mine seemed to appear everywhere. It was then that I encountered some faces and stories that are still branded permanently in my memory. I promised myself that if I ever could understand the value of suffering, if I ever uncovered the secrets of digging down deep inside myself and learning to grow through adversity, I would pass those discoveries along.

This book, then, recounts my discoveries about how people can move beyond being immobilized by tragedy and traumatic change, how people can use their traumas to enrich their lives.

The techniques I have developed to share with you are based on valid psychological principles, as well as on the experiences of individuals who have struggled successfully with crises.

As you read *Staying on Top When Your World Turns Upside Down,* you will be introduced to a step-by-step system for dealing with the stress of major traumas and changes in your life. If you learn this systematic process and use it as a blueprint for adjusting to life's ordeals, you will

1. grow mentally stronger and more physically capable of resisting the damage of stress;

2. increase your sense of self-control and confidence, even when dealing with events that you cannot control; and

3. discover the reservoirs deep within you that will ensure you stay on top, even when your world has turned upside down.

2

▲

When Coping Is Not Enough

Have you just lost your job? Gone through a divorce? Found out that someone you love has a drinking problem or a terminal illness? Are you faced with the pressures and demands of a financial setback? Perhaps you can't sleep at night or have no appetite worrying about that transfer that would mean relocating to a new city.

If anything like this is happening to you, one thing is for certain—your world is being turned upside down and you have a major adjustment challenge ahead of you.

LIFE-ALTERING STRESS

Dealing with life's day-to-day stressors, like traffic snarls and eleventh-hour deadlines, usually is much easier than coping with the stress traumatic change creates. By *traumatic change*, I mean any life trauma that robs you of the resources you need to stay healthy, be productive, and have rewarding relationships.

People who have unexpectedly lost lifelong jobs due to a corporate merger; who have suffered through a painful divorce, or the death of a husband or wife; who have discovered that they have AIDS, or cancer; or who are suddenly made aware that they are addicted to drugs or alcohol face life-altering stress.

These kinds of stress turn your world upside down, often leaving you overwhelmed, confused, and despairing. And major traumas can have a negative impact on your health. Such traumatic events as

the death of a loved one
divorce
marriage
being fired or laid off from work
retirement
major change in your financial situation
changes in business or line of work
major illness or injury

lead the list of stressful life events. They increase the probability that you will develop a health problem within two years of the onset of the event. Life traumas strain your capacity to cope and, if left unresolved, suppress your body's immune system. They leave you highly vulnerable to a wide variety of possible illnesses ranging from heart disease to cancer to skin problems.

If you don't deal effectively with major upheavals in your life, they can rob you of your motivation and enthusiasm, disrupt your family and work life, and trigger long-term depression. Each of us knows someone who has never quite recovered from the loss of a job or a loved one.

▲

CAN TRAUMA BE YOUR TOOL?

There is no doubt that the negative repercussions from traumatic life changes can be severe. And yet, stressful change is an inevitable part of all of our lives. Very few of us escape crisis. What then can we do to cope? Is there any chance of benefiting from traumatic stress? Can we make trauma our ally?

Just as we all know people whose lives have suffered from, or been ruined by, stressful change, we also know of people who have turned tragedy around and made it work for them. I have worked with countless people who have been able to grow from such traumas as lost love or career setbacks and have gone on to make their lives better than ever. The success of these people demonstrates that with the desire, the personal courage, and the right information, it is possible to avoid the stress damage associated with traumatic change. Even more importantly, it teaches us that trauma can be turned into a powerfully positive force in our lives. I believe that you, too, can benefit from upheaval.

What if you could take any of these circumstances or events just mentioned and deal with them so effectively that your life would be better than ever? Would you want to do that? Would you be willing to struggle—to spend time, energy, and effort—if you knew that you could turn chaos and upheaval to your advantage, to personal gain?

WHAT WOULD YOUR ANSWERS BE?

If your answers are *yes*, or if you are doubtful but willing, this book will be a valuable guide for you. It will support you and encourage you as you take on one of life's most difficult tasks: using the hurt, anger, disappointment, loss, and defeat of traumatic events as the sources for enriching your life.

MORE THAN A BAND-AID

All too often the only counsel and comfort we receive is from well-meaning people who offer us worn-out clichés like

"This may turn out to be the best thing that ever happened to you."

"You feel rotten now, but in a few months you will have forgotten all about this."

"Time is a great healer."

"Lightning never strikes twice in the same place."

"Every cloud has a silver lining."

"God only gives crosses to those who can bear them."

You know deep down inside that, at best, these affirmations are mere Band-Aids for gaping wounds. My system for growing healthier and happier through adversity offers you more than Band-Aids. It is a set of remedies that render emergency treatment in the initial stages of a traumatic event and then lead you confidently through the later stages of adjustment.

As a supplement to the case examples, I have studied the scientific literature for psychological insights that have helped people turn upside-down worlds right side up again. I have compiled my findings into a psychological coping system that is built upon two strategies fundamental to coping with adversity:

Strategy one

Learning how to evaluate the impact of your stressful life event on your health and happiness.

Strategy two

Learning how to reinvent your life by mastering the successive stages of adjusting to your traumatic change.

▲ MOST STRESSFUL LIFE EVENTS ▲

Several research teams have classified traumatic life events according to the degree of stress they trigger by gauging the extent of adaptation each requires of a person. There is broad general agreement among researchers as to the relative magnitude of stress associated with these events.

This list of the ten most stressful life events is scaled according to the magnitude of stress they generate. The research was done by Thomas Holmes and Richard Rahe of the University of Washington.

RATINGS OF STRESSFUL LIFE EVENTS

Rank	Life Event	Mean Value
1	Death of a spouse	100
2	Divorce	73
3	Marital status	65
4	Jail term	63
5	Death of close family member	63
6	Personal injury or illness	53
7	Marriage	50
8	Fired at work	47
9	Marital reconciliation	45
10	Retirement	45

SOURCE: Thomas Holmes and Richard Rahe, The Social Readjustment Rating Scale. *Journal of Psychosomatic Research* 11:213–218 (1967).

A BACKGROUND NOTE

When I first began to teach and consult about how to manage stress, I concentrated on showing people how to make the pressures of ordinary events in their lives work for them. In fact, most people have coping strategies for dealing with most minor stress. The stress of major life-altering events, however, is a completely different matter. Isn't that true for you, too? I am sure that for the most part you have learned how to cope

Each of these life events is traumatic and requires major adjustment because each causes us to lose something important: security, love, freedom, or self-esteem.

A research team headed by Barbara Snell Dohrenwend of the City University of New York similarly ranked traumatic life events. The high degree of correspondence between these two studies represents the research in the field; it reveals that certain life events are more stressful than others. Notice that most of the ten most stressful life events on this scale signify loss.

CLASSIFICATION AND RATING OF STRESSFUL LIFE EVENTS
Rank of Mean Scores

1. Child died
2. Spouse died
3. Physical illness
4. Went to jail
5. Divorce
6. Birth of a first child
7. Unable to get treatment for illness or injury
8. Convicted of a crime
9.5 Found out that cannot have children
9.5 Spouse relations changed for worse but no divorce or separation

SOURCE: Barbara Dohrenwend et al., PERI Life Events Scale. *Journal of Health & Social Behavior* 19:205–229 (1978).

with a traffic jam, a computer breakdown, job priorities that shift in midstream, broken appointments, flare-ups of temper, mass confusion. Almost anyone can adjust to those stressors by clarifying priorities, communicating in an assertive way, or stepping back and finding humor in the situation. You know how to think positively and relax under fire. Those stress-management techniques have served you well in controlling, eliminating, or relieving the immediate pressure of minor stressful situations.

But even when you know how to handle your reaction, you slip up occasionally and let minor stresses "get to you." Even though you know how to keep cool and stay in charge of your thoughts and feelings, you do sometimes feel your frustration rise and your temper heat up. Why? The reasons for your suffering at the hand of minor stressors can shed light on why you react as you do to traumatic stress.

INTERNAL VS. EXTERNAL CONTROL

We falter during stressful situations primarily because, for a moment, we let go of our focus on our inner power to control our behavior, mood, and thoughts. We focus instead on trying to change a situation that cannot be changed. If, for example, you view a traffic jam as responsible for your distress, it could become a circumstance you must eliminate or escape in order to feel better and reduce tension.

But strategies for *fighting or fleeing* a stressful circumstance aren't always appropriate. Most traffic jams are as immutable to your efforts to change them as acts of Congress and the weather. So, what can you do to ease your tension? Perhaps you breathe deeply, tune the radio to the news or to some soothing music, and plan your next step for when the jam clears. You are using your inner power to change your reaction to the stress. You are using the inconvenience as an opportunity to gain something. You hold yourself, not the circumstance, responsible for your stress reaction.

To deal successfully with traumatic change, you must go beyond these basic starting techniques of stress management and learn a more extensive process for managing your reaction to truly tough situations. Deep breathing may relieve frustration when you are caught in a traffic jam, but it cannot make one small dent in the despair and pain you feel upon the death of a loved one; nor could it ever soften the uncertainty of losing your job, or the horror of having a progressive illness.

For major stresses you require a process that will restore your focus on gaining internal rather than external control. You will benefit most by learning how to get out of a defensive and ultimately helpless posture into a position of inner power.

You can't change the traumas, crises, and upheavals; you can only change yourself.

YOUR GREATEST POWER IN THE FACE OF ADVERSITY IS YOUR POWER TO CHOOSE HOW YOU WILL REACT

When a major stress traumatizes your life, your only real choice is how you will react. You can treat it either as a *challenge* or a *threat*.

YOUR BEST CHOICE WON'T BE EASY

In the precivilized world, in the face of a life-threatening stressor, primitive humans survived by escaping or by over-powering a hostile force. Those instinctive reactions of *flight* and *fight* served our ancestors well. In a situation in which a tiger threatens our life or well-being, we must be able either to flee or to dominate the aggressor. But in our society we create problems for ourselves when we universally apply the primitive fight-or-flight reaction as a response to *all* stressful events. Most daily stresses in the twentieth century are not life-threatening. Even today's traumas that do pose a threat to our survival typically are not any we can flee from or dominate. Therefore, allowing ourselves to remain angry and afraid and, conse-quently, determined to fight or flee contemporary stresses is a big mistake.

For instance, when we become fixated on reacting only to the threat associated with losing a job or a loved one, our instincts are to *flee* or *attack*. Although those reactions are natural, they are not useful because we cannot carry them out. When we are unable to cope by physically escaping or conquering the threat, we may then try to do so psychologically. Psychological *flight* is an emotional denial of a trauma and its impact; psychological *fight* is vain retaliation against life for its injustice. When traumatic life events cannot be remedied by fighting or fleeing, an individual eventually harbors feelings of resentment and impotence. Such individuals arrest their own progress, lead disrupted lives, and become bitter and hopeless.

As I learned the hard way, it is impossible to avoid or to fend off the traumatic impact of stressful life events. We cannot cope with tragedy and change by mentally running away or aggressively trying to outsmart or beat them into submission. The great turmoils of life are cruel and immutable. You can actually make yourself physically ill, as well as rob yourself of enthusiasm and the motivation to live, by trying to fight or flee.

As I said before, to adopt the mental stance that trauma and crisis are threatening may be natural, but it certainly is *not helpful* in the long run. That is why it is so important to learn to adopt a perspective that will allow you to override anger and fear. You can accomplish this by developing the know-how for seeing life's most stressful events as challenges that can bring you self-enhancing results. In Chapter Six I will explain exactly how to do that. For now, promise yourself that you will not cling to your perception of threat, because from that perspective traumatic events have the power to spoil your life.

I have identified two major no-win styles of approaching stressful traumas that I want you to think about: the *victim* and the *aggressor*.

MORE ABOUT THOSE TWO NO-WIN STYLES OF COPING

If you adopt the style of the *victim*, you will cower and crumble under pressure. Because you are intimidated by the trauma, you will look to outside forces for a remedy. Then, because no one and nothing can rescue you, you will eventually become frustrated or perhaps depressed over the impotency of your approach.

If you adopt the style of an *aggressor,* you will feel like physically attacking or in some way annihilating the force responsible for your upheaval. You will take action, even decisively, but to no avail. Then you will become depressed over the impotency of that approach.

No matter whether your particular pattern of reacting to threat is that of a victim or an aggressor, eventually you will feel trapped by fate and doomed to suffer at the hand of the victorious trauma.

Anyone who fails to take responsibility for healing and growing in the face of major change, anyone who adopts the helpless course of either the victim or the aggressor, has chosen a path that leads first to worry, sleepless nights, confusion, frustration, and aches and pains, and eventually to major mental, physical, or emotional setbacks. Here are some examples.

THE VICTIM'S AGONY

Think of a victim as someone who spends a lifetime waiting for life to begin. The victim's dreams and hopes often remain dormant, with little chance to materialize because this style, in its extreme, encourages people to trust the power of outside forces more than their own. They doubt their capacity to make their life happen according to their own aspirations, so they wait to be rescued or blessed by good fortune. It is little wonder, then, that when trauma strikes, people who behave like victims under ordinary circumstances feel undermined and overwhelmed and become totally immobilized.

For now, review the following brief examples of how adopting a victim reaction to crisis and trauma leads to trouble. This review will give you additional insight into the plight of the victim.

▲

The Victim Stance in a Divorce

People who feel victimized by broken marriages believe that their spouse is the real cause of their pain and the dissolution of the marriage. They often see themselves as having done all that could be done to make the marriage work, and they see their partners as uncaring and unresponsive. It is not unusual for people like this to live on for years feeling that life has dealt them an unfair blow from which they can never recover, and that they have no chance of happiness.

The Victim Stance in a Job Loss

People who feel victimized by a setback in their career usually believe that they are the unlucky recipients of unjust treatment from a punitive system. They believe themselves to be cut off from financial security, achievement, and future career progress.

People who react like victims when they lose their jobs often rob themselves of the confidence they need to find other employment and advance their career goals. They continue to mistrust employers and life in general, and therefore take minimal risks. They frequently settle for a job with far less potential than they should be capable of pursuing.

VICTIM SUMMARY

If you usually feel on top of situations, a devastating loss or severe upheaval could be a such stark contrast for you that the experience will send you reeling into helplessness and retreat. Without realizing it, you could begin to behave and feel like a victim.

The tendency to feel victimized by life's turmoil is sometimes a natural first reaction, but you need to recognize that unchecked it can lead to long-term damage to your health and happiness. In Chapter Six, I will show you how you can let go of your fear and thereby your victim position when trauma strikes.

THE AGGRESSOR'S AGONY

Think of an aggressor as someone who lashes out at life in angry retaliation whenever turmoil or upheaval threatens. When the aggressor's vision of the way life should be is smashed by a tragedy or crisis, instead of reinventing a newer vision of what is possible, the aggressor will emerge from the trauma clinging to the life raft of outmoded goals that can never be realized.

Aggressors become angry and provoked at the outside forces that are to blame for ruining their accomplishments and chance at happiness. Aggressors do not retreat like victims. Instead, they retaliate against the perpetrators they see as responsible for their misery. In this way they, too, believe that external forces are more powerful than their own internal resources for ensuring self-fulfillment.

Review the following brief descriptions of how aggressors undermine their own health and happiness by focusing on what they have lost at the hand of trauma.

The Aggressor Stance in a Divorce

People who are threatened by a broken marriage and who react to that threat aggressively may believe just as most victims do that their spouse was primarily to blame for the demise of the relationship. Some aggressors are so intimidated by the failure aspect of the divorce that they strike out in an unconscious attempt to provoke their spouse into further misbehavior so there will be no doubt as to who is at fault. This enables aggressors to feel certain of their own virtue and of their partners' lack of any.

Other aggressors may bend over backward to try to fix a marriage to which they feel entitled. Such aggressors have difficulty taking *no* for an answer to any of their wishes. Over the long haul, however, if an aggressor remains threatened by a dissolved marriage, the anger triggered by the threat can easily turn into resentment and be generalized to all members of the opposite sex, to marriage as an institution, and to life as a whole.

The Aggressor Stance in a Job Loss

People who react with aggression to the very real threat to security that comes from losing a job pay an additional price for their trauma. Their continued anger at and blaming of the system can swell into a rage that cannot be vented or satisfied. Aggressors fail to realize that although their anger may be justified, it is not in their best interest to allow it to seethe for long. People who are unable to let go of their hostility and disdain after trauma are destined to suffer.

Some people feed their anger over a job loss to such an extent that they deplete themselves of the motivation needed to move on and learn from what happened. As a result, they turn into bitter, despairing people. In essence, they construct a win-lose scenario in which they are the big-time losers.

Perhaps you find it easier to see being a victim as a counterproductive coping style than to see the pitfalls of being an aggressor. Most of us believe that taking action against adversity is a sign of strength, but that is not always true.

SELF-ANALYSIS

As you can see, when trauma occurs, aggressors come out fighting. But because they choose the wrong battles, they end up losing face, health, and satisfaction.

How is it that you slip into the ineffective style of the aggressor? What do you do when you allow your threat to trigger anger for too long? Remember, aggressors often believe that they are pursuing a useful course of action by striking out instead of sulking, as the victim does. But the truth is the aggressor is equally ineffectual.

Now review the characteristics of a victim. Ask yourself how you may have exhibited the pattern of the victim in past circumstances that threatened you. What have you done to act like a victim when you have felt trapped, out of control, and disappointed by events?

SELF-EVALUATION

Which style predominates in your behavior? Do you know whether you lean toward being a victim or an aggressor when threatened by trauma? Answer the following questionnaire to find out.

VICTIM OR AGGRESSOR

Circle the numbers that indicate how well each statement describes you when you are *NOT COPING* effectively. The rating system is

(1) Rarely   (2) Sometimes   (3) Frequently   (4) Almost Always

When I am not coping well with stressful events and circumstances . . .	R	S	F	AA
1. I feel trapped.	1	2	3	4
2. I try to control things.	1	2	3	4
3. I find out who is to blame.	1	2	3	4
4. I won't rest until I fix it.	1	2	3	4
5. I feel like running away.	1	2	3	4
6. I act and think slowly.	1	2	3	4
7. I act and think quickly.	1	2	3	4
8. I feel like shouting.	1	2	3	4
9. I feel like crying.	1	2	3	4
10. I want to get revenge.	1	2	3	4

Ratings

Scoring to Determine Your Tendencies

Victim	Aggressor
Total your points for #1, 3, 5, 6, 9 _____	Total your points for #2, 4, 7, 8, 10 _____

Interpretation

If your scores on either dimension fall between
5–10, you are in the low range.
11–15, you are in the middle range.
16–20, you are in the high range.

Both victim and aggressor scores reflect your type and degree of emotional reaction, your tendency to think and act impulsively, and your propensity to take control. You may score somewhat similarly in both dimensions. This reflects your flexibility in response to threat. Sometimes you cower; other times you attack. Most people, however, have a tendency toward one extreme or the other.

▲

Now that you know more about how you react when traumatic change is getting the best of you, you can catch yourself in the act of making a self-defeating choice that leads to a position of helplessness. Let's take a look at how the divergent styles of victim and aggressor affect negative behavior when they converge in a marriage relationship.

WHEN VICTIMS AND AGGRESSORS COLLIDE

I was once asked by a married couple for some tips on how to improve their communication with one another. I needed only a few minutes of listening to them talk to understand that their problem was their opposing, but equally ineffective, responses to stress.

When Jack and Merideth were faced with family pressures,

▲ VULNERABILITY TO STRESS VARIES ▲

Recent research by Irwin G. Sarason of the University of Washington verifies that people's reactions to certain stressors differ in degree. For instance, job loss may produce a higher degree of threat in one person than in another.

Correspondingly, his studies show that people vary in degree of sensitivity to stressors. That is, an individual may be more threatened by a career setback than by a failed marriage, or vice versa.

It is important to realize that you are unique in your particular pattern of sensitivity to traumatic events. As you evaluate your tendency to be a "victim" or an "aggressor" when you feel threatened, remember that you may only exhibit these tendencies in circumstances in which you are particularly sensitive. It is instructive for you to reflect on which stressful circumstances are most threatening to you and lead to maladaptive responses.

Jack would try to *beat the problem into submission* and Merideth would *run for cover*. Their opposing reactions would then trigger anger in Jack and fear in Merideth. Those additional negative emotions exacerbated an already tough situation. It was only when a real crisis threatened that it became clear to them how counterproductively they functioned as a couple.

One day when Jack and Merideth came to see me they were both particularly upset. Jack's father had called from his Florida retirement home and intimated that he was contemplating suicide. Jack and Merideth tried to help, in their own way. But the eighty-one-year-old father remained despondent and the couple slipped deep into feelings of helplessness.

Jack approached the problem with harsh admonitions and a promise to be on the next plane to Tampa to *talk some sense* into his Dad if he didn't wake up on his own and see how foolish he was. Jack saw his father's depression as the *enemy*, and in typical *aggressor* style was trying to take charge, to dominate and prevail over the situation.

In contrast, Merideth cried and pleaded with her father-in-law to please not contemplate such a horrible act as suicide—it would ruin his entire family's life as surely as it would end his own. Merideth translated her concern into the common passive *victim* reaction.

There in my office, they were both very worried at the prospect of their father's death and were at a loss as to what to do to help him and themselves. We discussed how impotent they both felt and how little progress they had made in helping their father. Eventually both Jack and Merideth realized that they were allowing circumstances outside of themselves to control them. Had they confronted their circumstances as a *challenge* rather than a threat, they could have retained control and mitigated their helpless feelings. A challenge orientation to crisis leads to self-empowerment. They couldn't change their father, they could only change themselves. He alone could save himself. Ordering him to stop or whining about how he would ruin his life and theirs only aggravated the situation.

Once they saw their father's expressed wish to commit suicide as a challenge, Jack and Merideth were able to conclude that no matter what happened, they would live through it by finding some way to be strengthened—not beaten—by their father's decision.

A self-empowering attitude ensures that no matter what happens, you will put your life experience to good use. Oddly enough, it also makes you more effective in dealing with other people and events in the heat of the moment. Following our discussion, and my introducing the option of challenge rather than threat, Jack and Merideth called their father. In a carefully planned conversation, they told him how much they loved and cared for him, and how they hoped to have many more years with him. They expressed their concern for his depression and offered to help in any way they could. They began by calling his neighbors and fellow church members to ask them to visit and support him. Jack and Merideth took a trip to Tampa so they could encourage their father to live. Their approach actually calmed their father's agitation and helped him to believe that he had a reason to live—a decision directly influenced by Jack and Merideth's shift from *helplessness* to *empowerment*.

YOU HAVE ANOTHER CHOICE

You do not have to choose either of the two helpless positions in the face of traumatic change. That is, you don't have to be a victim or an aggressor. Instead, you can choose to view a trauma as a champion would. You can view your trauma as a *challenge* to be mastered, rather than as an *enemy* to be dominated or to be fled.

To make any of life's traumas work for you, it is fundamental for you to believe that any trauma can be a challenge. You must be willing to create a clear and specific vision of the benefits present in a stressful situation. You must make the trauma your partner and identify the personal rewards mastering it could bring you. Finally, you must plan and implement a strategy for earning those rewards.

A tall order? Yes!

A worthwhile one? Without a doubt!

The alternative choice, treating trauma as the enemy, is a course of self-destruction. Remember, in general, the greater the trauma, the greater the opportunity for you to gain or to be strained by the circumstances. So, for the sake of your health and happiness, choose to empower yourself.

A CASE IN POINT

Joan came to me for stress counseling because her nineteen-year-old daughter had been murdered while walking to her college dormitory. Finding someone to listen empathetically is a very difficult obstacle for an individual recovering from this type of tragedy. Because the survivor's suffering and loss are so horrifying, no one wants to hear about them. People need to pretend the event never took place. When Joan realized that, she made the appointment to see me. Joan needed an outlet, and a way to sort out her feelings. She knew how hard it was going to be to tell her story, to relive the horror out loud, in conversation, in order to grieve properly and avoid bouts of depression. But Joan wanted to process her trauma so she could resist the temptation to give up on life.

She began by describing the negative aftereffects she was experiencing. Joan reported that:

▲ She had a consistently short fuse at the office. She found herself snapping at the slightest provocations.
▲ She had no energy whatever and had to fight off sleepiness almost every hour of her day.
▲ She felt estranged from herself, and she lacked the motivation to do anything that was not absolutely necessary.
▲ She was shut down emotionally and wondered if she would ever feel alive again.

It wasn't until our third consulting session that Joan revealed to me that she was a recovering alcoholic. Naturally I was concerned that the murder of her daughter might trigger Joan's desire to drink again. When I asked her if she had been tempted to drink, she replied with an emphatic "No, I would never consider taking a drink, especially now, because my daughter was so very proud of my recovery. If I were to ever take another drink, it would be as if I had stabbed Deborah to death myself. It would be the ultimate act of disrespect. Deborah's memory helps me immeasurably to stay sober."

Joan was using the pain of her daughter's death as a positive force in her own life. The insight that her recovery demonstrated deep respect for her daughter's values brought some positive feeling back into Joan's life. She was allowing her child's opinion of her to be just as important after her death as it was during her life. And, when Joan realized what an accomplishment that was, she felt more in control and more hopeful about her capacity to adjust to her nightmare. Essentially she had created her first set of challenges in adjusting to her tragedy.

Gradually, Joan mastered the stages of self-empowerment. As she progressed, her symptoms began to disappear, and eventually she felt grounded and alive once again. Joan's pain over the violent loss of her daughter's life never disappeared. But Joan healed herself because she was willing to use the most terrible tragedy of her life to support herself, to learn from it, and to inspire herself to live more fully.

A WORD OF ENCOURAGEMENT

It is important that during the course of *your* adjustment process you remind yourself often that the road through trauma and crisis is risky and *never easy*. There will be setbacks and discouragement. Those who make strides during stressful times earn their rewards through guts and determination. To grow healthier and happier through trauma, you must be a true champion; you must be able to create a vision of what you need to restore your inner balance; *and* you must be willing to do whatever it takes to make that vision a reality.

Like Joan, each of us has the capacity to succeed against seemingly overwhelming odds. It is a matter of first believing that when your world turns upside down, it is an opportunity to achieve important gains in your life. Second, it is a matter of learning exactly what mental adjustment process will lead you past unavoidable suffering to personal fulfillment.

The process that I will outline at length for you in this book can be your major ally in dealing with life-altering change. It can be your key to dealing effectively with dramatic and traumatic change because I will show you exactly how to find and follow your own empowerment course.

▲

FOUR STAGES OF SELF-EMPOWERMENT

Stage I: Challenge
Stage II: Exploration
Stage III: Invention
Stage IV: Transformation

No matter what the traumatic event or circumstance, you must go through these four stages in order to earn the rewards of mastering your particular challenges. The four stages are actually your stepping-stones to success. For now, just read over the names of each stage, understanding that each holds the key for you to become a stronger, healthier person when your world turns upside down.

Choosing to be self-empowered says that *you are responsible for your own health and happiness no matter what happens to you.* Other people and institutions can support you in this effort, but you are the controlling factor. And that is what this book is all about.

I believe that just as you can *learn to be helpless*, you can now *learn to empower yourself.* So, if you would like to teach yourself how to thrive in spite of adversity; how to advance personally when setbacks occur; and how to benefit from the stress of changes that you do not welcome, get ready to read the chapters that follow. As you practice the exercises and adopt the attitudes outlined, your experiences will reward your efforts and you will discover for yourself

HOW TO

STAY ON TOP

WHEN YOUR WORLD

TURNS UPSIDE DOWN

3

▲

Your Balancing Act

THE PURSUIT OF HEALTH AND HAPPINESS

For years psychologists have been theorizing about what shapes our behavior, our ideas, our emotions. In 1900 Sigmund Freud published his classic text *The Interpretation of Dreams.* In it he set forth his revolutionary theories regarding the instincts that motivate human beings. Freud termed one of our most compelling instinctual drives the "pleasure principle." He stated that human beings instinctively seek to create a world for themselves that will provide them with pleasure and success.

Think about Freud's pleasure principle for a moment. Would you agree that you set out to provide yourself with a happy, rewarding life? Sometimes we feel it is a less-than-worthy goal to wish for and strive intensely toward. We have been taught to view self-sacrifice as more worthwhile than happiness. But this wish, this drive, this motivation on our part for satisfaction and happiness is a true sign of mental health. William James, another psychologist active at the turn of the century, believed happiness to be the secret motivating force that drives everyone.

Your drive to be a vital, healthy, happy, productive person is what will serve you best during the initial stages of adjusting to major upheaval. You will need to engage your traumatic circumstance to deal with your harsh new realities. It is that basic. Those people who have succeeded in benefiting from adversity and stress have developed and maintain internal resources that not only lead to health and happiness, but are critical for coping with crises and major change.

YOUR KEY INTERNAL RESOURCES

Everyone needs a wide array of resources from which to draw. Resources fall into three categories: Personal Resources, Productivity Resources, and Partnership Resources. All three are necessary to balance and maximize your well-being even when you are not under severe stress.

That is why I think of living life to its fullest as a *balancing act*. When your life is on an even keel and you are operating at your peak, you are, in effect, balancing the internal resources

---

▲ HEALTHY PLEASURE CENTERS IN THE BRAIN ▲

More than three decades ago, psychologist James Old discovered that laboratory animals would work to the point of exhaustion to have small amounts of electricity stimulate the pleasure-center areas of their brain. The animals gave up eating, drinking, and even sex to receive the pleasurable sensations that came from deep inside the brain's limbic system. Human beings have such pleasure centers, too; they not only provide us with intensely pleasing sensations, but contribute to health maintenance.

essential to your good health, optimum functioning, and fulfillment. Let's look at the elements in each of the three main resource areas:

Personal Resources

▲▲ Physical stamina, resistance to disease
▲▲ Mental clarity, flexibility, and creativity; self-confidence and optimism, sense of control, responsibility for self
▲▲ Emotional vitality, ease of expression, ability to feel love
▲▲ Spiritual groundedness, reflection; a sense of hope and fairness in life; strong commitment

Productivity Resources

▲▲ Worthwhile, purposeful vision
▲▲ Goal-oriented activity, challenge orientation
▲▲ Motivation for achievement, sense of mastery
▲▲ Sense of contribution, resourcefulness

Partnership Resources

▲▲ Supportive friendships, need for affection and love
▲▲ Intimate bonds, sense of autonomy
▲▲ Network affiliations
▲▲ Cultural identity, sense of coherence

This three-part categorization scheme for internal resources is supported by the landmark research of Suzanne Kobasa, who launched her career as a social psychologist at the University of Chicago. Kobasa and her colleagues investigated the elements that contributed to *hardiness* under stressful conditions. They studied middle- and upper-level executives at Illinois Bell Telephone Company, then a division of AT&T. Her research was conducted just before the divestiture of the operating companies of AT&T, which signaled one of the largest corporate reorganizations in the history of American industry. The preparation period of divestiture was a time of major change and upheaval.

While the operating companies prepared for divestiture, Kobasa surveyed nearly seven hundred Illinois Bell executives about the type and frequency of their stressful life changes and about the illness they had experienced in the three stressful years prior to the survey. She then examined a subsample of two hundred executives who reported high degrees of stress. Approximately half of those who were highly stressed also reported episodes of illness, while the other half of the sample remained healthy in the face of stress.

Why did some executives get sick and others stay healthy? That's what Suzanne Kobasa wondered and what her research was able to reveal.

One of the major characteristics that emerged to distinguish the healthy high-stress people from the sick high-stress people in Kobasa's study was *strong commitment to enriching oneself, one's work, and one's family—even under stressful circumstances.*

The executives who remained healthy were able to defuse their anxiety over job security by spending more time with their children; volunteering to head up fund-raising events for their favorite charities; and using their job uncertainty as a catalyst for searching out other career prospects.

▲ HARDINESS BUFFERS AGAINST STRESS DAMAGE ▲

If you have a sense of control over the course of events; if you have a commitment to meaningful goals; and if you see stressful change as a challenging part of life, you possess the three main ingredients of a hardy personality.

Suzanne Kobasa, now Associate Professor of Psychology at the City University of New York, has conducted extensive research verifying that people with hardy personalities cope better under pressure. Her research shows that hardiness is linked to psychological and physical health, and that hardiness can be learned. (See Chapter Four for detailed descriptions of the non-hardy and hardy personality.)

Although it isn't always easy, this balanced approach to dealing with adversity promotes satisfaction and rewards in multiple areas of one's life and leaves less time to dwell on the disconcerting pressure of the trauma.

Kobasa's findings substantiate my suggestion that by concentrating some of your coping energy on nurturing and replenishing your Personal, Productivity, and Partnership resources, you will increase your odds of mastering and gaining from stress-filled circumstances.

Another prominent stress researcher, Stevan Hobfoll of Kent State University, has developed a conceptual model to explain the phenomenon of stress. Hobfoll calls it the Conservation of Resource Model. He proposes that people feel stressed when there is a real or perceived threat to their internal resources, which are necessary for vital, balanced living. In other words, people's subjective experience of stress is directly related to the extent to which they feel that their current resources are being threatened or depleted.

My work supports Hobfoll's model. In fact, I believe that perceived threats to certain internal resources produce more intense stress than others when it comes to dealing with trauma. And, correspondingly, some internal resources are more basic to healthy normal functioning than others. The accompanying illustration represents the relationship among the various types of vital resources.

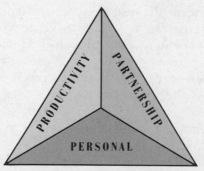

Your pyramid of resources

I have organized the three categories of internal resources into a pyramid shape to emphasize several points. First, as you can see, the category called Personal Resources is represented by the bottom triangle. I have made Personal Resources the *foundation* of the pyramid because I believe that our physical, mental, emotional, and spiritual resources, which are contained in this category, are *fundamental* to our well-being. Without Personal Resources, the other two categories are moot.

The research I have cited in this section and in sidebars throughout the book has begun to tell us which resources in this category are most important to stress resilience. The elements enumerated under Personal Resources have been shown to buffer the debilitating impact of stress (see page 35).

These Personal Resources are fundamental and support the other two categories of resources. For instance, Productivity Resources such as goal-oriented activity or achievement motivation depend on Personal Resources such as physical stamina and clear, flexible thinking. In the same vein, establishing Partnership Resources such as supportive friendships and strong family ties depends on your capacity to be in touch with your emotions and your ability to express your feelings, both of which are Personal Resources.

Countless people who are struck a stressful blow fail to realize that they need to give their first priority to restoring their Personal Resources in order to make headway on the other two important fronts of Productivity and Partnership. They relegate their personal needs for rest, exercise, emotional release, self-confidence, and the like to dead last on their list of priorities.

Take a few moments now to review the Personal, Productivity, and Partnership resources on page 35 that are key to your health, happiness, and ability to resist stress.

Each of the vital resources in the three categories has both instrumental and symbolic value. In other words, these resources help you to get what you want and need and contribute to your self-definition. For example, the resource of motivation for achievement of your goals also contributes to how you see yourself. If your achievement drive is high, you define yourself to be a high achiever. In this way these resources function as a powerful reinforcement. We need them in great supply to live well and to feel good about ourselves.

Everyone needs to focus on all three areas, but each of us has different degrees of need for Personal, Productivity, and Partnership resources at different times and under specific circumstances. For example, certain career-related traumas may rob you of vital Productivity resources, and a divorce may exact its heaviest toll in Partnership resources.

The role of this model in managing traumatic stress is more fully explored in Chapter Eight. For now, let's look at a prime example of how these three interlocking sets of resources work to keep a person healthy and effective under one set of especially adverse conditions.

THE GREAT ESCAPE

When I was a teenager, my father took me to a movie that showed how he had lived for eighteen months as a prisoner of the Germans during World War II. The movie was *The Great*

▲ HOPE, TRUST, AND LOVE: ▲
INGREDIENTS FOR GOOD COPING

In recent years stress researcher Richard Lazarus and his colleagues at the University of California at Berkeley have consistently found that positive emotions such as hope, trust, and love have a positive effect on coping with stress.

First, they act as time-out periods in which people take a break from the demands of coping. Second, positive emotions like hope and trust can help people sustain and persist in coping efforts. And, finally, Lazarus and his research team suggest that positive emotions can help people restore their depleted resource pool. (Citations for these studies appear in the Bibliography.)

Escape. I didn't realize then the significance of what was unfolding on the screen, but later I understood that the story revealed a brilliant formula for how to survive—even thrive—in any dire circumstances. In the movie the Allied prisoners developed a variety of activities that bolstered their Personal, Productivity, and Partnership resources. Officers with advanced educational degrees taught courses to the men to keep their intellectual curiosity alive and their goals before them. The men competed in bridge and chess tournaments, and those contests were as stimulating to them as any tournament involving grand masters. They participated in athletic events to keep themselves physically fit and their competitive spirits high. They held religious ceremonies, which bolstered their emotional and spiritual well-being by stimulating their faith and hope and reconnecting them to the mysteries of life. A talented group of writers, directors, and actors put together original stage performances, which provided tremendous comic relief from the anxieties of the moment.

To stay productive, the men reassembled an odd collection of mechanical parts and built radios. They used the radios to gain information from the outside world, which kept their motivation to escape high. They established an in-camp news service to communicate Allied strategy, and they never stopped believing that the day of victory and their release would come.

In the midst of all this, the prisoners were engaged in digging

---

▲ FAMILIES ARE STRESS RESOURCES ▲

At Johns Hopkins University, Caroline Bedell Thomas investigated how psychological factors contribute to long-term health by studying 1,337 medical students who graduated between 1948 and 1964. Her research showed that the best predictors of cancer, mental illness, and suicide were a lack of closeness to one's parents and a negative attitude toward one's family.

escape tunnels. They improvised tools and used slats from their bunks for supports and beams in the tunnels. My father's barracks competed with others to reach freedom, and in order to throw the guards off the course, each barracks team would dig diversionary tunnels that led nowhere.

They were playing a very dangerous cat-and-mouse game, because the prison guards were aware of the tunnels. Every time the prisoners tunneled under the walls—to what they thought was freedom—the Germans were waiting for them. Despite being unable to escape, the prisoners found that digging the tunnels provided a dimension of self-worth and bonding that was critical if they were to survive their captivity. They strengthened their Productivity and Partnership resources.

My father, who is six feet tall, weighed just 120 pounds at the end of his captivity, but was otherwise in great spirits and sound health. The scars of captivity have healed, and he now speaks of the prison camp as having had a major positive impact in his life. He used the period to solidify his values and to strengthen his character.

What is the lesson here? It is that my father and the other men stayed as healthy as they did in captivity because all of them concentrated on building their resources as a *person,* a *producer,* and a *partner.* They invented ways to stay in balance under tremendous and unusual stress. Their ability to restore their resources and to achieve inner balance was the key to their successful survival.

WHEN YOU LOSE INNER BALANCE

In Chapter Eight I will show you how to estimate the negative impact of your own trauma on each of the three categories of resources. But for now let's take a broad perspective on the damage produced by major life change.

When you go through a major change, trauma, or crisis, you can be certain that you will lose some of your internal resources. By this I mean that trauma can rob you of energy and enthusiasm, a sense of accomplishment, companionship, and an emotional support system. The sudden loss of these will throw you off balance.

When you evaluate the impact that comes from minor daily stressors such as arguments, missed deadlines, traffic jams, spilled coffee, or whatever, you notice that while they can cause temporary disorientation and strain your resources, they do not usually deplete them. However, when you encounter the stress of significant adversity or loss, for a time your life will be full of upheaval and you'll believe your world will never again be the same.

Robert Frost paints a vivid image of what a major state of imbalance feels like in his poem "The Armful":

> For every parcel I stoop down to seize,
> I lose some other off my arms and knees,
> And the whole pile is slipping, bottles, buns,
> Extremes too hard to comprehend at once,
> Yet nothing I should care to leave behind.
> With all I have to hold with, hand and mind
> And heart, if need be, I will do my best
> To keep their building balance at my breast.
> I crouch down to prevent them as they fall;
> Then sit down in the middle of them all.
> I had to drop the armful in the road
> And try to stack them in a better load.

Restoring your resources, and thus your balance, must be your primary goal in recovering from any trauma. To be healthy and happy again, you must recover the resources you have lost, and as Robert Frost says, "try to stack them in a better load."

INNER BALANCE COMES FIRST

A man we will call Bill, who was suffering through a major setback in his business, came to me for stress-management training. At our first meeting Bill was agitated and visibly distraught. His face was deeply lined, and he had dark circles under his eyes from lack of sleep. He paced back and forth as he described his situation. He'd had an appliance dealership for thirty years that had been very successful, but due to economic conditions sales had begun to lag. Bill said he could handle normal ups and downs well enough, but a new regional manager was dissatisfied with his work and had conceived a plot to replace Bill with one of his friends. Bill found it impossible to cope with that kind of stress.

At our first meeting, I zeroed in on improving Bill's physical and mental well-being before we tackled his employment problems. The upheaval in his life was causing him to lose his self-confidence and was robbing him of sleep and enthusiasm. Bill's crisis-triggered threat was creating an imbalance for him. The first priority for Bill, and for anyone who is faced with a change of major proportions, was to determine what he needed to restore inner balance.

Once Bill realized that he could not effectively solve his business problem until he took care of himself, he started to make some progress. The first positive change Bill made to restore his depleted energy and self-confidence was to give himself a break from the routine by taking a well-earned vacation. He hadn't taken time off in five years. When he returned from his white-water rafting excursion in Colorado, he was mentally alert and physically robust. While he was away, he had decided that he was ready to sell his dealership and move on to a new business venture that promised less conflict and more reward.

What Bill's story emphasizes is that *your first priority is to commit yourself to restoring and maintaining the resources you need so you can be healthy and fully functioning again, given your world as it is at the moment*. Then, and only then, will you be able to proceed with empowering yourself to meet your needs and to master the challenges of your situation.

THE IMPORTANCE OF "SELF-CENTERING"

Anyone who successfully restores him- or herself in all three resource categories—Personal, Productivity, and Partnership—has achieved a state of inner balance that yields optimum health and functioning. Think of pursuing an inner state of balance as a process of *centering* yourself. The late mythology-scholar Joseph Campbell retells a captivating Japanese folktale that makes this point. It is a tale about the value of being in a self-centered state, especially when adversity strikes.

In the old days a young person desiring to learn swordsmanship in Japan would be left by the master largely unattended for a time, doing chores about the school, washing dishes, and so on; and every now and again the master himself would come popping out from somewhere and give him a smack with a stick. After a season of that sort of thing, the victim will have begun to be prepared. But that will be of no use to him either; for when ready for the blow to come at him, say, from over there, he will get it from back here; and next, from nowhere at all. At last the baffled youth will arrive at the realization that he will do best not to ready himself in any specific direction, because if one has a notion of where the danger may be lurking, he will be attentive in the wrong direction. *The only protection, then, is to be in a perpetual state of centeredness in undirected alertness, ever ready for sudden attack and immediate response.* [Emphasis added.]

Campbell recounts an amusing anecdote that is kindred to the first.

A certain master told the young men of *his* school that he would, himself, bow before anyone who, in any way whatsoever, could catch him by surprise. Days passed, and the master was never caught. He was never off-guard. But then, one day when he had returned from an afternoon in the garden, he asked for some water with which to bathe his feet, and it was brought to him by a ten-year-old. The water was a bit cold. He asked the youngster to warm it. The little fellow returned with it hot, and the master, without thinking, put his feet in, quickly pulled them out, and went down on his knees in a very deep bow before the smallest boy in his school.

One of the secrets to thriving in adversity or crisis lies in the drama of these Japanese stories. The stories instruct us to be perpetually in a state of inner balance so that stressful change will be unable to knock us too far off course. That's what self-centering is all about.

The concept of *self-centering* is the guiding principle in personal growth during trauma. Working toward centering yourself gives focus and direction to your Empowerment process as you adjust to the demands of stressful change. In the system of adjustment to trauma that I teach:

SELF-CENTERING MEANS

To pinpoint and restore
the resources you need for
health and happiness.

The term *self-centering* may leave you feeling a bit uncomfortable because most of us were taught that being self-centered is selfish, that we should instead reach out and give to others. Generosity is a socially important value, of course. What I mean by the term *self-centering* is highly compatible with a generous spirit. In my system self-centering refers to the net result of restoring all of the resources you need to be healthy and happy. When your resources are fully restored, you are living out of your center, out of the core that is you, which makes your life worthwhile. Self-centering supports generosity because, unless you have a strong sense of inner balance, there is not much of you available to give away.

▲

YOUR INTERNAL AUTHORITY

My definition of self-centering implies that the responsibility for determining what constitutes health and fulfillment rests ultimately with you. Although others can advise, inform, and support you in your quest for health and fulfillment, your internal authority in these matters is the last word. No one, not the greatest expert or the closest loved one, is capable of knowing better than you exactly what can enhance or satisfy you.

In order to be responsible for what will lead you to health and fulfillment, you must turn inward and examine yourself very closely. You must thoroughly know your abilities, interests, needs, and desires in order to set goals for the Empowerment process. This *internal focus* is essential and often difficult to achieve.

I have found that people who grow stronger and balance themselves during times of significant transition or crisis are strongly focused on their private experience. They are modern-day pioneers who realize that their foremost priority for dealing with upheaval is to know themselves. Once they have accomplished that, they use their knowledge to formulate objectives that, in turn, make change a catalyst for personal advancement.

Some people have profound insight into themselves, but I have found that most of us are tragically limited in this area. As a rule we are completely unaware of our actual feelings and the extent of our needs—and especially so when we are under stress. To compensate, we search anxiously for external rules and regulations to guide us. The popularity of call-in radio talk shows with "expert" guests may help prove the point. Many people who listen to and call in to those shows rely more on the advice of the guest psychologist than on their own opinions. If you listen closely, you will hear how anguished and perplexed the callers' voices often sound. The callers are disconnected from their innermost feelings and are therefore at a loss about how to reduce their stress. They trust *outside* authorities more than they trust their own *inside* experience.

A PROBLEM COMPOUNDED

This problematic preoccupation with searching for external authorities is compounded by our culturally sanctioned longing for instantaneous solutions and for masking our internal turmoil from public view. Although our institutions and traditions teach the value of finding solutions through experience, these lessons are often lost in practice. Rules and rituals become divorced from their original intent, taking on magical qualities that do not help us tap into what we really think and feel. Many people follow ritual mindlessly or dismiss it without giving it a chance to relieve their pressure or help them find solutions. As a result, our culture is full of people who are so alienated they will try almost anything that promises to calm their frightened, tumultuous inner experience during trouble and upheaval.

The use of drugs and alcohol in our society to relieve tension is an obvious sign of this incessant drive to find some sort of peace. The *Pharmacy Times* has ranked the prescription tranquilizer Valium among the top fifty drugs prescribed in the United States for the last twenty-five years. Only four other drugs of the two hundred rated hold that distinction. Despite the recent evidence for Valium's negative side effects, it has, in the last decade, continued to be among the ten most frequently prescribed medications.

The Valium prescription rate is not the only evidence of our desire to medicate away our stress-related ailments. The *Pharmacy Times* also reports that from 1979 to 1989 Inderol, used to treat high blood pressure; Tagamet, for stomach and digestive disorders; and Valium consistently accounted for approximately forty percent of all new and refill prescriptions.

These statistics on the high rate of prescription of medicines for stress-related problems confirm both that stress is taking its toll on us and that our culture promotes drugs as a primary cure. Is it any wonder that so many people self-medicate to ease their stress-related pain—insomnia, anxiety, and depression—with over-the-counter drugs, alcohol, caffeine, and the so-called recreational drugs?

Despite this cultural push for quick external cures, current attempts to medicate away stress damage cannot work. However, there are alternative solutions that do. Learning how to empower yourself to gain from adversity is one such solution. Once you have mastered the skills, you will be able to swim against the cultural current.

YOUR COMMITMENT TO KNOWING YOURSELF

A willingness to know yourself may turn out to be one of your greatest assets in coping with trauma. The commitment must extend beyond discovering your strengths and personal assets to uncovering the shortcomings and weakness of your dark side.

The quest for deeply honest self-knowledge will make it easier for you to master the goals at each stage of your adjustment. I recommend that you record your insights about yourself in a private journal and that you use it to complete the assignments and exercises I will suggest in Part II of this book (Chapters Five through Twelve).

Many of my students call this notebook their *Empowerment Journal* because it has value as a record when they are mapping out their sometimes complicated path to self-fulfillment. By keeping a record of the spontaneous thoughts, feelings, and images that occur to you either during the day or at night, you tap into a rich reservoir of self-help.

Your thoughts and emotions are housed in multiple levels of the mind, some more conscious than others. Most people learn more about their innermost desires and feelings by reading their journal notes on their dreams and other mental activity than they can learn by trying to figure things out analytically.

The practical evidence for the value of your day- and nighttime imagination in helping you to adjust and grow is borne out by major psychological theories and research. Sigmund Freud and Carl Jung believed that insights from one's

---

▲ DREAMS ▲

People dream every night, whether they remember their dreams or not. About ninety minutes after we fall asleep we begin our first dream sequence. Electrical signals from the brain stem trigger the release of chemicals into the upper front portion of the brain. There, a flood of images and thoughts produces rapid eye movements (REM). Scientists have verified that REM periods of sleep produce not only darting eye movements, but also muscle paralysis and irregularity of breathing and heart rate. There is no question that dreaming is a significant physiological event.

---

dream life and having an active imagination (visualizing or daydreaming about something while in trancelike, wakeful state) are essential to everyone's healthy psychological development.

Current scientific evidence gathered by such notable researchers as Robert Ornstein, president of the Institute of Human Knowledge in California, substantiates that we are bombarded daily by a veritable sea of suggestions and symbolic messages from our dreams and trances. If we pay attention to them, we can shape our thoughts and behaviors and promote our well-being.

Your Empowerment Journal will help you put both your symbolic messages and your logical thought to good use. As you learn the system for recovery and as you plan how you can benefit from your trauma, I will suggest types of experiences you may want to record in your journal. The journal itself should be a convenient size so you can carry it in your pocket or purse and keep it at your bedside. Many people fill multiple journals in the course of their work.

This is the time for you to select a journal that is right for you and to begin recording your thoughts, feelings, and dreams. Save your entries for later analysis.

▲ REMEMBERING YOUR DREAMS ▲

Often the toughest part of learning from your dreams is remembering them. Here are a few tips that will aid your memory of your dreams:

1. When you wake up in the morning or in the middle of the night, write down *any* detail from your dream(s) you can remember. Do not eliminate anything. All the details are relevant.

2. If you don't remember the details of a dream, write down whatever is on your mind when you awaken. Those thoughts may be related to a dream sequence and may be helpful in retrieving it later.

Note: Some people prefer using a cassette tape recorder for documenting their dream notes.

As further preparation, let's look at how the value of inner balance helped some of my clients prevail over adversity by first restoring their Personal, Productivity, and Partnership resources.

A TEAM BALANCING ACT

I was invited to consult with the president and executive team of a major corporation that was in deep trouble. Because of a series of market shifts, all but one of their product lines had been rendered obsolete. Furthermore, the viability of the last product line was in jeopardy because of an investigation by a U.S. regulatory agency. However, the company's president refused to cave in to adversity and instead went on the offensive. He regarded the atmosphere of intense, continuous pressure as an opportunity for him and his management team to learn how to produce under fire. The president and the ten executives who reported to him came to me for personal training in how to master their severe upheaval.

For fourteen months I had their lives under a microscope. My initial findings showed that historically the executive team had existed as a team in little more than name. Each executive had pursued his own projects, acting out a businessman's fantasy of the macho Marlboro Man.

I suggested that they adopt a different way of doing things. I organized the executives into a mini–think tank that met weekly to share responsibility for handling such thorny problems as how to counter the unfavorable publicity they were receiving—publicity that might make customers reluctant to purchase their remaining product. Then I instituted a rugged organized schedule of exercise for each executive, designed to build physical stamina and promote mental sharpness.

Before the executives began exercising and sharing the responsibility for decision making, their physical health had been poor. Take, for example, John, one of the most senior people on the team. John had had several severe attacks of hyperventilation during late-afternoon planning sessions. His symptoms were diagnosed by the corporate physician as a direct result of unresolved tension. When those bouts of anxiety struck, they frightened the entire group. To make matters worse, no sooner had John's symptoms appeared than two other executives experienced severe stress-related symptoms. One developed a bleeding ulcer, the other had a mild heart attack.

The executives' spouses, who are too often forgotten as a prime ingredient in their partners' success, were assembled in a support group to hear and exchange news, information, and opinions. Their first meeting took place in my conference room. The chairs were arranged in a semicircle. We shared afternoon refreshments as the president explained, frankly, the breadth and depth of the company's problems. As the spouses listened and discussed the business pressures, I helped them to draw conclusions about how those pressures would affect the home front. I told them, "Lower your expectations of spontaneous, friendly conversation and casual, playful interactions." They unanimously agreed that the business tasks that lay ahead would detract from the amount of attention they could expect from their partners, who would not be too easy to live with.

Although the spouses had little previous contact with each other, several of the women quickly formed informal alliances to help themselves survive. In fact, it was John's wife who invited the first small group to her home for a brainstorming and support session. She had been particularly worried about her husband's hyperventilation attacks. Her stress led her to seek support from her peers as a coping strategy.

I attended these informal group sessions and taught the spouses how to use the concept of balance in planning their adjustment strategies. I reminded those present that their families were a rich source of support and a good release valve for pent-up business pressures. I advised them to take simple but crucial steps, like preplanning periods of family recreation in which everyone could and would participate.

The women were most creative in their inventions for family outings. Each household had different interests, but ideas flowed freely and stimulated unusual solutions: roller-skating, cooking sessions, and outdoor adventure courses are just a few examples. The children were included, too. The women notified schools, teachers, and other agencies, such as day-care facilities, about the potential strain on their family, asking the professionals involved to report any early warning signs of behavior problems. Finally, because stress exacerbates existing difficulties, any family that was already suffering from marital strain, adolescent adjustment problems, and the like took advantage of intense counseling.

Throughout the fourteen months, winning the regulatory issue and responding to market demands remained extremely important to the executives. However, those goals were secondary to the goal of empowering themselves to withstand pressure by achieving a *balanced* lifestyle. Their relationships at home and on the job were key sources of support that had been underrated. Rest, relaxation, and conditioning were essential

---

▲ TIES THAT BIND ▲

Feeling loved intimately and having a trusted confidant contribute to our self-esteem and our sense of mastery—even during high-stress situations. Studies by Irwin Sarason and his colleagues at the University of Washington also reveal that intimate ties with one's spouse make a special contribution to stress resistance. Sarason's work is cited in detail in the Bibliography.

---

to prolonged effectiveness. Morale remained high throughout the period of chaos and uncertainty because the primary objective was to excel personally—even when the company's future was in question. The men took charge of the only variable they could expect to control: themselves. Their priority was to maintain balance.

The regulatory battle is still going on. However, the executives have learned their lessons well and have created several new product lines and diversified the company's financial base. Most important, several of the executives have reported improved marital and family relationships. The individuals involved converted a negative situation into a positive one.

Now that you are aware of the importance of knowing *what* you need to do to restore your *inner balance*, it is time to move on to the steps to take toward your own successful Empowerment.

4

▲

Preparing Yourself
for Progress

By now you see how important it is to have the right mental attitude in order to make adversity work for you. To prepare yourself mentally to meet the demands of your stressful circumstance, you need

1. *to accept* that your world has, indeed, been turned upside down by whatever traumatic event may have occurred; and

2. *to believe* that opportunities for your growth do exist within your new circumstances; and

3. *to have confidence* that you will be able to take advantage of those opportunities and become healthier and happier as a result.

In this chapter I will show you mental exercises that will encourage you to adopt these outlooks that are so crucial to your actual recovery program.

ARE YOU MENTALLY PREPARED?

Recent research not only supports my suggestions about the best mental attitudes for fostering your growth, it defines the *payoff* that occurs once you adopt those productive frames of reference. For instance, researchers Michael Scheier of Carnegie-Mellon University and Charles Carver of the University of Miami have found that people who are optimistic about how stressful life events will turn out have fewer physical symptoms. Also, people who score high as optimists on the Life Orientation Test* show better recovery from such major surgery as a coronary bypass.

Once again, the extensive research of Susanne Kobasa and her colleagues sheds light on what makes people *hardy* when they are assailed by life stress. Dr. Kobasa has determined that people who feel in control of themselves and their reactions to events are the most resilient under pressure.

Other studies show that poor physical and mental health are associated with the attitude of the victim and the aggressor discussed in Chapter Two. People who believe that life's ups and downs are beyond their control (the belief system of a victim) tend to develop illnesses when their lives are traumatized. In fact, people who see themselves as having little, if any, control over their environment and over what happens to them on a daily basis are likely to show severe symptoms of depression and anxiety when confronted with the stress of a traumatic life event.

People who have what psychologist David McClelland of Boston University calls a "chronic stressed power motivation" (the motive to dominate and control everything, which is associated with the aggressor), suffer more respiratory infections

---

*The *Life Orientation Test* is a twelve-item questionnaire that measures a person's inclination to anticipate the best possible outcome in the course of life events.

and hypertension. They actually weaken their immune defenses when faced with traumatic circumstances.

These findings leave little question that when it comes to the ultimate impact of traumatic life events,

What You Expect

Profoundly Influences What You Get.

If you expect that your life change or crisis offers you an opportunity to become stronger and healthier, and if you expect to be able to find out how to accomplish that growth, it is more likely to happen. But if in response to trauma you expect dire consequences and feel out of control over your life, you will tend to cope effectively in the short term but run the risk of suffering unforeseen long-term damage to your health and performance.

You can put your mind to work for you in the face of trauma. But *how* exactly can you cultivate the mental attitudes crucial to your resilience and progress during life's upheavals? Here are some mental exercises that show you how.

YOUR MENTAL CONDITIONING PROGRAM

Because bedrock optimism and feelings of being in control of yourself are such critical preliminary ingredients to your success in dealing with adversity and trauma, it is important to start to encourage them in yourself even before you approach the formal stages of adjustment and growth I will describe.

If you currently are experiencing the *initial* impact of a major loss or disappointment, you may question whether cultivating an optimistic attitude is possible for you. You may feel hopeless and beaten by your circumstances. However, I believe you can muster an optimistic attitude even now, when things are the most chaotic. In fact, I believe that anyone who wants to create more positive expectations about how things will turn out can do this for him- or herself—now or at any time in the process of adjustment. It is a matter of *programming positive messages into your mind, using words that describe what you think, say, and see.*

POSITIVE MESSAGE PROGRAMMING

Few of us realize the powerful influence of the spoken and printed word on our thoughts, our feelings, our behavior, and ultimately on our physiology. What we say to ourselves can

---

▲ THE PLACEBO EFFECT: ▲
THE SELF-FULFILLING PROPHECY IN MEDICINE

The placebo effect usually refers to the healing power of sugar pills or pills that are chemically inert. The placebo's positive healing effect is due to the patient's *belief* that the treatment has the power to heal. The history of medicine is filled with remedies, even surgeries, that turned out to be ineffective in themselves but actually helped patients get well because of their faith in the procedures.

The placebo effect is a dramatic example of the self-fulfilling prophecy. In their book *The Healing Brain: Breakthrough Discoveries About How the Brain Keeps Us Healthy*, Robert Ornstein and David Sobel devote an entire chapter to the subject.

> Medicine has not actually had such a great run: Most discoveries throughout medical history have actually been unexplained by the usual canon of medicine. It was not in most cases the specific medical remedy that usually cured the patient. It was the *belief* in the remedy and in the healer (or in something else) that seems to have mobilized powerful innate self-healing mechanisms within the brain.
>
> The long history of medical treatment is, for the overwhelming part, a history of how strong belief heals. [p. 77; emphasis added]

---

provoke optimism and enthusiasm that leads to logical and creative problem-solving behavior; or what we say to ourselves can equally powerfully provoke pessimistic thoughts and feelings of depression that spawn confused and erratic behavior. I will now review for you some of the startling research that reveals how our verbal messages to ourselves can trigger thoughts and emotions that impact on the functioning of all our major organs and even on our body's immune system—for better or worse.

YOUR MIND IS A HEALER

Current research is making medical history because it has pinpointed how the mind actually heals or produces a toxic impact on the body. For example, well-documented research that links our belief systems and our moods to how well our immune system fights off invading organisms and toxins that can damage the body has been reported by Robert Ader of the University of Rochester and Steven Locke and his colleagues at Harvard Medical School. These landmark studies assure us that our immune system, although it is an automatic system, is also pliable and can learn. The immune system communicates directly with the brain and has a kind of memory and decision-making capacity all its own.

Robert Ader, a leading authority in psychoneuroimmunology, made one of the major breakthrough discoveries in this area while conducting a novel and elegant conditioning experiment with laboratory animals. In his study Ader trained a group of laboratory rats to associate the taste of sweetened water with becoming nauseated. He gave them the drug cyclophosphamide, which induces nausea, every time they drank sweetened water. The rats learned to make the association very quickly and many of them, after only one trial, became nauseated after drinking sweet water.

What Ader had not realized initially was that cyclophosphamide not only induced nausea but also suppressed the rats'

▲ THE MIND-BODY CONNECTION ▲

Psychobiologists and immunologists are just now beginning to map out the biochemical steps by which our thoughts and feelings can influence molecules at the cellular level of the body.

It appears that what goes on in our central nervous system as thoughts or images is evidenced by neural impulses in the frontal cortex of our brain. These neural impulses then travel through the area of the brain called the limbic-hypothalamic, or endocrine system, which is responsible for emotions. There they are changed into messenger chemicals called neurotransmitters and hormones that regulate the activity of our autonomic nervous system, which governs such vital functions as heart rate, breathing, and digestion.

The autonomic nervous system is then stimulated by those neurotransmitters to secrete additional neurotransmitters; they in turn activate the receptors on the cells of body organs such as our heart, lungs, pancreas, and intestines. This is what excites you and prepares you for fight or flight.

It is now also believed by some researchers that the central nervous system and the endocrine system communicate directly with the body's immune system, which is responsible for fighting off microbial invasions.

For those of you who are interested in pursuing how the mind modulates the function of cellular activity, entire organ systems, blood flow, the immune system, and even the coping process, see Robert Ornstein and David Sobel, *The Healing Brain: Breakthrough Discoveries About How the Brain Keeps Us Healthy.*

immune systems. This fact was responsible for the most startling results of his experiments: the rats learned to become nauseated at the taste of sweet water, and they learned to suppress their immune systems. There is no question that the rats were trained to control the functioning of their immune systems by behaving in a certain way. Indeed, further research has verified that many different aspects of our immunity can be conditioned by our expectations and beliefs. The impact of our mood on immune-system functioning has also been well documented.

With regard to traumatic stress, Steven Locke and his associates found that people's ability to cope emotionally influenced the immune system's functioning. In their study people who were anxious, fearful, or depressed in response to stressful life change showed a decrease in the activity of the immune system's natural *killer cells*, while people who were coping well emotionally with traumatic events had higher natural killer-cell activity.

Many studies now show that relaxation and mental imagery can have healing effects. In her doctoral dissertation at North Texas State University, Barbara Peavey reported that successful relaxation training improved the functioning of neutrophils, the most prevalent type of white-blood-cell defenses in our immune system. And in another fascinating series of studies investigating the impact of mental activity on innate immunity, J. Schneider and his research team at Michigan State College of Medicine found that after six sessions of imagery training, students could greatly increase or decrease the number of neutrophils circulating in their bloodstream, depending upon whether the images were positive or negative ones.

These examples of well-controlled experimental studies herald the *good news:* What goes on in your mind truly matters when it comes to creating negative or positive conditions in your body following trauma. Now let's begin to learn how to take advantage of the power that your mind can exert over your well-being.

PUT YOUR MIND TO WORK NOW

In this stage of preparation for learning how to empower yourself to gain from adversity, you can begin to telegraph success by inundating yourself with positive messages that will boost your mood, improve your attitude, benefit your physiol-

---

▲ MATTERS OF THE HEART MATTER TO HEALTH ▲

Research psychologist David McClelland and his colleagues at Boston University conducted a series of studies in which feelings of love and affection for other people were seen to create a stable increase in salivary immunoglobulin, an immune function response.

This could very well mean that, over time, loving thoughts and images can increase our resistance to getting sick.

---

ogy, and give you a sense of control over what happens. To do this type of programming you will need to generate a set of phrases that engender the three empowering outlooks: *acceptance* of what has happened, *faith* in the future, and *confidence* in your ability to cope. The messages should be in the form of real phrases that are meaningful and memorable for you. Think of these phrases as *superior-awareness* statements because they take you beyond your current logical understanding of yourself and your circumstances and direct you to a state of superior awareness. Here are some samples:

▲ I can learn to accept life the way it is for me.
▲ I am in charge of my own thoughts and feelings.
▲ I have the courage to go on with my life.
▲ I know that I will have all I need to be successful.

A HIGHER POWER

If you are a spiritual person, you may believe that God, or some powerfully positive cosmic force, is feeding your courage to accept your fate and build self-confidence. All the better! People who believe in a power greater than their own that operates in the world for good are always a step ahead in the process of self-empowerment. This deep spiritual faith in an

61

abiding, loving, benevolent universe yields you hope in the future and the invaluable comfort that you will not be alone in getting there.

I mention this here to assure you that both the preparation for and the process of my system for taking advantage of trauma are compatible with traditional religious belief systems. In fact, many Jews, Christians, and Moslems have remarked how well their religious beliefs and practices dovetail with this secular psychological program for thriving in the face of adversity. This compatibility is valuable because your spiritual faith can only enhance the results of the system you are about to learn.

Make your list of superior-awareness affirmations here in the space provided, or keep a similar list in your Empowerment Journal. You will be adding more statements to the list during your adjustment process. Some students of my system prefer to create a different superior-awareness statement for each day or week, as a kind of motto to live by during that period. So feel free to experiment with the number of statements you generate and how often you change them.

MY SUPERIOR-AWARENESS MESSAGES

_____

_____

_____

_____

_____

_____

I want you to be certain that you repeat these phrases to yourself in the morning when you first wake up; during downtime in your day, such as when you are commuting or showering; and just before you fall asleep at night. Many people actually write out their positive messages and display them on desktops, refrigerators, bed stands, car visors—wherever they will be noticeable and can trigger the thoughts they suggest.

For those of you who are thinking of skipping over this suggestion because it feels awkward or silly to coach yourself with positive verbal messages, please don't dismiss the technique so easily. Remember the evidence for how positive messages can influence your health. Try it for one week. After a week you will be more able to determine if positive verbal programming gives you the encouragement and affirmation you need throughout the Empowerment process.

CHARTING YOUR PROGRESS

Now I want to show you a chart that depicts the characteristics of each of the four stages that are part of every person's process of Empowerment. It is also a scorecard you can use to keep track of your own progress.

The history of this chart, or scorecard, dates back to when I began analyzing case histories and research material for this book. I had formulated those data into charts and graphs I could carry with me to study whenever I had a spare moment. They traced the mental adjustment process of hundreds of people who had succeeded in growing by coping with life-altering change.

As I examined the data, I found that although individuals' personalities and life situations were unique, as were the circumstances surrounding change, and although a wide variety of traumas had been encountered, the essential approach everyone had used to capitalize on change was the same—often strikingly so. But what had their approach been? What is the secret to triggering the process of adjustment and growth?

▲ WORD POWER ▲

The powerful effect that words can have on us, although unnoticed in living our everyday lives, is highlighted in the etymology of words. For instance, the Latin root of the verb "to obey" is *obedire*, which is a composite of *ob* and *audire*, "to hear facing someone." Thus, when we listen to someone face-to-face, the words spoken have the power to make us "obey" or to influence us.

The printed word has power over us, too. The very word *authority* (implying someone who has power, or who is an expert) stems from medieval times and is now applied to someone who *authors* the printed word, thus emphasizing the power of even the written word.

Let's use this brief digression about the power of spoken and written words as additional evidence that what we hear and read can indeed directly affect our thoughts, emotions, and actions—for better or worse.

Here is a list of words, some of which we use every day, that may have a greater positive impact if you think about their linguistic roots:

re-create	co-operate
no-thing-ness	re-mind
re-pair	dis-ease
re-cognize	aw(e)-ful-ness

No matter what happens to cause a critical change and no matter what type of person is confronted by the change, the people who succeed in taking advantage of traumatic circumstances follow a predictable course of recovery. As I said in Chapter Two, I call these stepping-stones to personal growth the *four stages of self-empowering growth:*

Stage I: Challenge
Stage II: Exploration
Stage III: Invention
Stage IV: Transformation

YOUR SCORECARD OF PROGRESS

The chart on p. 66 summarizes the goals and characteristics that are specific to each *stage* of your self-empowering growth after any traumatic change. Memorize it. Then use it again and again as a scorecard to evaluate your progress as you empower yourself to succeed during periods of traumatic change.

As you can see, each stage is characterized by a goal one hopes to accomplish, as well as by a series of mental and emotional reactions. As progress is made, the goals become more far-reaching and the adjustment more positive. Some sample time frames for each stage are also noted to give you a sense of how long it will take you to master the goals at each stage. Finally, I have included information about the coping resource that is most beneficial at each phase of progress and how much of a demand will be made on your supply of adaptive energy.

It is important for you to note that many people backslide during their recovery process and may even float back and forth between the stages before they have completed the system. Some people actually skip over the initial stage of crisis and seem to go immediately to Stage II, Exploration, without harming their recovery. And it is true that your ethnic heritage and particular family culture can influence your pace and style in moving through the stages of recovery. The general pattern for restoring health and happiness is adapted by each person according to his or her particular needs and circumstances.

You will learn exactly how to negotiate each stage in subsequent chapters. For now, I want you to feel the flow of progress and understand the *big picture*. Let me illustrate the entire process for you by tracing each stage of adjustment during a dramatic upheaval in my career. I followed the four-stage process in order to benefit eventually from a business trauma.

▲

SELF-EMPOWERMENT SCORECARD				
	Stage I *Challenge*	*Stage II* *Exploration*	*Stage III* *Invention*	*Stage IV* *Transformation*
Mental *and* *Emotional* *Reactions*	Shock, Disorienta- tion, Fear, Anger, Drive	Confusion, Curiosity, Risk, Clarity, Direction	Creativity, Experiment- ing, Progress, Achievement	Satisfaction, Mastery, Meaning, Growth
Goals	To identify dangers and opportunities	To confront rules of the new reality	To verify success strategies	To stabilize new achievements
Sample *Time* *Frame* *for* *Mastery*	4–8 Weeks	8–12 Weeks	12–16 Weeks	12–20 Weeks
Demands *on* *Adaptive* *Energy*	Intense	Moderate	Moderate	Mild
Primary *Adjustment* *Assets*	Courage	Curiosity	Creativity	Commitment

A BUSINESS DOWNTURN MADE GOOD

After a nine-year working relationship with St. Louis University, I made the leap into my own corporate psychology practice. I made the decision with confidence because the Stress Center I had developed at the university had been so successful I had earned a national reputation as an expert in the field of stress management. As a result, I had many corporate clients who would continue to hire me as a speaker, trainer, and consultant.

I was attracted to setting up my own business because it was an opportunity for me to set my own goals and to be my own boss. I weighed the exhilaration of being an entrepreneur against the continued security and, yes, prestige of directing a department in a medical center in making my decision to leave, but the lure of the entrepreneurial adventure eventually won out.

The career shift was, in itself, a traumatic change—from working in an environment that spanned ten square blocks with sixteen multistory buildings and five thousand employees, I went to a three-person office suite.

I hired lawyers to incorporate my business and accountants to set up my books. I purchased a computer, a word processor, calculators, and typewriters. I leased the office space for two years, hired two support staff, and signed professional agreements with four psychologists.

One week after the ink had dried on the last legal document that established me in my own business, I received a series of three phone calls that canceled seventy-five percent of the projected revenue for my first year of operation. The calls were from three divisions of a Fortune 500 company that had decided to save money by closing their management-development schools for twelve months. As a result, forty-five stress seminars were canceled. What had appeared to be a well-thought-out career move had turned into a potential disaster.

I was stunned.

Suddenly I couldn't sleep. I would wake up frequently during the night with racing thoughts and images of catastrophe. My temper was short, and I had a difficult time just exchanging simple pleasantries with my staff. These were distress signals that told me I was in the grip of a traumatic change. My symptoms in the initial days were natural because I was viewing my canceled business as the *enemy* and as an unwelcome intrusion in my new career adventure. I was allowing myself to feel threatened.

Fortunately I had already established a procedure for dealing with traumatic change, and so I knew what I had to do. In order to face this severe downturn of my business and make it work for me, I focused on accomplishing the two objectives that compose Stage I of taking advantage of trauma.

CHALLENGE: STAGE I OF SELF-EMPOWERING GROWTH

OBJECTIVE ONE: MINIMIZE THE THREATS

OBJECTIVE TWO: MAXIMIZE THE CHALLENGES

Clearly, I had plenty of threats to overcome in light of the amount of canceled business. Spelling them out was the first step to reducing or eliminating their hold on me. My economic stability and the financial security of my business and of those who counted on me for an income were clearly jeopardized by those phone calls. My enthusiasm for building my own business was threatened. My confidence and business judgment were called into question. When I let those threats occupy my full attention, they immobilized me. I knew that I had to overcome them and challenge myself if I wanted to make progress and capitalize on the setback.

But what was there about the situation that was challenging? Hidden within the crisis, right alongside the list of threats, there were opportunities for me. And as soon as I uncovered them, I could feel challenged enough to take advantage of them.

For instance, I had the opportunity to rethink my desire to be an entrepreneur (after all, small businesses often take rollercoaster rides. I had a chance early on to see if I was really cut out for the *downs* as well as the *ups*); to identify new corporate clients; to research what new programs would appeal to the marketplace; and to redesign my sales plan. And, as one clever friend of mine put it, "You had an unexpected opportunity to take a lot of time off!"

I found a way to challenge myself by focusing on each of the opportunities that came my way by virtue of my canceled seminars. The challenges kept me moving toward staying on top of my situation. That is the essence of Stage I: challenging your spirit and enthusiasm to make the most out of any situation. This quality is kept alive and even expanded when you create challenges that mean something to you personally. The exact procedure for turning your threats into challenges we will explore in detail later, but for now realize that once you have worked through this stage, you are ready to move on to Stage II.

EXPLORATION: STAGE II OF SELF-EMPOWERING GROWTH

Stage II involves a thorough investigation of the ways in which the traumatic event has changed the "rules of the game" in your life. In my case canceled business shifted the reality of my world in many ways. Almost immediately after the shock wore off, I realized that my reduced economic security would require a change in my pattern of spending and saving money. It also meant that my staff and I would need to redirect our efforts in order to be productive.

Unfortunately, as the scorecard predicted, Stage II also initially brought with it feelings of confusion. My office environment went from one that made people feel sure of themselves and excited about the growth of my company to one that made them anxious about the present and the future. Furrowed brows and serious expressions replaced smiles and the flushed glow of expectation. During Stage II it wasn't fun coming to work each morning for any of us.

I was constantly trying to sort out the ramifications of my

traumatic loss—on my finances, on my staff—and my prospects for recovering and regaining a healthy financial status. The loss of business made it necessary for me to arrange for a line of credit so I could meet my monthly payroll and bills. I canceled all of my nonessential developmental projects, such as reformatting my workshop manuals, and put every noncommitted dollar into marketing efforts.

My staff and I refocused our attention from expanding a healthy business to saving a floundering one. We realized that group meetings and individual efforts were needed to develop strategies that could sustain us. I told myself more than once, and my staff as often as I could, "Never again will we depend so completely on one customer." I could see the real impact of the lost business. It wasn't a very uplifting sight, but at least I knew what I was facing.

My honest appraisal of the situation gave me renewed confidence and a sense of direction. Now I could tackle finding the remedies. I was eager to get started. That's how you know when you are ready to move on to the third step. When you are clear about the new rules and new reality that have been brought about by change, you have completed the goals for Stage II. You'll find that you are energized and excited about inventing the strategic objectives that will help make you successful in the long run.

INVENTION: STAGE III OF SELF-EMPOWERING GROWTH

Stage III is an intensely creative period. You already have a sense of what is possible in light of your changed circumstances; in Stage III that sense crystallizes into strategic objectives. You become a kind of scientist experimenting with systems to achieve success, testing them to verify the winning ones and eliminating those that don't pan out.

The following is a partial list of objectives I put to the test during Stage III of my self-empowerment.

Stage III: Strategic Objectives

▲▲ To identify at least ten potential Fortune 500 corporate clients

▲▲ To secure financial support for at least twelve more months of operation

▲▲ To develop new programs and services based on market research results

▲▲ To improve team spirit and increase individual confidence levels

▲▲ To gain consultation, support, and encouragement from key individuals

By this time in the process, I was just as happy to know which strategies would fail as I was to discover the ones that would work. The elimination of nonproductive approaches helped me to concentrate more effort on the approaches that yielded some gain. I was so busy experimenting with new strategies to accomplish my financial, business, and personal objectives, I had no time or energy for being angry or afraid anymore; nor did I care to focus on the whys or wherefores of my predicament.

That will happen to you, too, during Stage III. At that point in the process of self-empowerment, you are swept along by the momentum you have worked diligently to create. The challenges you gained in Stage I combine with the confidence and sense of direction you accomplished in Stage II; they thrust you ahead, making you look forward to testing your strategies in Stage III.

As your strategy testing gives you results, you will begin to realize success. As you have probably already imagined, the success you achieve after setbacks and in response to traumatic change is more rewarding than any more easily gained. In my case my efforts to identify new corporate clients uncovered numerous companies that were interested in my services and in some of the new programs I had on the drawing board. I was thrilled by their reaction and encouraged by the broad base of interest in my work.

My business crisis was very useful to me because it prevented me from building my business on too narrow a base—both of clients and services. This narrow foundation would inevitably have had negative repercussions for the business that might have proven more disastrous later, when it would have been more difficult to be flexible.

TRANSFORMATION: STAGE IV OF SELF-EMPOWERING GROWTH

In Stage IV I was able to achieve permanent changes in the way I ran my business that were true advancements, promoting both the stability and the growth of my company. Two of the most salient business transformations were my new marketing approach and my new diversification of service.

As the result of my major financial setback, I instigated marketing strategies that targeted multiple industries. My corporate interviews suggested that I expand my services to emphasize keynote speaking in addition to my workshops and consulting. And, most important of all, I was able to reconfirm my commitment to being an entrepreneur. It was a terrific feeling to be on firm ground again.

That feeling of arriving home again, of being on firm footing, safe and secure, is always part of the transformation process in Stage IV of self-empowerment. It is the period during which you will restabilize your life and be forward-thinking once again.

THE BIG PICTURE

The four-stage process of *Challenge–Exploration–Invention–Transformation* involves the stepping-stones to successful personal growth no matter what changes you may have to master. And you will see that progress from stage to stage is only possible when you are ready.

Most people who follow the objectives and learn the skills of this system find that their progress is not linear. In one week you may take three steps forward only to find that the next week you have gone one step backward. My system is developed in such a way that you can always refer to earlier adjustment techniques to reinstate your progress if you slip back into a trouble spot.

Although everyone has a unique time frame for progressing through the stages, as you will observe from the case histories I give, there is some value in knowing what the average time span is for each stage. As I have noted on the Self-Empowerment Scorecard, many people find that it takes a full year or more to work successfully through the progressive stages of adjusting to a life-altering trauma.

Most people take four to eight weeks to master the crisis of Stage I. The demands on adaptive energy are most intense during that initial period. In contrast, Stages II and III are longer than Stage I and can last on the average from two to four months each to accomplish the work of exploring and inventing. The degree of demand on your adaptive energy will be moderate throughout both of those stages.

The final stage of growth, Stage IV, is far less intense but usually lasts the longest—on average six months. This is so because any true transformation in your behavior, beliefs, attitudes, and feelings requires time to become an automatic, well-integrated response.

I want to make very clear that the time frames are only general guidelines. You will progress at a rate that fits you and your circumstances. Because you will want to chart your progress, this book includes a list of Readiness Signals that indicate when you will be ready to move on to the next stage. The Readiness Signals are a much more reliable gauge of your progress than the sample time frames. The signals that you are ready to move from Stage I to Stage II are found in Chapter Six; from Stage II to Stage III in Chapter Eight; from Stage III to Stage IV in Chapter Ten. Chapter Eleven includes signals that confirm growth and recovery in Stage IV.

Now that you have the big picture, you are ready to delve

into a thorough exploration of what *self-empowering growth* is all about. In the following chapters you will learn in detail what to expect of the experiences you will have as you move through each stage of recovery and growth. You will learn how to gauge the extent of negative impact from traumatic changes and events and how to use that evaluation to establish short-range and long-range goals for how to restore your health and happiness. You will invent and adopt the coping strategies that work the best at each stage for accomplishing both ranges of goals. Throughout the process, you will encourage yourself to plan and pursue your own best approach to turning your world right side up again.

UNDERSTANDING AND USING PART II

In Part II of this book two chapters are devoted to each stage of recovery and growth. The first of the chapters is primarily *descriptive*. It offers a detailed account of what you are likely to think and feel. It answers typical questions and concerns and suggests appropriate goals and expectations during that stage. The second chapter of each pair is primarily *prescriptive*. It delineates the skills and strategies you will need to complete the objectives of that particular stage. You will learn ways of accelerating your progress and techniques to verify that you are on the right path. The second chapter concludes with a list of criteria that signal that you are ready to move to the next stage.

The following chart summarizes the organization of Part II.

		Description	*Prescription*
Stage I:	Challenge	Chapter 5	Chapter 6
Stage II:	Exploration	Chapter 7	Chapter 8
Stage III:	Invention	Chapter 9	Chapter 10
Stage IV:	Transformation	Chapter 11	Chapter 12

Preparing Yourself for Progress

You may be wondering about the best way to master the information and skills contained in Part II. Those chapters are the heart of this training program in how to grow after your world turns upside down. I recommend that you start at the beginning and work your way thoroughly through each chapter, no matter which phase of adjustment you may be in at the moment. That approach will give you a comprehensive overview of the process, a glimpse of what's in store for you in future stages. Most people find that knowing about the stage to come is reassuring—it reduces the uncertainty of what tomorrow may bring and provides hope that life will be rewarding again. Then you can go back to focus intensely on and practice the skills that pertain to your current stage of recovery.

As you work through Part II, your automatic reaction will be to concentrate on the chapters that pertain to the phase of progress facing you. This emphasis is natural and beneficial. When you focus on the material that meets your most salient needs you will accelerate. I cannot recommend too strongly the value of keeping in touch with your daily experiences and nighttime dream sequences as additional fuel for your growth process. Writing notes in your journal and discussing the feelings, thoughts, and images that emerge during each stage with trusted confidants and mental health professionals will ensure that you are taking full advantage of the conscious and subconscious opportunities that are part of your particular trauma—every step of the way.

Good luck with your self-study program. Remember, in addition to understanding the concepts and strategies I present, you must *practice* them. Put them to the test in your everyday life and discover what works for you. This testing to assess what works for you is an essential part of learning how to empower yourself. My system is designed to help you tap into your own best answers, to establish and reach *your* goals.

Think of this system that you are about to learn as a detailed map, complete with alternate routes and instructions for reaching *your* destination for growth and fulfillment. With this map you are both navigator and driver, the best judge of which routes and strategies will help you to make the best progress possible toward your goal of

STAYING ON TOP

WHEN YOUR WORLD

TURNS UPSIDE DOWN.

PART

II

▲

CHAPTER

5

▲

When Your World Turns Upside Down

KEYS TO UNDERSTANDING TRAUMA

We can use a lighthearted metaphor to describe the experience of major change. Peer through the "looking glass," as Alice did before she began her adventures in Wonderland, and you will find yourself falling down a long, dark rabbit hole. Landing with a thump in a heap of sticks and dry leaves. Lost and surrounded by doorways that are all apparently locked. Shrinking to only ten inches tall. " 'That was a narrow escape!' said Alice, a good deal frightened at the sudden change, but very glad to find herself still in existence."

Alice's story is a remarkably accurate account of what it is like to encounter a major life trauma. It is frightening and overwhelming, with much of our fear stemming from the uncertainty of our new reality. We are confused by trauma in part because the world as we knew it is shattered and because we were robbed of some of the resources we depended on to stay healthy and happy.

TRAUMA SHATTERS YOUR WORLD AND YOUR RESOURCES

Like most people, you can probably remember the most traumatic day of your life. Think about that day for a few moments until your memories are vivid. Do you remember feeling helpless or hurt or angry? Did forces outside of your control blindside you with pain, heartache and worry? Do you recall asking yourself questions like

"Why me?"
"What did I do to deserve this?"
"Will my life ever be normal again?"
"How long can I take this?"
"Is this a bad dream?"

If so, you can be certain that you experienced a traumatic, life-altering change. The painful emotions and haunting questions you had on your worst day were actually signals that whatever happened to you robbed you of resources that were critical to your vitality. The traumatic event may have obliterated some of your intimate ties; it may have destroyed your career path or taken away your financial security; or it may have damaged you mentally or physically.

If you lost these kinds of precious resources, your world and your way of operating in it were severely shaken. You were helpless to stop the emotional upheaval. You lost your vital resources for health and happiness, and as a result, you lost your inner balance.

The loss of vital resources is the key to why traumas are so difficult and damaging unless you know how to recover. Stevan Hobfoll, director of the Applied Psychology Center at Kent State University, contends that traumas involving loss of vital

---

▲ SUFFERING OPENS THE MIND ▲

In his treatise *Primitive Mythology: The Masks of God*, Joseph Campbell cites various myths that deal eloquently with the subject of suffering. This one, a primitive Eskimo maxim, is my favorite:

The only true wisdom lives far from Mankind, out in the great loneliness, and it can be reached only through suffering. Privation and suffering alone can open the mind of a man to all that is hidden to others. [p. 54]

---

resources for health and happiness are the most psychologically threatening. His contention is substantiated by the fact that stressful loss is responsible for ninety percent of situational depressions. Barbara Snell Dohrenwend and her research team at the City University of New York found that people who lack resources are particularly vulnerable to additional trauma-induced losses, or *loss spirals*.

So, no matter whether you are suffering from the shock of a single trauma or of multiple crises, Stage I is a time of major upheaval. You didn't expect the trauma and surely you didn't deserve it. In essence, your whole world has been shattered. Let's look at the hallmarks of what happens during Stage I of adjusting to traumatic life events. Review Stage I in the following chart. You might call it a Scorecard of Progress. (See page 66 for the complete Self-Empowerment Scorecard.)

As you can see, the first set of experiences you will have during Stage I are mental disorientation and perhaps shock, along with strong feelings of fear or anger and the drive to *end* the crisis.

▲

	SELF-EMPOWERMENT SCORECARD			
	Stage I Challenge			
Mental and Emotional Reactions	Shock, Disorienta- tion, Fear, Anger, Drive			
Goals	To identify dangers and opportunities			
Sample Time Frame for Mastery	4–8 Weeks			
Demands on Adaptive Energy	Intense			
Primary Adjustment Assets	Courage			

STAGE I: A MIND-BODY EMERGENCY

A good way to begin to understand the impact of trauma on your mind and body is to learn what happens to your mental and physical status when you encounter minor stress. Under day-to-day circumstances, your mind and body usually remain relatively stable, with minor ebbs and flows of excitation. The ordinary stresses of living, such as deadlines, decisions, disagreements, mistakes, and conflicts cause you to mobilize the resources of your mind and body to meet the demands of those minor troubles. You then *promptly* restore yourself to an even keel mentally and physically once you meet the demands.

This instinct to seek an internal equilibrium is natural. In fact, your mind and body will go to great effort to maintain your internal equilibrium against any intrusion or change from the outside world. Walter Cannon, regarded as one of the most creative and authoritative scholars in physiology, termed this propensity to restore ourselves to an inner state of balance *homeostasis*.

The concept of homeostasis can be a comforting one for you during this early stage of upheaval. Be assured that your subconscious mind and your body systems are now and will always be dedicated to restoring your vital resources as a response to stress. In a short time you will also become willfully and consciously dedicated to restoring your equilibrium by *directing* your thoughts, feelings, and behavior. This conscious effort on your part will assist your innate drive toward homeostasis.

YOUR ALARM REACTION

Now let's look closely at exactly what happens when something traumatic makes your normal world disappear. When major trauma occurs, the restoration of our internal equilibrium as well as our other vital resources for health and happiness is not such a routine matter as it is during coping with ordinary stressful events. When severe upheaval occurs our task is to mobilize more than the usual amount of *adaptive energy* in an effort to recover and cope.

Hans Selye, founder of the International Institute of Stress, and one of the earliest and most prolific stress researchers, coined the phrase *adaptive energy* to describe the physiological assets that are part of the human body's well-orchestrated defense system. This adaptive energy comes into play to protect our bodies from harm when our welfare is being severely threatened, as it is during traumatic upheaval.

On a practical level, when a death or divorce, a job termination or business failure, a financial setback or dreaded illness upsets our life, it is natural and beneficial for us to rise to meet the extreme demands of those crises with our adaptive energy at peak levels. Selye referred to this first set of physiological responses to the crisis of traumatic events as the *Stage of Alarm*. He identified two subsequent stages of responding to unresolved stress as the *Stage of Resistance* and the *Stage of Exhaustion*. Selye termed the entire process of our physiological defense system the *General Adaptation Syndrome*. (We will examine Selye's final two stages as part of the discussion on the pattern of ineffective coping with traumatic stress in Chapter Thirteen.)

Hans Selye's pioneering concept that the body responds in phases, or stages, to prolonged stress has helped us immeasurably to chart the body's physiological process of coping. His theory was a direct outgrowth of the findings that physiologist Walter Cannon made public in 1932. In Cannon's book *The Wisdom of the Body*, he concluded that prolonged exposure to severe stress leads eventually to a breakdown in our biological systems. However, during the early stages of exposure to harsh environmental stressors, the body prepares itself to *fight* or to *flee* the noxious invasion of the stressor by virtue of its adrenaline response.

Selye's concept of the *stage of alarm*, combined with Cannon's breakthrough discovery of our *fight or flight response*, gives us a strong foundation for our current and more vivid picture of what happens inside the body during the first stage of responding to any traumatic stress. Technically, when our body prepares to fight or flee a stressful circumstance, a receiving center in our brain stem, called the *ascending reticular activating system,* sends emergency messages from our senses to higher centers in the brain. Those messages signal the *sympathetic nervous system* directly to stimulate the heart to beat faster and the peripheral blood vessels to clamp down. The signaling is accomplished via neurotransmitters called epinephrine and norepinephrine. As a backup, another area of the brain, the *adrenal medulla,* is also instructed to release those same neurotransmitters toward the same target organs. This process of *alarm reaction* increases muscle strength, alertness, endurance, and our overall energy level both mentally and physically.

Make a mental note of the fact that this natural and historically beneficial physical preparation for fight or flight in response to stress is the physiological underpinning of today's two most frequent *maladaptive psychological reactions* to stress—i.e., the response style of the victim and the response style of the aggressor.

As we learned earlier, the victim style of attempting to escape threat originates with the flight reaction; while the aggressor style of attempting to control and dominate stems from the fight reaction. These two styles are primitive and for the most part not applicable to most modern traumas.

Both the flight reaction of the victim and the fight reaction of the aggressor are triggered by feelings of threat and are brought about by our preoccupation with the fact that the trauma has taken vital resources away from us. Although this preoccupation with what we have lost is natural, it is not productive.

To cope most productively and effectively with crisis and upheavals, we need to minimize our perceptions of the *threatening* aspects of our stressful circumstances and next to turn our attention toward the *challenging* aspects. This shift in perception is what channels our emergency response system in a direction that builds stamina, resilience, mental alertness, and emotional control.

I will show you in detail in the next chapter how to accomplish this perceptual shift to yield such beneficial results. For now, let's focus on the impact of the alarm reaction on your learning and memory. Our focus illuminates the physiological and psychological mechanisms that cause a perception of challenge to bring benefit and a perception of unresolved threat to spawn damage.

YOUR KEY LEARNING MOMENT

Thanks to the flow of stress hormones, you are charged up to meet the emergency at hand when trauma strikes. What is even more intriguing, perhaps, is that, in addition to the physical arousal, you enter into a kind of spontaneous hypnotic mental state while your adrenaline is flowing.

A good way to understand what it means to enter a hypnotic mental state induced by trauma is to try to recall a stressful emergency you have had, such as a car accident. Seconds before the collision happened you may have felt that time was suspended—events seemed to move in slow motion and there was a dreamlike quality to the whole experience. You may also recall having been very mentally alert. In essence, when anyone experiences the onset of such an emergency, it triggers a mental state that can be considered a form of hypnosis. This is what we mean by a trauma-induced trance.

Two very important things occur while you are in this altered state of consciousness:

1. No matter what the trauma is, if you are experiencing fear or anger while you are in your hypnotic state, those emotions are recorded and encapsulated in a memory process that continues to have a negative impact on your entire system until you resolve the threat. As time goes on, you will exhibit symptoms that stem from that particular traumatic circumstance if the threat remains unresolved.

2. While you are in this trauma-induced hypnotic trance, your brain may also trigger memories of any incidents you have previously experienced that are similar to the stress at hand. So, for instance, if you are about to have a car accident, and you had one at an earlier time, your body's emergency response to the stress at hand may be compounded by your brain's association of the two events. The alarm response triggers the deeply ingrained memory of the earlier accident.

Because your mind works in these two ways during the initial period of a crisis, it is critical for you to confront your anger and fear associated with recent traumas as soon as possible. That will enable you to disengage the negative emotions from the memory of the event and thus heal those mental wounds. It is equally critical for you to learn the skill of deprogramming your emotional memory of any past traumas that are still smoldering so that you don't exacerbate your feelings of threat with memory-encapsulated anxiety and rage during a future crisis.

If you are *unable* to break the connection between the traumatic event and your feelings of anger and fear early in the recovery process, your body will remain in a heightened state of physiological arousal due to that unresolved threat. This is how you put yourself at risk for extended damage. Without specific effort to minimize the threatening aspects of your trauma, you are planting time bombs of anxiety and rage that will explode during future traumatic episodes in your life.

WHEN ALARM SYMPTOMS APPEAR

Most people start out their process of adjusting to trauma in a state of unresolved threat. This state of unresolved threat is recorded throughout your body and can have a negative impact on your immune system because it accelerates your sympathetic nervous system and endocrine system. Over a period of weeks

▲ TRAUMAS: A CHANCE TO BECOME AWARE ▲

There is a true spiritual value in the experience of trauma. Theologian Matthew Fox speaks to this point in a passage in his treatise on creation spirituality, *On Becoming a Musical Mystical Bear*.

> Life is at many crucial junctures a question of chance. Perhaps a chance exposure to poliomyelitis puts someone in the hospital at a critical moment in his life, forcing reflection and recollection on him; perhaps the sudden death of a friend; perhaps the loss of a friend; perhaps a chance encounter with a stranger; perhaps an unexpected article or book we read, a movie we see, a record we hear. Who can predict or catalog such critical occurrences? Yet, who can ignore them or cut them out from the process of our becoming aware of life and its mysteries? [p. 122]

if your condition of physiological arousal remains high, you will trigger symptoms that stem from an alarm reaction that has gone on too long. Your memories of similar past traumas that continue to threaten you will heighten symptoms, too.

Each of us exhibits a unique pattern of symptoms from unresolved alarm reactions. Just remember that the signals are natural and will dwindle in strength as you minimize your threats by restoring your lost resources and maximize your challenges by understanding what profound lessons and opportunities your trauma has to offer.

Now look at the following lists of possible symptoms that you may experience during the initial part of Stage I of adjusting to trauma before you have minimized your threats. Remember, these symptoms will only last until you have mastered the goals of this stage. They may reappear in later stages if you perceive additional sources of threat, but usually they are much less frequent and intense.

Unresolved alarm occurs for almost everyone. You are not alone. The typist who worked on an earlier version of this manuscript was so struck by what she read she made copies of alarm symptoms for two friends. She wanted to assure them that what they were experiencing was not only natural but common.

Review the different types of symptoms associated with Stage I reactions to trauma. Check any that may apply to you.

MENTAL ALARM SYMPTOMS

These signals primarily result from the traumatic disturbance of the communication between your nervous system and other parts of your brain that are responsible for thinking, learning, and memory:

- ▲ Feeling of being in a daze
- ▲ Distractibility and inability to concentrate
- ▲ Sense of timelessness
- ▲ Memory failure
- ▲ Preoccupation with the past
- ▲ Preoccupation with what might have been
- ▲ Startle reactions
- ▲ Hyperalertness and intense concentration
- ▲ Rumination over loss
- ▲ Daydreaming
- ▲ Mental reenactment of the moment of impact
- ▲ Hallucinations
- ▲ Frightening dreams

PHYSICAL ALARM SYMPTOMS

These signals primarily result from traumatic disturbance of the communication between your nervous system and your major physiological systems:

- ▲ Chronic fatigue or exhaustion
- ▲ Heaviness in limbs and trunk
- ▲ Sweating
- ▲ Rapid heartbeat
- ▲ Digestive disorders
- ▲ Hyperactivity or lethargy
- ▲ Eating disturbances
- ▲ Sleep disturbances
- ▲ Surges of energy

EMOTIONAL ALARM SYMPTOMS

These signals result primarily from the traumatic disturbance of the communication between your nervous system and other parts of your brain that are responsible for your feelings and mood states:

- ▲ Numbness
- ▲ Emotional attacks or pangs; waves of feeling overwhelmed
- ▲ Fear of losing control over aggressive impulses
- ▲ Shame or guilt
- ▲ Rage at the source of loss or those exempted from it
- ▲ Episodes of sadness and crying
- ▲ Episodes of euphoria and excitement

ALARM SYMPTOMS CAN BE SEVERE

Occasionally people experience horrendous traumas that are outside the range of usual human experience. Examples of these horrors include the sudden destruction of one's home or community; witnessing someone who has been or is being seriously injured or killed; torture; kidnapping; and combat.

When these types of events occur, a person may experience a severe and persistent collection of alarm symptoms called *post-traumatic stress disorder (PTSD)*. Anyone who displays this syndrome is in need of immediate medical and psychological help.

The system for coping with trauma presented in this book will be effective for people who have been so severely traumatized as a supplement to extensive, direct therapy. (See the appendix for the diagnostic criteria for PTSD, which were published in the latest edition of the *Diagnostic Statistical Manual III*. You will be able to distinguish in it the alarm symptoms often triggered by more normal human trauma—bereavement, chronic illness, business losses, and marital conflict—from the more pathological pattern of symptoms associated with unusually terrorizing events.)

For our purposes here, we will examine the character and pattern of alarm symptoms that occur in response to typical upheavals in everyday living. Even the trauma of positive changes can trigger your alarm system to go off.

ALARMS SOUND EVEN DURING WELCOMED UPHEAVAL

You may have an initial alarm reaction in response to being promoted to a new job, just as you would if you were fired. Both events can trigger sleeplessness, hyperactivity, tension, and even confusion and distractibility. However, feelings of euphoria would accompany the promotion, while being fired would likely trigger anxiety, anger, or both.

Our immediate response to either negative or positive upheaval is somewhat similar. In fact, if you entered a room filled with people who were agitated but you had no idea what had happened to trigger the alarms, it would be difficult to determine if they were reacting to a positive or negative experience. For example, as the camera scanned the viewing stands during the *Challenger* space shuttle disaster in 1987, it was difficult to read the faces of the onlookers. Many of them understood that the explosion meant disaster, while others were still in awe. It was difficult to separate the initial reactions of horror from those of awe and delight. In much the same way, a million-dollar lottery winner could be mistaken for someone who has received devastating news—but only for a moment.

Positive traumas never trigger alarm reactions for very long. Alarms are sounded and then dissipate because we understand the challenge to be nonthreatening. On the other hand, negative traumas do very often trigger overextended alarm reactions because at first we feel threatened by the blow to our vital resources. It is unresolved threats that trigger the symptoms. You should feel some comfort, however, in knowing that alarm signals are valuable for you. You actually need them to move you to action in the initial stage of a trauma.

ALARM SYMPTOMS ARE PRECIOUS

Please don't make the mistake during this initial adjustment stage of trying to *treat* or eliminate the alarm symptoms themselves. You may be tempted to treat the symptoms, especially if they are extremely painful, unpleasant ones. You may want desperately to tame confusion, relieve tension, alleviate sadness, or calm hyperactivity to restore balance. Resist the impulse to make symptom relief your primary goal. It is okay to get some temporary relief from a prescription drug, or from a massage, or perhaps a funny movie, or a good jog. But be careful not to make eliminating the symptoms your chief priority.

REASSURE YOURSELF

Bear in mind that your alarm symptoms are a *normal, natural,* and even *helpful* part of the initial stage of traumatic change. You may think you are disintegrating before your very eyes, but you should not worry. An emotional *falling apart* or *letting go* is necessary for reintegration and growth. Not literally of course, and not to a dangerous degree. There is a huge chasm between the *symptoms of alarm* and the *symptoms of mental illness*. With alarm symptoms, you may be exhausted and robbed of a fundamental joie de vivre, but it will pass. People with symptoms of mental illness often have a chronic feeling that life is pointless

▲ THE BLESSINGS OF ANGER ▲

Anger is a signal and one worth listening to. Our anger may be a message that we are being hurt, that our rights are being violated, that our needs or wants are not being adequately met, or simply that something is not right. Our anger may tell us that we are not addressing an important emotional issue in our lives, or that too much of our self—our beliefs, values, desires, or ambitions—is being compromised in a relationship. Our anger may be a signal that we are doing more and giving more than we can comfortably do or give. Or our anger may warn us that others are doing too much for us, at the expense of our own competence and growth. Just as physical pain tells us to take our hand off the hot stove, the pain of our anger preserves the very integrity of our self. Our anger can motivate us to say "no" to the ways in which we are defined by others and "yes" to the dictates of our inner self. [Harriet Goldhor Lerner, *The Dance of Anger,* p. 1]

and may have active impulses to end their life on a regular basis. With alarm symptoms, you might miss work because you can't concentrate and don't care much about your productivity. That is very different from *hearing voices* that warn you about vicious people who are trying to ruin or kill you, or from contemplating suicide—which are symptoms of extreme mental disturbances.

Do not make eliminating alarm symptoms the sole focus of your attention, regardless of how uncomfortable they may be. Eradicating uncomfortable symptoms can cloud the real issues that need attention. Let me give you a vivid example of how one of my students used alarm symptoms to guide her to the source of her feelings of devastation. This story will help you to see how you can use your own confusion, anxiety, and depression to illuminate the path to a full recovery.

AN UNCOMMON DETECTIVE STORY

At our first counseling session, Gloria stared blankly over my right shoulder as she recounted her daily crying episodes. She had no idea why she cried, sometimes every hour on the hour. She compared her sadness to an "evil spirit" that enveloped her entire being. This demon sadness was robbing her of control and, she felt sure, it would gradually overtake her sanity. Gloria could no longer concentrate on her job, and she had withdrawn from her husband and daughters. To her, the family was on one side of a great wall, and she was on the other—distant, apart, lonely.

By the time Gloria came to me, she was almost completely unnerved by her symptoms. She began to panic and thought that she was "losing her mind." Gloria decided, on her own, that she had developed these troubling feelings and behaviors because there was a history of mental illness in her family. She recalled an uncle who was hospitalized for severe depression. Gloria's mother had been diagnosed as schizophrenic. She felt out of control, in great turmoil, and was convinced that she must be suffering from a major mental illness.

Before Gloria came for her first visit, she had been under the care of a psychiatrist who, although puzzled by her case, was sure she was not mentally ill. He called me and asked if I would work with Gloria to help her out of her crisis. In the first session we looked for what might be triggering such extreme alarm. She insisted that nothing significant had changed in her life, nothing that could have created such fears. In order for us to be able to explore what might be at the source of her mysterious alarm, Gloria agreed to my request that she write in a journal any events that bothered or excited her.

When she returned for the second session three days later, she had no entries in her notebook. She explained that whenever she tried to recall what specifically had occurred to trigger her upheaval, the very process made her so anxious that her symptoms flared while she was writing. These flare-ups made her shut down her thoughts and put down her pen.

I surmised that Gloria's logical, conscious mind might be so threatened that she dared not directly face her *enemy* at all. I asked her to doodle for five minutes, three times a day, on a roll of shelf paper. She could do her drawings at any time and in any mood. Doodling would allow Gloria to express herself by indirectly addressing whatever happened to upset her.

After four days of drawing, Gloria rolled out about eight feet of images across the floor of my office for us to look at. Many of her initial markings were geometric shapes that abruptly gave way to animal-like figures that filled the page. Here is a reproduction of what Gloria had drawn:

It was in these simple drawings that Gloria first saw the hidden sources of her problem. Her own detective work allowed her to break through to the cause of her distress. We discussed her ideas. I usually asked the questions and she searched for her answers. I asked her what the animal shapes on her paper looked like to her.

She vacillated between saying "I don't know" to "I should know." After twenty minutes, she said, "Maybe some kind of bird. Yes, that's it—a sort of bird. No particular kind—just a little bird."

Then I queried her more: "If you had to guess what type of little birds, what would you guess they were?" She hesitated and then she said, "Okay, I'm not sure, maybe chickens. Yes, right, exactly . . . chickens!"

I wondered out loud, "And what does the word 'chicken' mean?" Gloria looked at the floor. "Well, 'chicken' normally means afraid—afraid of something."

Then I asked, "What are you afraid of? Maybe you are scared of something?"

Gloria, gaining confidence in the importance of her drawings, began to scan the paper for clues as to what fears might be hidden inside her. She finally zeroed in on a series of arrows clustered all around the chickens. She decided that the arrows resembled the symbol for the male gender.

Over a period of time we analyzed all her images. Gloria's insights into her drawings led her to the painful truth that she no longer loved her husband. She had been living with that fact buried within her for some time but was afraid to admit such a horrible thought. Gloria's symptoms were coming from her fear of facing the fact that her intimate *world* had changed. She was being altered by going through the emotional trauma of losing communication and love from her husband, and she was angry about what she had lost.

As she became more and more consciously aware of the nature of her crisis, the exact path to how she could adjust and what she could do to restore herself to balance also became more and more clear. For Gloria to grow and to lessen her alarm reactions, she had to face reality. She had to accept that it was her responsibility to confront the truth and to find out how she could become happy and healthy once again in spite of her marital upheaval.

One of the strategies for restoring her lost intimacy that Gloria pursued was a painstaking year in marital counseling. This caused stress for Gloria's husband, too. But in dealing with their trauma, these two chose to face how they had grown apart. They chose to learn how to grow back together again. It was difficult, but the rewards were great. Gloria and her husband succeeded in reinventing their marriage.

Through your study and application of the system of self-empowerment, you will come to realize that the beginning stage of every adjustment to trauma is fraught with alarm signals.

You can benefit by recording your spontaneous thoughts and feelings and by letting your imagination doodle information as Gloria did.

EMPOWERMENT JOURNAL NOTES

While working your way through Stage I, you will have a myriad of feelings, thoughts, daydreams, and night dreams that may seem chaotic, fragmented, and disconnected. This is normal. But you can gain some measure of control over your untamed mind and emotions by recording in your journal whatever seems important.

Don't be surprised if your entries don't make perfect sense to you at the time you record them. It is not uncommon for people to be stumped by the significance of a doodle, a note, or a dream at first, only to have the meaning dawn on them at a much later stage.

One of my favorite examples of a significant Stage I dream was recorded by Sara, a woman who was in the first week of a divorce. One night she dreamed that she was traveling out of town by car. As she was leaving she passed a white Spanish Mission church with a neon sign that flashed "Live Well."

During the dream Sara remembered thinking, "How strange it is to have a women's health spa in this location." In her journal notes, Sara surmised that in her dream she had associated the neon sign with a national chain of health clubs called Living Well Lady and left her analysis at that.

In her work with me two months later, Sara realized another, deeper significance of the dream. Her later insights led her to believe that "traveling out of town" symbolized getting out of her marriage, and that the Spanish church was a metaphor that radiated her *mission* in life, which is to *live well*.

Sara felt quite a positive vote of confidence from her unconscious mind about her decision to divorce once she understood the significance of her crisis dream. It is important to point out here that although Sara's understanding of her dream came later, she experienced some relief from her initial anxiety *just by writing it down.*

Assure yourself now that you will experience relief and you, too, will gain helpful insights from recording your dreams. You do not need a magical formula or a manual to learn how to interpret your dreams. Practice is the best teacher. Most people find that as they begin to keep journal notes on their dreams, they are better able to remember them, and their dreams are richer and more vivid. These improvements in memory and dream images will give you deeper insights into how dreams might help you to recover and grow.

In preparation for reading Chapter Six, I would like you to be aware of one more reason why you feel disturbed when something traumatic happens to you. It will help you appreciate more fully the terror of traumatic stress in the first stage of adjustment.

TRAUMA OFTEN TRIGGERS YOUR MOST BASIC FEAR

If you find that you are disturbed and confused about life in general when traumatic things happen, most likely it is because in the first stage of coping with a crisis of any kind, in addition to the immediate sense of loss and disappointment, you are reminded that you are mortal. During the initial stage of the onslaught of any loss, you catch a rare glimpse of what it may be like when you die—to lose touch with all that you have been given, with all that you have worked so diligently to achieve.

Our fear of dying is so great that most of us go to fantastic lengths, mentally and emotionally, to hide from it. We go about our everyday lives *pretending* that we're immortal so that we can forget about dying. Not only do we refuse to think about death, many people spend incredible energy to keep themselves looking and feeling as young as possible—not solely because it is healthy, but to ward off the evils of aging and its inevitable outcome. We all want to hang on to what we know, and we know life—not death.

▲ NIGHTMARES ▲

As your dream develops, if your anxiety escalates, your normal psychological defenses against becoming overwhelmed will break down. At the point where your defenses are insufficient, you will have a nightmare.

Nightmares are frequent in Stage I because even in your waking state your defenses are overwhelmed by your trauma. If you do wake up startled and in a state of panic over a nightmare, reassure yourself that it was only a dream. Have something soothing to drink or eat and write down the main events of your dream. You may want to discuss the feelings you had in the dream with someone so you can release the negative emotions.

The underlying emotional source of all suffering is mortality itself. After all, if our life is altered so dramatically by trauma that we can hardly recognize it as our own, we naturally might think of it as a *death* experience. In a small but real way, our life as we once knew it has died. This small but real death certainly is reminiscent of the ultimate of all traumas—our own death.

Extremely stressful life events rob us of our masks, the devices that ordinarily shield us from the fact of our own death. So, when our life undergoes upheaval, not only do we suffer from the losses that are associated with that specific trauma, we quake at the reminder that one day we will lose our most precious possession—our very own life. It is important to realize that the terror of trauma gives us a great opportunity to resolve the primordial fear we all experience.

▲

COMING TO TERMS WITH LOSS

You can lessen the trauma of future life events by facing your fear of dying whenever you have the opportunity to do so. The less you fear death, the less threatened you will be when faced with traumatic loss and the more easily you will be able to challenge yourself by the circumstances. Let me show you exactly what I mean by illustrating a popular method for controlling and eliminating worry.

Worries can be calmed by asking the question, "What's the worst that could happen?" When that question is applied to most worries, the answer is, "This concern may cause me great disappointment, but it is *not life-threatening*." This realization typically reduces the threat involved in the worry-come-true.

But what if your worry *was* life-threatening? What if you were told you have a killing cancer? And what if you found out that you did have a grave illness that left you with a short time to live? Could you eventually be at peace with that news? Could you come to say, "The worst that could happen is that I will die, and that's not so bad"?

If you honestly could be at peace, knowing that your death might be imminent, you have already achieved an exceptional accomplishment. It will prepare you to empower yourself to grow through adversity. Believe me, the more comfortable you can become with your own death, the less fear you will experience when traumatic events happen, *and* the more at ease you will be in mastering any stressful situation.

Coming to terms with your own death is so freeing and powerfully positive that Bruno Bettelheim, founder of the Orthogenic School for mentally disturbed children in Chicago, once said: "Children will not be afraid to live, whose parents are not afraid to die."

My favorite example of this point I am making about the benefits of being at peace with your own mortality is to be found in a story about an elderly, frail Jesuit priest who was hospitalized with a severe coronary condition. Within days of his admission, this Jesuit had captured the attention and hearts of the entire staff and many patients on his floor. They flocked to his room because, despite his critical condition, he maintained both an incredible sense of humor and empathy for the overworked nurses and physicians. He was so congenial, the other patients actually stood in line to talk with him.

Another priest, a professor of mine, told me that one afternoon he visited the old Jesuit and found thirteen people gathered around his sick friend's bed. After the crowd dispersed, my professor asked the dying priest, "How can you be so positive? Where do you get such energy? Aren't you worried about your heart failing?" His friend smiled and said, "Even though ice cream tastes like mush to me, and my hearing is almost gone, and I can't read the newspaper anymore even with my glasses, and I grow weaker each day, I feel very much alive. The way I look at it, God is removing from me all of my distractions, one by one!"

▲ ON DEATH AND DYING ▲

When we look back in time and study old cultures and people, we are impressed that death has always been distasteful to man and will probably always be. From a psychiatrist's point of view this is very understandable and can perhaps best be explained by our basic knowledge that, in our unconscious, death is never possible in regard to ourselves. It is inconceivable for our unconscious to imagine an actual ending of our own life here on earth, and if this life of ours has to end, the ending is always attributed to a malicious intervention from the outside by someone else. In simple terms, in our unconscious mind, we can only be killed; it is inconceivable to die of a natural cause or of old age. Therefore death in itself is associated with a bad act, a frightening happening, something that in itself calls for retribution and punishment. [Elisabeth Kübler-Ross, *On Death and Dying*, p. 2]

Think about what the Jesuit was saying. What he called his *distractions* are our treasures. We cling to our sight, our hearing, our health, and all of our senses so we can stay tuned in and live fully. We only know our world through our senses. And yet, at some point in life, it is our job to prepare ourselves to give up our senses. We must prepare for a time when we are no longer anticipating life as much as we are death.

This holy man's story proves that it is possible to face death without fear. It shows how his graceful acceptance of his coming death freed him to accept the loss of his faculties and his failing health.

How can each of us accomplish this degree of comfort and peace with death? Why not plan to use each stressful event you encounter as an opportunity to consider that life is sometimes very short. Shorter than we may wish. Let's face it, we all know that there is nothing like a brush with death to wake us up and help us get our priorities clear. A line from William Saroyan's famous short story "The Daring Young Man on the Flying Trapeze" makes this point eloquently. It describes the experience of the main character, who was nearing death: "It was then that he became thoroughly awake: at the thought of dying."

It is the great losses, the small deaths in life, that wake us, that sound the alarms, and that give us an opportunity to search and to grow more alive.

6

▲

Turning Threats into Challenges

Now that you have a deeper understanding of the perils inherent in Stage I, you are ready to learn the skills that will help you to survive its upheaval. With your inner fears and hostilities calmed, you can learn the strategies to challenge yourself to become stronger and healthier through adversity and loss. You can place yourself on the productive course that leads directly to the second stage of your growth process.

With the ultimate goal of making yourself ready for Stage II, your objectives for this chapter are to learn how to *minimize your threats* and *maximize your challenges*.

HOW TO CALM YOUR INTERNAL CRISIS

The internal chaos and external demands so characteristic of the crisis atmosphere during Stage I can take their toll on you in the form of alarm-system symptoms. You read about those symptoms in Chapter Five. I suggested then that you don't want to numb yourself completely to the mental and physical signals of your trauma because they are important to your growth. However, you and those around you do deserve some relief from your nervousness, sleepless nights, short fuse, and other assorted trauma-induced symptoms.

How do you achieve legitimate, long-standing relief from negative symptoms? There are two basic ways. First, you can learn to comfort yourself enough to take the *edge off* the pain and disturbance of the symptoms; and second, you can eliminate the primary sources of your alarm reaction altogether—which also lessens the symptoms.

Let's begin with looking at ways of taking the edge off your symptoms, since that will give you the most immediate relief. By this time, I find that what most people who are trying to master the tasks of Stage I need most is immediate relief.

NORMALIZING YOUR INTERNAL RHYTHMS

Under ordinary circumstances all of us experience a kind of rhythmic ebb and flow of energy and activity level. You may have noticed, for instance, that you have a typical pattern of daily activity that begins at a certain hour, say 8:00 A.M., and then after that, about every 90 minutes or so, you feel like taking a break—at mid-morning, lunch, mid-afternoon, quitting time, dinner, etc.

Scientists who have studied the physiological pattern of these energy ups and downs call these cycles *ultradian rhythms*. In 1957 two researchers, W. Dement and N. Kleitman, found that this 90- to 120-minute cycle of activity runs in our bodies continuously throughout our twenty-four-hour day—even during sleep. They called this rhythmic pattern the *basic rest-activity cycle*.

When this basic rest-activity cycle is operating on a regular schedule, it signals the normal, healthy activity of your auto-

▲ RELAX AND RESTORE ▲

Ernest Rossi, an expert on therapeutic hypnosis, proposes in *The Psychobiology of Mind-Body Healing* that psychosomatic symptoms develop because of stress-induced distortions of the normal periodicity of ultradian cycles. He also suggests that hypnotherapy facilitates healing because it restores and normalizes the ultradian processes.

You can restore your own natural ultradian rhythms by taking a relaxation break at various intervals (60–90 minutes) throughout your day. These breaks can range from three to five minutes with good results. Practice relaxation with any method that works for you. The method of Reflective Focus is outlined in Chapter Eight. For other relaxation techniques, see Herbert Benson's *The Relaxation Response,* or Bernard Siegel's *Love, Medicine, and Miracles.*

nomic nervous system and your endocrine system. This means that the presence of ultradian rhythms is associated with the healthy functioning of your body's metabolism, hormones, and major organ systems. However, when traumatic stress occurs, the acute activation of your autonomic nervous system, in response to threat, disrupts your 90- to 120-minute basic rest-activity cycle.

Therefore, when you are experiencing a biological alarm reaction to trauma, as one does during Stage I, your ultradian rhythms are thrown off. It seems as though your normal rest periods in the cycle are reduced or eliminated, while the periods of activity or excitation in the ultradian cycle are exaggerated. This disturbance is thought by some scientists to be the key reason we develop symptoms in response to trauma.

The logic here is that when your ultradian rhythms are disturbed by traumatic events, it necessitates a disturbance in the functioning of your cell metabolism, neuron firing, hormonal secretions, and major organ activity. It is little wonder with all of this physiological upheaval and deregulation that you develop such symptoms of strain as sleep disturbance, indigestion, weight loss, depression, and aches and pains.

Now that you understand how stressful trauma disturbs your basic rest-activity cycles, it will be easy for you to see that the rest portion of your cycle is vital to your healthy recovery. Restoring your natural rhythms of *rest* and *activity* will also take the edge off your symptoms of alarm.

How can you accomplish this? There are a variety of ways to quiet and comfort your agitated rhythms so that your body cycles will evidence a rest period and promote health once again.

QUIETING COMFORTS

When a baby cries, what helps to calm the infant's distress? Being held, rocked, and fed, of course. A soothing touch, the slow rhythm of a rocking chair, or a warm breast seem to offer reassurance and the alleviation of whatever discomfort the baby was feeling.

That which gives comfort to a crying infant contains important guidelines for adults. Similar quieting techniques can benefit you, too, by giving your agitated system a moment of rest and recuperation.

You can bring relief from tension by something as simple as a warm bath. Submerging in warm water for more than five minutes produces a soothing effect. Many people find that short walks, when accompanied by pleasant, calming music, provide a quick respite from their gnarling insides. Although we still, as a culture, shy away from the idea of adults being comforted by a soothing touch, who could deny the sheer delight of a gentle back rub or an extended hug as an antidote for the distress of life's most fretful moments? It is important for you during this first stage of adjustment to be as gentle with yourself as you would be with an emotionally exhausted infant.

Follow your instincts. Have meals that remind you of pleasant, comforting times. Sleep when you are tired. To the extent that it is possible for you to do so, surround yourself with the people and conditions that reassure and calm you.

Many songs, prayers, and meditative chants have a soothing effect during times of crisis. There is a certain universal cadence, rhythm, or vibration, if you will, in that music that leads you to experience inner harmony and peace when you hear it. The

---

▲ QUIET YOUR HOME ▲

Every person and every home needs to balance times of great activity with periods of rest and reflection. This practice helps us find pause and renewal in a busy world. Whenever you feel tension building in yourself or your home, you can use music to help regain peace and attunement. Cultivate stability and joy by playing some of these musical selections:

Pachelbel—Canon in D
Grainger—Blithe Bells, Country Gardens
Grieg—Lyric Suite
Mozart—Concerto for Flute and Harp
Telemann—Flute concerti, Concerto for Three Violins and Orchestra
James Galway (soloist)—*The Magic Flute,* Annie's Song
Gluck—Dance of the Blessed Spirits
Debussy—Clair de Lune
Susann McDonald—Miscellaneous harp music
Mendelssohn—*A Midsummer Night's Dream*
Chopin—Polonaises
Tchaikovsky—Waltzes from *Sleeping Beauty, Swan Lake, The Nutcracker Suite*
Kreisler-Dvorak—Humoresque

These pieces are especially good as accompaniment to "coming down" after the day's work when loved ones come together. They are valuable in treating stress, worry, and high-strung emotional states. (Hal A. Lingerman, *The Healing Energies of Music,* p. 85)

---

mantra *om,* when repeated over and over, is a good example. When you say it out loud, repeatedly—*om, om, om*—you are reproducing the fundamental frequency of calm.

You can detect this same sound by listening to the repeated pattern in the noise of wind through the trees or the constant pounding of the ocean's surf. Try this self-calming method by listening to *your* most comforting rhythms.

A personal acquaintance, whom I'll call John, discovered his greatest comfort was from walking-and-singing jaunts during a traumatic time brought on by a divorce. John went for a walk and sang his favorite songs whenever his symptoms began to appear. He walked miles and miles alone, sometimes crying all the way. He often called me for company, and frequently we covered a sizeable territory together. John believed that his walking sing-along was key to his emotional survival. In this inventive walk he had found his own method for keeping in touch with his feelings and rhythms and for releasing his anger.

Immerse yourself

You can achieve welcome moments of respite from your crises and you can lessen your pain and induce some peace by *immersing* yourself in any activity that provides an outlet for your emotional and physical tension and that promotes the physiological rebalancing of your internal rhythms. Choose pastimes that absorb your full attention and at the same time relax you, such as

dance	music	yard work
sports	walking	movies

If you give yourself the opportunity to experience the trance-like quality that these types of activities trigger, you actually can begin to normalize your basic rest-activity cycle.

You will find that reading for pleasure is not easy during Stage I because the crisis has cut down on your ability to concentrate. That is why most people find the most benefit in activities that involve body movement.

▲ EATING CARBOHYDRATES CAN HELP YOU RELAX ▲

If you eat carbohydrates alone, without protein, more tryptophan will be made available to your brain, which will use it to make more serotonin. As a result, you will feel less stressed, less anxious, more focused and relaxed. [Judith J. Wurtman, *Managing Your Mind and Your Mood Through Food,* p. 22]

RESTORING YOUR INNER RESOURCES

If you are like most other people, Stage I also is the time when you feel as though your vital resources are in short supply. The strengths that you normally count on to help you function well—your patience, energy, optimism, and self-control—have dwindled. You lost them to the trauma itself or you have used them up trying to hang on and cope with your upside-down world. No matter what the source of your trauma, during Stage I your Personal, Partnership, and Productivity resources are usually very disturbed and severely depleted.

So, here you are, trying to survive your upheaval without your full supply of inner strengths, just when you need them the most. How are you to solve your problems if you are out of patience, motivation, and creativity? How do you expect to be able to feel happy and alive if you don't have the relationships you want and the work that satisfies you? Just when you need them most, your resources are gone.

That's why I want to teach you a mental technique that will help you to feel hopeful about the restoration of some of your lost resources. It will allow you to get the most out of the strengths you do have left, so you can at least begin the process of coping with your trauma.

▲

CONSTRUCTIVE SELF-TALK

When you spontaneously evaluate your inner strengths during Stage I, you may find that they fall short of what you want and need. For instance, after reviewing your internal resources, you may end up saying to yourself

"I *don't have enough* patience." (I've been waiting too long.)

or

"I'll *never have enough* energy to go to work, clean the house, pay the bills." (I'm feeling so depressed.)

or

"I'll *never, ever have enough* happiness to enjoy life again." (I've lost so much.)

These statements may be true, but they are very discouraging, especially during times of intense upheaval. In fact, phrases like these promote the *negative self-fulfilling prophecy* discussed in Chapter Three. Although these statements may accurately reflect how you feel, they are *not helpful.*

So what *can you do* to make the most out of your waning strengths? You can talk constructively to yourself. Tell yourself you have *"just enuff"** of the resources that you need to make *some* progress; perhaps not to reach your ultimate goals by tomorrow, but to make a positive move toward them right now. For example, you can assess your internal resource reserves and make such truthfully positive progress statements as

"I have *just enuff* patience to wait ten more minutes."

---

*I have purposely misspelled the word *enough* (enuff) so that you will be able to better remember this mental strategy.

110

or

"I have *just enuff* energy to work for one more hour."

or

"I have *just enuff* good humor to delight in this joke."

Can you see what these positive, encouraging progress statements reflect? They reflect the deficit in your *ideal amounts* of
inner strengths while they focus on what you *can do* with the
amounts remaining. This positive approach assesses what you
have left to work with, not what you have lost. Be sure to make
a list of constructive self-talk messages in your journal notes.
This will assist you in remembering and visualizing them when
you need their help.

Encouraging words

When the going gets tough you will benefit most from actually
saying to yourself, out loud, while you visualize, "I have *just
enuff* _____ to _____ ."
     (resource I need)   (reach my goal)

   Without exception, the people whom I have counseled
through the crisis stage of adjusting to major change have
found this subtle mental reframing process invaluable to their
progress. In Stage I, perhaps more than during any of the
other stages, you need to engage in constructive self-talk. You
need to *encourage*, not *discourage* yourself. You have to believe
that you have the inner resources you need to stay in the game.
With this foundation, you can feel enough in charge of yourself
to challenge yourself to meet your tragedy.

"JUST ENUFF" LOVE

The following brief story illustrates how powerful this simple
just enuff perspective can be in reducing the inner turmoil of
crisis. Last year during the break time in one of my seminars,

I spoke with an aerospace engineer in his fifties. He was a man with a strong love of family who was struggling with mid-life fulfillment. He told me that he was at a very low point in his struggle.

For twenty years Joe had been married to a woman he respected, but did not love. In their mid-forties, as a couple, they agreed to divorce. Joe immediately sought a new relationship and married a much younger woman. She left him only three years later.

"You know, Dr. Cramer, I've got it all," Joe told me. "The house in the suburbs, the pool, the cars, the club memberships, a solid career, fulfilling work. I have it all except someone to share it with. I don't have enough love in my life and I don't know what to do."

I responded by encouraging this dejected gentleman to refocus his evaluation. "What do you have '*just enuff*' love and support in your life to accomplish now?" I asked. "Do your connections with other people provide you with friendships, or intellectual collegiality, or companionship?"

During this line of questioning, Joe began to realize how many relationships he *did* have. He seemed almost surprised. And the realization that he did have some relationships of value gave him confidence. It held out some promise that he could look forward to developing an in-depth, loving relationship in the future.

Naturally our brief exchange did not solve all of Joe's problems, but he did feel more hopeful and motivated to pursue his goals. Why not do what Joe did and look at which inner strengths are present and working for you, instead of concentrating on what is missing as a result of your trauma? Encouraging yourself about your inner resources will help you calm your internal crisis. The resources you do have left will become clearer to you as you learn the next skill critical to Stage I, minimizing threats and maximizing challenges.

▲

THE REWARDS OF CRISIS

As a foundation for learning how to skillfully turn your attention from the *threats* of a situation to the *challenges* it provides, let's consider a couple of ancient meanings of the word *crisis*.

In the Chinese language, which is written in ideograms, the symbol for the word *crisis* denotes a *"moment of danger and of opportunity."* Through this symbol, the Chinese communicate that every crisis is a paradox, a true representation of the duality of our temporal lives. Where crisis offers danger, in threatening our vital resources, it becomes the dangerous *enemy*—a perspective that will trigger your *fight* or *flight* responses. But crisis also offers you an opportunity to feel challenged, to grow, and to master its requirements. And in this way, crisis is an *ally*.

With the vantage point of challenge you couple yourself to the momentum of the crisis, you flow with it and direct it toward results that will restore your health and happiness. Thus, in crisis, the perspective of challenge coexists with the perspective of threat but stands in stark contrast in terms of its consequences. It is critical for successful coping that the perspective of challenge prevail. But how do you achieve and maintain the challenge perspective?

The Greek meaning of the word *crisis* is *"moment of judgment,"* a helpful denotation because it emphasizes that crisis is a moment of choice. When you face crisis, you make a judgment about whether to concentrate on the dangers or on the opportunities. You may not even be aware that you have a choice of perspective during trauma, but it is true that you do. If we combine the Chinese and the Greek meanings, the implications of these two messages inherent in the word *crisis* are intriguing. The combined message becomes: *During trauma, you will encounter both danger and opportunity and you are free to choose your point of focus.*

Although both of these focal points are equally rational, you know by now that if you select the perspective of threat that encourages fighting or fleeing the enemy, you will strain and damage yourself. However, if you selectively engage opportunities and create challenges, you will be resilient and grow stronger through trauma.

Learning how to shift from threat to challenge also relates to recent research findings made by Susanne Kobasa and her associates concerning highly stressed executives—some of whom remained healthy and some who suffered debilitating illness. Kobasa found that executives who felt *challenged, not threatened,* by their traumatic circumstances remained healthy.

If you will recall, Kobasa's landmark study revealed two other characteristics associated with the healthy highly stressed executives: *a sense of control over their own reactions* and *a strong commitment to self, work, and family.*

Dr. Kobasa has published profiles of these stress-resilient and *hardy* executives. She has also published characterizations of the non-hardy types.

Reprinted here are two of the executive interviews that were part of Dr. Kobasa's study at Illinois Bell Telephone. The first report characterizes someone low on hardiness traits; the second describes someone who exhibits a high degree of hardiness. As you read these cases, you will get a good impression of how a sense of control, commitment, and challenge manifests itself during times of trauma.

Case Description 1:
A Low-Hardiness Executive

"I'm thinking of making a major change; I'm thinking of leaving the phone company and going to this little electronics company that's a much more risky operation, and I figure if what you're going to do is free, I'll come and get the advice. Maybe it'll be helpful." This man's protocol showed high stress and high illness. He was only in his thirties, but he had hypertension, peptic ulcer, and migraine headaches: many symptoms as well as diseases.

What stands out from his personality questionnaire is *alienation, not only from himself but also from other people. He also shows some low control, but the main factor is the alienation, the lack of commitment that is striking.*

He arrives forty-five minutes late, trench coat flying behind him, papers under his arm. Then he makes a beeline for my secretary's desk and begins calling people. He's got to call many people to let them know where he's going to be in the next forty-five minutes, while I'm in my office waiting, hearing all these phone calls. He comes in and I've prepared what's going to be a fairly difficult conversation with him about his alienation from other people, but it's difficult to do that because the phone keeps ringing and every time it does he jumps up because he's convinced it's for him and he can't talk in my office so he has to run out to the secretary's office. This happens three times and we're not getting anywhere.

He says to me, "Look, I really need to take all these calls, they're very crucial. But you may have something here. So why don't you talk into my tape recorder?" So he pulls out a tape recorder, puts it on my desk and says, "I'll listen to it at night when I have a chance."

Case Description 2:
A High-Hardiness Executive

Bill B. is the kind of person who has an immediately reassuring effect on those around him. At fifty-five years of age *he has a twinkle in his eye and an easy, relaxed manner.* He seems to have all the time in the world as he asks the interviewer what the research is about and how it is done. *All the details seem interesting to him.*

When he begins to describe his work at the phone company, the curiosity he has for what he does not know shades over into *zest* for the familiar. He embellishes his descriptions, all the while making his role in planning commercial telephone services come alive. Although he has a *clear sense of the importance of broader social issues* concerning his work, and certainly feels that his role requires innovative planning, *it is the moment-to-moment activities of the day that intrigue him the most.* He claims to *learn fairly continuously,* even when the task appears at first to be routine.

When asked his views about the company reorganization, he expresses a clear sense of the magnitude of the changes in the offing. But he shows no signs of the panic we saw in other subjects. He is not more certain than they are about what the changes will mean for him specifically. But he is so involved and interested in the evolutionary process going on that he almost welcomes it. *Whatever his new role turns out to be, he is sure he will find a way to make it meaningful and worthwhile.* He recognizes the hard work and possible frustrations involved in the company's reorganization, but he treats it all in a day's work. He looks forward to rolling up his sleeves, working hard and learning new things—he is involved with the company and wants to help with its reorganization.

Bill's wife died seven years ago in an accident while they were on vacation. He can still evoke the pain and shock of that unfortunate event. Her death depressed him for more than a year, though he showed few signs of guilt. He missed her more than he felt guilty. . . . Since his wife's death, Bill has lived alone. Although this was difficult at first, he has long since developed a satisfying routine. When he wants company, he invites friends for a meal he enjoys cooking, or visits his children or grandchildren. Often, however, he spends time alone, reading or building furniture, and does not feel lonely. . . . *He enjoys satisfying social interactions yet is not bored when alone. Even when he relaxes, he finds much in himself and the passing scene that is of interest.*

Reflecting on the early part of his married life, Bill recounted some fortunate and unfortunate events—his son's hernia operation, the deaths of his grandparents, a fire in the family home. Although he discusses these events vividly, *he experiences them as part of life, the things that helped make him the person he is now. He sees the negative and positive events in balance, the regrets mitigated by the satisfactions. . . .*

Bill remains basically quite healthy. Signs of mental and physical strain are mild to nonexistent. Despite the reactively high number of symptoms typical of people in his age category, Bill has avoided a serious illness. [emphasis added]

Can you see yourself in either of these two characterizations? Hopefully you are more in line with Bill B. than with the first man described. But no matter how you rate yourself now, it is part of your foundation to realize that you can bolster your hardiness quotient—and therefore your stress resistance and resilience—by learning how to shift out of a mental stance of threat into one of challenge.

YOU ARE WHAT YOU THINK

In the wake of a traumatic upheaval you have two mental options. Take a look at the accompanying diagram. It offers a vivid representation of your fundamental interpretive choice in evaluating the demand of any life-altering change.

Review the Dynamic Model of Traumatic Change. Notice the major steps involved. Be certain that you understand the important role that perception plays in setting your course toward self-enhancement or self-diminishment.

Remember, in any stressful situation the prospect of *challenge* is just as real as the prospect of *threat,* even though you may not readily be able to identify the challenges. The challenges will become apparent when you find in your trauma the opportunities that exist alongside the dangers. When you are able to see both, they will be distinct focal points: positive aspects that foster *challenge* and negative factors that spawn *threat.* If you want to empower yourself to grow stronger and healthier, I will show you a procedure that will help you to maintain a primary focus on the challenging, positive aspects of your crisis.

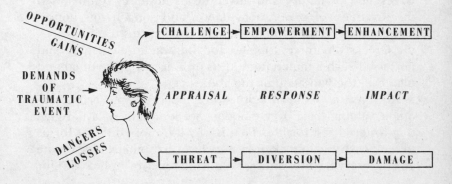

OPPORTUNITIES GAINS → CHALLENGE → EMPOWERMENT → ENHANCEMENT

DEMANDS OF TRAUMATIC EVENT → APPRAISAL   RESPONSE   IMPACT

DANGERS LOSSES → THREAT → DIVERSION → DAMAGE

YOUR CHALLENGE OPTION

Think of perceiving the challenge of your crisis as bringing into play your inborn attraction to seek positive pressure. This type of rewarding stress has been called by several theorists, including Hans Selye, *eustress*. Eustress is associated with the excitement and thrill of victory. It is the pressure of victory that turns people on. It releases energy. It electrifies life with positive feelings of joy, hope, and happiness that stem from a challenge well met. It stands in stark contrast to the *distress* factors of anxiety, anger, and depression that are associated with the threats of great loss and disappointment.

I believe the pursuit of eustress overwhelmingly helps you to unlock your reservoirs of motivation to be challenged during times of upheaval. Your capacity to engage in a positive partnership with trauma, through perceiving what you stand to gain from the situation, is the key to your success. And just remember, your drive to pursue the challenges of trauma is a drive as natural and instinctive as the drive to ward off threat. Because this is so, it's just a matter of emphasizing your drive to seek eustress and de-emphasizing your fixation on fending off the distress in your trauma.

Historically this human urge to take productive action—this fire in your belly to meet the demands of any challenge—is characterized in mythology as Dionysianism. Dionysus, the Greek god of nature and adventurous impulse, commanded the invention of celebration, dance, and song in his honor. Greek theater is said to have emerged from this tradition. For the Greeks this force, this lust for life, was so elemental, and possessed such a momentum of its own, it was personified and placed in the Pantheon of the gods.

However, as Western culture developed an intellectual tradition valuing logic over emotion, we lost sight of a heritage that fostered zest for life. That is why it is more difficult for us to seek eustress, to make the pursuit of happiness a legitimate goal in everyday life, much less during times of upheaval. Our culture breeds in us a stronger tendency to repel the thunderstorm than to search for the silver lining.

> The mind is its own place, and in itself
> Can make a heav'n of hell, a hell of heav'n.
>
> —John Milton, *Paradise Lost*

What you are learning here not only often goes against your instinct to be threatened by trauma, it also flies in the face of an intellectual tradition that promotes the fixing of problems over the seeking out of opportunities. You will need to train yourself carefully. Take as example of learning over instinct a driver on an icy road. When the car begins skidding on ice, the driver can choose to fight the slide or turn into it. Inexperienced teenage drivers invariably fight the skid, hit the brakes, and end up flying in circles all over the road. But with experience the mature driver learns to make the life-saving choice automatically. This retraining of your natural instincts is what you are after in Stage I.

A FOCUS ON SUCCESS

Let me give another illustration of how pressure-filled situations always offer two distinct perceptual paths of threat and challenge. As you read the following recapitulation of how a client of mine viewed the stress of a lifelong ambition come true, put yourself in *his shoes* so you can fully appreciate his dilemma.

Late one morning David waited motionless behind the curtain in a brightly illuminated corporate television studio in Cupertino, California. Finally he heard the voice of the announcer say, "Ladies and gentlemen, it is my pleasure to introduce you to our commentator for this program on how to manage the marketplace, David Washburn." David took a deep breath. He was about to host his first hour-long, live telecast. In seconds he would walk out on the stage to perform before a live studio audience of four hundred and for nine thousand cable viewers scattered in offices throughout the country. What great exposure for his message.

This event was full of pressure because it signaled a turning point in David's career. If he performed well, he would take a big step forward. If he performed poorly, his career would be set back severely. David's moment of awareness of his risky circumstances caused two mental currents to explode inside him simultaneously, *threat* and *challenge*. He was threatened by the possibility that he might fail, while the chance that he would excel fueled his momentum and challenged him.

As David stepped out of his safe hiding place, he could feel the threat and challenge at war inside him. In one vision he saw himself tripping over his words and losing his train of thought. Laying an egg! Bombing! Simultaneously he imagined his verbal fluency, heard his own eloquence exciting the crowd with his message.

David could only wonder which image would prove true. If the current of threat won out, he would want to run. It would take all the energy he could muster to resist the fear and the flight. But if the feeling of challenge prevailed, he would be filled with enthusiasm. He would engage the momentum of the challenge to putting all his effort into communicating with his audience.

> If you think you can or
> you think you can't,
> you're right.
> —attributed to Henry Ford

That memorable morning, as he accepted the microphone and scanned the crowd, David reported to me, he intentionally zeroed in on his possibilities for success. He refused the temptation to dwell on any aspect of threat. If the lavaliere microphone went dead, or the cue cards fell over, or technicians scurried around behind the cameras ignoring his efforts, it would make no difference. He decided to focus on his enthusiasm and use his experience to amuse and inform the audience. As as result of his ability to direct his mental focus, David delivered his message beautifully under difficult circumstances. He met his challenge.

In any traumatic situation, you can choose the current of thought that will serve as your focal point. It is your major task in the first stage of self-empowerment. If you select the current of threat, you will set yourself up for losing ground. If you decide for the current of challenge, you set yourself up for advancement.

FEELING CHALLENGED IS MORE DIFFICULT THE GREATER THE JEOPARDY OF THE TRAUMA

It was not uncommon for our grandparents to remain in one job for their entire working career. But in contemporary culture, buy-outs and corporate mergers have made sudden job termination an everyday occurrence in the work force. We naturally focus on the threatening aspects first: lack of income, lost security, low self-esteem, and more. But losing a job has opportunities and a challenging side also. More and more people are realizing that if it hadn't been for losing a job, they would never have considered branching out to a new, more stimulating career, or found an employer that better matched their needs. *Even though the opportunities are difficult to discover sometimes, change always provides some aspects of challenge that lead eventually to real gains.*

▲ OPTIMISM LEADS TO BETTER
COPING AND BETTER HEALTH ▲

If you tend to look on the bright side of things and you usually expect things to go your way, you can consider yourself an optimist. Michael F. Scheier of Carnegie-Mellon University and Charles S. Carver of the University of Miami have been studying the impact of being optimistic on coping and on health for the past decade. They have concluded from their studies that when people who are optimists are under stress they engage in effective problem solving and seek support from others more often than pessimists do. These two positive coping behaviors lead to better health.

To challenge yourself is the first step in gaining benefit from adversity. It begins in Stage I, when the impact of life-altering change is at its height. As you feel the shock and disorientation of any change, your adrenaline will flow freely. You will feel the demand to adapt to the situation intensely. This is exactly the time to begin looking for ways to challenge yourself. Knowing what you might gain from a situation in this early stage will give you a sense of direction.

EVALUATE YOUR ADRENALINE IMPACT

You may know almost immediately whether you are focusing on the threatening or challenging aspects of a stressful event. However, if your attention is consumed by *what* is happening to you, you may forget to monitor your own reactions. This over-reliance on external focus can lead to unwanted and unnecessary complications. Therefore, during the stress of upheavals, assess your mental perspective as quickly as possible. Only then can you ensure that you will choose to be challenged (the mental perspective that yields progress).

How do you perform this evaluation? I have devised a short questionnaire you can use to evaluate your perspective on any crisis (see p. 124). Fill out the questionnaire a few times. Then you won't need to use it directly anymore. You will find that you can complete your self-evaluation mentally and jot down a record of your assets and liabilities in your journal every week or so.

Answer each item on the self-test in terms of how you are *currently* reacting to Stage I of your trauma. You will see that the questions are divided into two columns, one marked *Adrenaline Assets* and the other *Adrenaline Liabilities.* The asset items correspond to the impact of taking a challenge perspective; the liability items reflect the impact of assuming a perspective of threat. My research indicates that these two types of adrenaline impact are distinct from each other.

Remember to rate yourself in terms of how you are reacting to a specific traumatic circumstance. Do not use this questionnaire to assess your response to life in general. Your self-evaluation results will be most helpful to your recovery plan if they reflect your disposition relative to your stressful trauma only.

Your scores on these dimensions allow you to calculate the relative effects of your judgments on challenge and threat for specific stressful circumstances. Your goal is to maximize your view of the challenges and to minimize your concentration on the threats in order to progress through Stage I and move on to more growth and fulfillment. If your quotient of liabilities is *moderate to substantial,* you will intentionally want to shift your perspective away from threat and focus it toward challenge. I have devised an effective way for you to accomplish that important shift.

HOW TO TURN "THREATS" INTO "CHALLENGES"

Now we are ready to begin the heart of your Stage I skill building. It is time for you to learn a systematic way of shifting away from threat toward challenge. *You will use this system over and over again in later stages whenever you feel more threatened than*

SELF-EVALUATION OF ADRENALINE IMPACT

Scoring key:

   AA—Almost always
   O —Often
   S —Sometimes
   R —Rarely
   AN—Almost never

Instructions:

   Circle the number that reflects how frequently you experience these Adrenaline Assets and Adrenaline Liabilities.

Adrenaline Assets	AA	O	S	R	AN		*Adrenaline Liabilities*	AA	O	S	R	AN
A. Enthusiasm	5	4	3	2	1		J. Frustration	5	4	3	2	1
B. Hopefulness	5	4	3	2	1		K. Anxiety	5	4	3	2	1
C. Motivation	5	4	3	2	1		L. Resentment	5	4	3	2	1
D. High energy	5	4	3	2	1		M. Fatigue	5	4	3	2	1
E. Stamina	5	4	3	2	1		N. Muscle tension	5	4	3	2	1
F. Resilience	5	4	3	2	1		O. Hyperactivity	5	4	3	2	1
G. Creativity	5	4	3	2	1		P. Worry	5	4	3	2	1
H. Concentration	5	4	3	2	1		Q. Indecisiveness	5	4	3	2	1
I. Clear priorities	5	4	3	2	1		R. Self-criticism	5	4	3	2	1

Adrenaline Assets
Total Score   _____
    (Add up your points A–1)

Adrenaline Liabilities
Total Score   _____
    (Add up your points J–R)

Interpretation

36–45: Assets Excellent
21–35: Assets Moderate
 9–20: Assets Minimal

Interpretation

36–45: Liabilities Substantial
21–35: Liabilities Moderate
 9–20: Liabilities Minimal

challenged by your circumstances. The skills at each stage of adjustment are not confined only to that stage; they are to be applied and reapplied all along your way to restoring health and happiness.

You will see that your progress does not always follow a linear path forward. You will experience setbacks. It is natural. Do not let it dishearten you because you will know what to do to regain your forward momentum.

Whenever you feel threat overcoming challenge, review my description of the three-step process for turning threats into challenges and then work through each step in your journal notes.

Step 1: Reveal the Dangers

The process of shifting out of a mental zone of threat into a mental zone of challenge begins with asking and answering the questions that confront the source of your trouble. It is important to give the devil his due before attempting to focus on the positive side of your trauma. Those questions are probably some variation and combination of the following:

"What is disturbing me?"
"What are the dangers?"
"What are my losses?"

If you zero in on and thoroughly examine the very real sources of threat, you will be able to isolate and confront exactly the aspects of the trauma that trigger fear and anger. Most of us think we *know* what frightens us and makes us angry about a trauma, but we rarely fully understand our negative emotions until we scrutinize their sources. This scrutiny and resultant understanding will make you feel in charge of yourself; at the very least, you will understand yourself and your situation better. Those insights are a good foundation for productive action.

I recommend that you do this self-investigation privately and then talk it over with a trusted friend or, ideally, with a professional counselor. On your own, you can write down your fears and hostilities and what is triggering them. For example, when his spouse died, one of my clients wrote in his journal:

What Is Disturbing Me?

"I am scared that I will be alone."
"I am angry that my wife suffered."
"I am resentful that medicine couldn't save her."
"I've lost faith that God is fair."
"I have no more desire to go on."

Emotions like these are legitimate and natural, so their existence must be acknowledged. Unless you register your truly disturbing feelings, they will have you in their clutches and continue to generate alarm signals.

Once you give them some *expression* in writing or in conversation, they lose some of their power to hurt you. In effect, you have released the fright and anger from deep inside of you, given them form in words, and then *expressed* them. The Latin root of the word *express, expressus,* means "push or force out." This definition can remind you that once you have expressed your feelings, they are not inside, but outside you, where they do less damage and don't hurt so much. And so you can see them more clearly and actually let them go or let them be.

As a case in point about how it can be a source of renewal for you to ventilate your feelings, I will tell you about another person who suffered the sudden loss of her husband.

Martha spent many bleak, wrenching hours literally screaming and swearing that if life got no better for her, she was going to end it all and find out if things would be better on the *other side.*

Any talk of suicide, or the thought of suicide, is always serious and calls for immediate professional help. But, as it turned out for Martha, this way of ranting at the universe in Stage I of her painful loss became her emotional salvation. Martha had such deep resentment and rage at losing her husband that she absolutely had to express it or it would have devoured her.

By volubly expressing her most violent emotions, Martha relaxed her worn-out system and sank into a period of incubation that led eventually to her renewed trust in and enthusiasm for life. If you need to expel such ravaging emotions, be certain, as Martha did, that you have help from a competent professional. If you have less volatile feelings, you can afford to sort them out for yourself in your journal entries and in conversations with trusted friends.

Just remember that once you have realized the sources of your disturbance; once you admit that you are frightened and angry—and justifiably so—you will come to the point of wondering what you can do about it. You could dwell on your troubles and tragedies, but wouldn't you rather find some more rewarding activity?

It's up to you. If you feel strongly attracted to focusing on the threats and troubles—those things about the situation that are scaring you and making you mad—go ahead and explore them until you are weary of them. Just as a child can only have a tantrum for so long, you will run out of energy for examining the *enemy*. And, as soon as you do, you will know that it is time to make a shift.

Step 2: Identify Opportunities

Now continue your process of shifting away from threat toward the focus of challenge. Ask yourself, "In light of my trauma,

WHAT ARE MY
POSSIBILITIES
AND
OPPORTUNITIES

for growing, for learning, for becoming wiser, stronger, healthier, more loving, and more productive? In essence, what key resources can I seek out of this crisis? What benefits and gains are hidden in my trauma?"

My client whose wife died answered Step 2 questions like this:

What Are My Opportunities?

"I can learn to be more independent."   (Personal Resource)

"I can celebrate my fortunate past."   (Personal Resource)

"I can search for new ways to love."   (Partnership Resource)

"I can feel a strong connection, even in separation."   (Partnership Resource)

"I can find more meaning in my life."   (Productivity Resource)

The responses to Step 2 will vary from person to person.

Your responses and point of view toward the possibilities hidden in your loss experience, in your trauma, are the only *right* answers. But sometimes other people's input can help. Someone else may not be as blind as you are to the rewards intrinsic in your traumatic stress situation. But be sure that you focus only on those rewards that *ring true* with you. No matter what another person thinks is valuable, you must sense that value, too. Otherwise, it will not work as a positive force for you.

Step 3: Challenging Yourself

Out of your opportunities and your possibilities come your challenges. In pursuit of *opportunities, challenge* yourself; your *benefits* will always call you to action.

In this third and final step, ask yourself to complete the phrase "In light of my opportunities, what if I were to _____ ."
(Action) Steps)
The answers of my client whose wife died flowed like this:

CHALLENGING MYSELF

In light of my opportunity to	What if I were to
be independent	live alone for at least six months?
celebrate my past	review picture albums and letters for their joyful memories?
search for new love	become a Big Brother to a child in need?
feel connected in separation	meditate each day on my continuing awareness of my spouse?
invest more meaning in my life	volunteer to help the cancer society?

You will need to generate a hypothetical action for each of the opportunities that is associated with your trauma.

Let me emphasize that the answers you develop in Step 3 are only *possible action steps*. Your answers and actions must remain dormant for a while. These possible actions are only meant to give you a sense of direction right now, as well as the hope that in the not-so-distant future you will be able to act. These thoughts provide a feeling of positive momentum. DO NOT ACT NOW! In fact, during Stage I you have *JUST ENUFF* energy to do *positive thinking* about your options. Be assured that the capacity to glimpse opportunities is more than ENUFF.

At this juncture in your progress, notice that Step 3 in the process presents you with prospective challenges you may engage in if you wish. Step 2 is the step that ignites your Dionysian spirit, that excites you about the possibility that you can grow and gain from your painful adversity. Feel the benefit of challenging yourself to seek your opportunities and possibilities.

YOUR OWN PERSONAL SHIFT

Now that you have learned the three-step process of turning threats into challenges, you can begin to progress. Some people find it helpful when they feel threatened to go through the three steps mentally and ask themselves:

STEP 1: What is troubling me? Scaring me? Making me angry now?

STEP 2: What possibilities and opportunities do I see for myself now? How can I benefit?

STEP 3: What if I were to _____ ?
(Action Steps)

I highly recommend that you try this internal dialogue each time you feel a bout of anger, fear, disillusionment, or sadness coming on.

COACH YOURSELF

You can be a good coach for your own progress during Stage I, by repeating a statement such as "I choose to be challenged," whenever you feel yourself slipping back into the disturbing position of feeling threatened by your trauma. Repeating such a statement both out loud and silently will bring you the encouragement you need to *let go* of your preoccupation with the situation's inherent dangers. It will also point you in the direction that has the most momentum: the direction that focuses you on the opportunities hidden in your crisis.

ONGOING CHALLENGES

Use your Empowerment Journal to keep an ongoing log of your shifts from feeling threatened to feeling challenged. You will find that over time your understanding of those shifts will deepen.

Set up a chart, or charts, like the one shown here. With every entry you will become more aware and in control of your negative feelings and more capable of distinguishing opportunities and challenges.

Resources	Minimizing Threats (What is disturbing me?)	Maximizing Opportunities (What are my opportunities to benefit?)	What-If Statements (Possible action steps?)
Personal			
Productivity			
Partnership			

Many of my clients make entries on this chart even in much later stages of adjustment and growth. This may be the case with you, too; people can only deal with a threat—and an opportunity to be challenged—when they are ready to do so. Your capacity to deal with progressively more threatening and challenging aspects of your trauma will increase as you become healthier and happier.

Remember to use these three steps *whenever* you need to. Now let's look at how a woman whose world had been shattered by a mid-life marital crisis managed to turn her threats into challenges.

A CASE OF MID-LIFE TRAUMA

Emily was a fiftyish mother of eight when she first ventured out of the house and into the workaday world. She had an alcoholic husband who had finally agreed to move out. At about the same time her husband left, Emily went on an initial round of job interviews. The world as she once knew it was over, forever. Emily felt afraid.

During the first stage of her traumatic shift in life-style, Emily was nagged by self-doubt. Some days she would wake up threatened by being middle-aged and lacking work experience. She was strongly tempted to stay in the house, or even in bed, on those days. Her at-home life-style beckoned her like a comfortable *cocoon.*

On other mornings she would be terrorized by the thought that her decision to seek a career might trigger a destructive flare-up of alcoholic behavior in her husband that would jeopardize her child-support payments. Each of these sources of threat was real for Emily, so that is where we began our work together. We examined her threats before we looked for her opportunities. Per my formula the first question to be answered was the following one:

What is disturbing about the situation?

When Emily asked herself that question, she found that she feared feeling guilty and responsible for provoking her husband to drink. As we examined the fear more closely Emily realized that she didn't have to be accountable either for protecting her husband or fixing his alcoholism. It was his problem to manage, not hers. She had plenty to handle just taking care of herself.

Emily also identified a growing *fear of failing* in answer to the question: What is blocking you from feeling good about seeking a new job? Revealing this specific fear helped Emily to realize that her alternative to failing at a career was to *die on the vine* at home. Once she saw that alternative, it was even more frightening to her than job failure, and she felt propelled to take the risks associated with finding a career niche. Seeking out a career would help her to minimize the greater threat of having an empty life.

The second step, of turning a threat into a challenge, involved asking another question:

What are the opportunities to benefit in light of the circumstances?

As Emily and I pressed on in Stage I of her adjustment process, she identified multiple opportunities present in her job search: establishing new goals, learning new skills, increasing self-worth, providing additional income, and gaining respect from others. They became Emily's focal points for challenge. When she reminded herself of the benefits associated with her job search, it took on an attractive and exciting quality.

She challenged herself into Step 3, which, you will recall, is to complete a phrase.

If these are my opportunities, what if I were to _____ ?

Step 3 is a call to action. If you will brainstorm the possible action steps in light of the opportunities, you will have a list of strategic moves you can make. Emily's list of *what if*s looked something like this:

CHALLENGING MYSELF

In light of my opportunity to	What if I were to
earn more income	assess my current career skills?
improve my self-image	identify my interests and talents?
learn new skills	participate in retraining?
set new goals	prepare a five-year plan?
gain respect from others	network with key, influential people?

Once Emily broke her fixation on her fears and saw instead her actual opportunities, her list of *what-if* action steps came quickly. As she developed the list, she gave the steps a priority ranking. Of course some of Emily's *what if*s might turn out to be rewarding, but others might be dead ends. Of real importance to Emily was that she was spending her energy to maximize her challenges and to minimize her threats. This is the essential work of Stage I.

THE RESISTANCE FACTOR

The cases I have reviewed with you so far have demonstrated how you can move smoothly through the prescribed steps out of threats into challenges. You may find in practice, however, that it is not easy for you to negotiate the steps. The first is especially difficult. You may even think that you have eliminated or minimized your fear and anger over the threatening aspects of your situation when in reality you have only momentarily *resisted* facing them squarely. The temptation to deny or to mask in some way the threats of a trauma rather confront them and examine your apprehension and hostility is human. If you are tempted, go back and do Step 1 again.

CONFRONT THE DANGER

It can be very difficult to be patient and persistent enough to confront such dark nights of the soul. When we encounter a crisis, we always wish we could resolve it immediately, for we desperately want it to be over. We yearn to get on with living in ordinary, familiar, and safer times. So, we look for shortcuts. We attempt to quell the crisis by treating it as an *enemy* to be annihilated or fled. We resist becoming a *partner* of the trauma, and we refuse to acknowledge both its true dangers and its opportunities.

As I highlighted in Chapter Two, this tendency to treat

trauma as the *enemy* is harmful; it puts you in a position of helplessness, wherein you act as either a victim or an aggressor. Most people have a tendency either to treat trauma as an *enemy* or *resist* coming to terms with it. Whichever your tendency is, you'll see that it influences you off and on during Stage I.

When these occasional internal contests between your *helplessness* and your *hero*—between your drive to avoid, escape, and ward off the dangers and your drive to approach, engage, and take advantage of opportunities—occur, your internal resources (Personal, Productivity, and Partnership) will be devastated. You will just have to have confidence that you will rebuild whatever resources you will need in later stages.

▲ FREEDOM IS JUST ANOTHER WORD FOR ▲ NOTHING LEFT TO LOSE

If you are free enough to act independently of your environment, you will possess great stability in the face of deprivation, failure, and loss.

The humanistic school of psychology, represented by such theorists as Rollo May, Carl Rogers, Erich Fromm, and Abraham Maslow, espouses the view that a sense of autonomy contributes to self-esteem and that both help one to remain strong and healthy in the face of hardship.

ARE YOU READY FOR STAGE II?

You will welcome the signals that tell you that you are ready for Stage II. One day you will realize that you want to look to the gains of the future more than you want to dwell on the losses of the past. You will feel yourself locking into focus on *challenge* and overriding your preoccupation with *threat*.

How will you know for certain that you are ready? By comparing how you once felt and acted out of threat with how you feel and behave now out of challenge. The following lists will help you to distinguish whether you have indeed chosen to be challenged and are ready to move on to Stage II.

	DYNAMICS OF THREATS	DYNAMICS OF CHALLENGES
Perspective	Trauma as the "Enemy"	Trauma as a "Challenge"
Assumptions	The world is doing it to me.	I am the author of my life.
Dynamic	<u>Me</u> against the trauma. Combative/Passive Resisting Self-diminishment	<u>Me</u> joined with the trauma. Cooperative/Progressive Empowering Self-enhancement
Role	Victim or Aggressor	Master and Champion
Experiences	Angry Fearful Ineffective Helpless Rejecting Resentful Annoyed Anxious Lonely Burdened Detached Hopeless Exhausted	Excited Courageous Competent Powerful/Potent Accepting Appreciative Enthusiastic Serene In Partnership Gifted Involved Hopeful Energetic

Evaluate yourself according to each list of dynamics. Count the characteristics you recognize in yourself that stem from a challenge approach to trauma. Compare those to the characteristics in you that result from approaching trauma as a threat.

If you have more challenge characteristics than you have threat characteristics, you are ready to move ahead to the next stage in your process of advancement and growth. If you still need to subdue your experiences of threat, go back through the exercises in this chapter as often as necessary. *You will want to return to the strategies for calming your inner crisis and for eliminating your focus on threats whenever you notice that you have alarm signals or any of the experiences of threat.* This can happen at any time during your adjustment process—even up until the final stages.

The experience of challenge also continues throughout the process of coping and growth. You will encounter more and more challenging aspects of your ordeal as you progress. They will always enliven you. During Stage I they inspired you to

READINESS SIGNALS

☐1. seek your inner balance.

☐2. have confidence that you can eventually grow stronger and healthier.

☐3. feel more in control of yourself again.

Now you are ready for Stage II.

7

▲

Discovering
What Is Real

As you enter Stage II, you will have a well-earned sense of accomplishment at having survived the upheaval and crisis atmosphere of Stage I. Your achievements during that initial phase of adjustment were truly remarkable. Praise yourself for having chosen to be challenged, not threatened, every time you felt burdened or beaten by your trauma.

You have made a courageous beginning. You've said *yes* to living and growing stronger when it might have been easier for you to say *yes* to dropping out and giving up. You have refused the temptation to wallow in your disappointment or to feel bitter and resentful because fate struck you an unfair blow. Now you are tapped into your own inner power.

▲

THE REWARD OF CHALLENGING YOURSELF: ENTERING STAGE II

You tapped into your inner power by learning how to shift out of a perspective of threat into a perspective of challenge. Having mastered the process, you are able to shift from threat to challenge whenever you need to do so. Throughout Stage II you will again have confrontations with what is threatening you. One reward for using the shifting method to remain challenged during Stage II is that your perspective on challenge keeps you moving closer to restoring your health and happiness. In turn, your forward momentum gives you a sense of progress and self-control. It is in Stage II that you begin to sense that you have a grip on yourself and on your life again, even if only in small measure.

Another reward for having successfully coped with Stage I is relief from its constant tension and internal turmoil. You'll have fewer sleepless nights and bouts of anger and tears to endure. You are calming down inside.

In the beginning of Stage II, you will notice that you are already more curious about how to take advantage of this *new world* your trauma has enabled you to fashion. In fact, the most common question you will ask at this stage is "*What now?*" Back in Stage I you were asking yourself "*Why me?*"

The difference in those questions is one of the hallmarks of growing past Stage I into Stage II. Stage II signals a shift away from focusing on the *why*s of past events to concentrating on the *what now*s of present circumstances. You will notice that you are beginning to wonder exactly how this *new world* of yours works. As your curiosity builds, you will explore how you might restore the resources your trauma depleted. You will sense that you are more capable now of knowing which routes to inner balance your trauma closed off and which remain available to you.

So now, just as you did in Stage I, begin to master this new phase of adjustment by reviewing your scorecard. See what is in store for you mentally, physically, and emotionally. Preview the goals you will accomplish during this period, and discover the time frame for completing Stage II as well as the primary coping resources you will need. (See page 66 for the complete Self-Empowerment Scorecard.)

SELF-EMPOWERMENT SCORECARD				
		Stage II Exploration		
Mental and Emotional Reactions		Confusion, Curiosity, Risk, Clarity, Direction		
Goals		To confront rules of the new reality		
Sample Time Frame for Mastery		8–12 weeks		
Demands on Adaptive Energy		Moderate		
Primary Adjustment Assets		Curiosity		

CREATING MENTAL COMPARTMENTS

As you can see from the scorecard guidelines, you begin to focus on the present in Stage II. Your burgeoning curiosity about learning the rules of your new reality is your motivation. Your curiosity sparks a spontaneity in your thinking and imagining during Stage II that makes it easier for you to concentrate on the here and now.

That special mental process of which I speak is the creation of separate *mental compartments* for each of your worlds—one for the old and one for the new. Because you are now ready to close out an outdated episode of your life and to open up and explore current options, you will feel yourself doing mental gymnastics. You will notice that gradually you begin to let go of your focus on the past by relegating memories to a compartment you have mentally sealed off. Your past life experience cannot invade the boundaries of your here and now.

Let me illustrate how this process works by recounting the story of how one person found herself creating separate mental compartments for the past and present.

BLIND ALLEYS OF THE PAST

On February 22, 1987, Joyce found out that she had cancer. Up until that time, she had enjoyed an energetic life filled with the demands of an exciting career and a growing family. Joyce was an accomplished actress. She performed in a repertory company that toured to many cities. As a result, Joyce was away from her husband and two teenaged children for weeks at a time. She was devoted to her career, but disliked the fact that she had to sacrifice a normal home life to develop her talents.

Joyce had always made certain that she took enough breaks in her schedule so that the family could be together to make up for lost time. When Joyce was told that she was too ill to travel anymore and that she needed at least six months of chemotherapy, she went into shock. For weeks she walked around in strained silence. She couldn't eat or sleep. The initial period of crisis was fraught with anguish over her lost career and anxiety over the possibility of dying.

As the reality of her severe illness began to sink in, Joyce gradually moved out of a state of panic and mourning into a more curious frame of mind. She could almost feel her mind seal off the thoughts and feelings that belonged to the episode of her life as an entertainer. She no longer awakened in the morning wondering where her next engagement would be. Instead, her first thoughts were of her therapy and how she was going to manage to save her life. This was a sure signal for Joyce that she was advancing to Stage II in her adjustment to her trauma. She was creating a new mental compartment for the reality she had to face. To keep relying on the compartment that suited her past would have led her nowhere.

What happened to Joyce happens to everyone who advances to Stage II. If you allow the demands of the new reality to challenge you, you automatically will begin to create a mental compartment for mastering the challenges of that new reality. However, just because you have sealed off one episode of your life doesn't mean that it will always be closed to you. Joyce, for example, made a complete recovery. About a year after she learned she was sick, she was reestablishing her career as an entertainer. When she was ready to go back on the road, she needed to access the mental compartment that contained information about how to balance her hectic travel schedule with her family concerns.

MENTAL COMPARTMENTS AS BUILDING BLOCKS

Most of the concern you will have for yourself during this second phase of adjustment revolves around how you will ever establish a rewarding life again. You will find yourself wondering about what Einstein suggested was our most important concern as a human species: "Is the universe a friendly place?" Will I ever feel comfortable and at ease again? How can I muster the courage to explore how this newly wrought world of mine works?

Even though you may wish that your world had never changed, and despite the fact that you may be skeptical that your new role will ever be as good for you as the past one was, in Stage II you will begin to accept it, explore it and learn what it has to offer you. You will know that you have fully entered Stage II when you act as if you are a *partner* with your new reality—a reluctant one perhaps, but a partner ready for a give-and-take relationship with an unknown world. Let me give you an example of what I mean.

A RELUCTANT PARTNERSHIP WITH ADVERSITY

In his recent autobiography, corporate wizard Lee Iacocca recounts the crushing experience of his dismissal by Henry Ford II. He rages over being exiled from his Ford Motor Company home and executive dominion. More important, however, he dramatizes how he channeled his rampant anger at his losses into a positive force for his career and his whole life. He molded his aggression into a partnership with his new reality. In the Prologue Iacocca writes:

> There are times in everyone's life when something constructive is born out of adversity. There are times when things seem so bad that you've got to grasp your fate by the shoulders and shake it. I'm convinced it was that morning at the warehouse that pushed me to take on the presidency of Chrysler only a couple of weeks later . . . *In times of stress and adversity, it's always best to keep busy, to plow your anger and your energy into something quite positive* [p. xvi; emphasis added]

Iacocca demonstrates here what has been dubbed by psychologists the *Pollyanna principle*. He confirms that as human beings we can selectively emphasize the positive aspects of a traumatic situation in our thoughts, feelings, and behavior, even if we are angry and despondent over what we have lost.

Fortunately this built-in capacity to dwell on the *plus* rather than on the *minus* will emerge in you during Stage II of your recovery. This is the time you will gain the momentum you need. You will create the vitally important partnership with your traumatized world that will help you to survive and prosper.

Remember Nietzsche's incantation, "That which does not kill me, makes me stronger." And, so it is with you—you can make yourself stronger when you allow yourself to be a partner with the very forces that turned the world you loved upside down.

THE BRIDGE FROM OLD TO NEW REALITIES

Closing one life chapter and putting it in its own mental compartment requires emotional release, especially if you close a chapter of life that you have enjoyed. Opening a new life chapter with its own mental compartment will recharge your emotional battery when you've found the courage to face what's in store for you. After experiencing a traumatic life event that causes you grief and disappointment, *closing* and *opening* are extremely painful jobs. But you will find yourself doing it without much, if any, instruction. That is part of your natural healing process.

There are four transition signals that will tell you you are already moving from a *past* to a *present* focus in your adjustment to any trauma:

1. Positive denial.
2. Emotional release and recharge.
3. Paying attention.
4. Exchanging questions for comments.

Let's examine each transition signal in detail.

Transition Signal 1: Positive Denial

As someone who has just experienced life-changing crisis or life-threatening illness, you may have an advantage if you are able to deny certain facts about the situation and affirm others. Does that surprise you? There is research to support this startling statement. Recent discoveries on the value of denial run counter to the well-respected schools of thought holding that the hallmark of mental health is a person's ability to distinguish what is *real* from what is fantasy or wishful thinking. For example, M. Scott Peck, in his book *The Road Less Traveled,* suggests that to be psychologically healthy, "We must dedicate ourselves to facing reality at all costs."

It is true that most of the time knowing what is *real* is a characteristic of mental health, but *not* in the early stages of adjusting to traumatic change. In practice the pursuit of knowing reality following a traumatic life event should be made in progressive stages. A partial denial of reality actually eases the initial stages of adjustment; a full acknowledgment of reality is essential only in later stages.

During this early stage of exploration, then, you'll be better off allowing yourself to zero in on the gains that are presently possible for you, ignoring the exact consequences of the downside of your losses. You can assimilate the harsh details later. Consider it a temporary reprieve.

WHEN IGNORANCE IS BLISS

Psychologists Richard S. Lazarus and Frances Cohen of the University of California at Berkeley completed a study of sixty-one surgery patients and found that those who avoided asking about all of the particulars of their operation fared better than those who were alert to every detail.

Those who were alert to their surgical risks, potential post-operative complications, and likelihood of disease recurrence were labeled *vigilant* by Lazarus and Cohen. When the researchers compared the people who were vigilant with those who avoided details, they found that the *avoiders* had a lower incidence of such complications as nausea, headaches, fever, and infection. Also, those less vigilant were released from the hospital sooner.

In another series of studies with people who were hospitalized for heart problems, psychiatrist Thomas P. Hackett of Harvard Medical School found that the cardiac patients who minimized their illness and were calm about their fate tended to survive more often than those who were chronically worried about their condition.

Do these research studies mean that you are better off not knowing about possible risks, complications, and negative consequences of such traumas as grave illness? Not exactly. It seems that what the research on the benefits of denial does support is that you are better off if you do not focus on all the nerve-racking details and potential for harm linked to your trauma.

These studies and others like them support the mental attitude I have found among my most successful clients. I have found that people recover best from a trauma if they search only for the information and facts they need to solve their problem or to take advantage of an opportunity. Knowing the gory details of losses and risks you can do nothing about only increases your anxiety or anger. It encourages either the vain attempts of the victim to escape or those of the aggressor to control.

You will reinforce your challenge perspective and cement your partnership position if you can control, or at least influence, the amount of information and insight into the circumstances of your trauma.

STRENGTH BOMBARDMENT EXERCISE

Take a few moments now and reflect on how you can use positive denial to view your new reality as a *friendly place*. In fact, take positive denial one step further and ask yourself what

---

▲ THE POSITIVE SIDE OF DENIAL ▲

Denial functions as a buffer after unexpected shocking news, allows the patient to collect himself and, with time, mobilize other, less radical defenses. This does not mean, however, that the same patient later on will not be willing or even happy and relieved if he can sit and talk with someone about his impending death. Such a dialogue will and must take place at the convenience of the patient, when he (not the listener!) is ready to face it. [Elisabeth Kübler-Ross, *On Death and Dying*, p. 39]

---

might be in store for you as you learn to live as fully as you possibly can in this new world. This is your chance to see what positive illusions are lurking within your Stage II imagination. Use the work you did in Chapter Six on identifying opportunities to supplement your thoughts, if you wish. However, during Stage II you will come up with many more ideas because you have positive denial working for you and have gained some distance from your tragedy.

I. **How do you see yourself growing *personally* from this trauma?**

What are the mental benefits? _____
_____
_____

What are the physical advantages? _____
_____
_____

Emotionally, how will you grow? _____
_____
_____

Spiritually, how are you enhanced? _____
_____
_____

II. How do you see yourself becoming *productive* as the result of this trauma?

Has your sense of purpose been expanded? _____
_____
_____

Can you contribute more? _____
_____
_____

Can you achieve better results? _____
_____
_____

How are your goals improved? _____
_____
_____

III. How do you sense that your *partnerships* will be strengthened?

Your intimacies? _____
_____
_____

Your friendships? _____
_____
_____

Your collegial relationships? _____
_____
_____

Your affiliations and networks? _____
_____
_____

Jot down whatever thoughts come to mind. You will want to record these in your Empowerment Journal. Give yourself plenty of space to write. Accept whatever occurs to you as often as you find yourself coming up with positive illusions. Don't be concerned if you only have a few ideas during this period. Remember, you have just recovered from the shock of your crisis in Stage I. Some people only gradually see the positive illusions of their new reality.

You will practice deeper exploration of what your new world has to offer in the Stage II skill-building section in the next chapter. For now, relax and reflect only on what occurs to you spontaneously. Fantasize what might be the true benefits of living through your devastation. This is a fruitful method of capitalizing on your Stage II tendency to be more intensely curious about the long-term positive impact of your trauma.

DENIAL AND ILLUSIONS HELP US TAKE RISKS

People often use the strategy of positive denial and illusions to cope with high-risk, but welcome, life change. Think about how positive denial can benefit you in the traumatic but desirable upheaval of marriage, a promotion, turning twenty-one, moving to a new city? In those moments of exciting change, it is exceptionally easy to create the illusion of the gains that are present; your mechanism of positive denial operates to block out the strenuous demands that accompany any one of those events.

When you think about it, there is little doubt that positive denial helps us take risks. How many times have you heard someone say, "If I had known how much stress and effort this particular life change would bring [in parenting, career advancement, relocation, etc.], I would probably never have done it." So it is common that during dramatic but positive life change we agree to take the risk of growing and accomplishing our goals; we do it in part because we don't realize what the extent of the demands on us will be. This is another example of how fooling yourself can be an advantage.

NEVER DENY SYMPTOMS

Positive denial is a valuable coping tool, but *never* use it to block out life-threatening symptoms. Symptoms such as breathing difficulties, severe depression, and cardiovascular irregularities

▲ HOPEFUL STORIES ▲

Psychologist Daniel Goleman interviewed Shlomo Breznitz, the director of the Center for the Study of Psychological Stress at the University of Haifa, for *American Health*. Dr. Breznitz is a leading researcher and authority on traumatic stress.

In the interview, Dr. Goleman asked Dr. Breznitz about the psychology of hope, how it differs from denial, and how it works as a coping mechanism. Dr. Breznitz answered:

> The major difference between hope and denial is that in denial you try not to pay attention—not to see, not to hear, not to think about the negatives. But in hoping you look at the situation, no matter how negative, to seek out the few remaining positive elements and build on them. It's the patient who tells himself, "I may be in the coronary care unit, but lots of people recover with what I have. I'll be home next week."
>
> That's why hope takes work: one has to dwell on the situation, think it over, weave some possible scenarios, tell oneself some stories with happy endings—all kinds of things. [p. 60]

need recognition and attention. Guard against denying acute distress signals that indicate you need to take some well-earned time out. They are red flags signaling you to get the help you need to heal and return to a productive, fulfilling life. Rarely are our acute distress symptoms indications of personal weakness. Rather they are the result of profound trauma. So be sure to slow down and get the professional help you need.

If you are wondering about whether your symptoms are serious enough to warrant professional assistance, they probably are. If other people have told you that they are concerned because you show such symptoms as weight loss, depression, frequent crying, or physical ailments, then by all means see your family physician and a mental health specialist.

A competent physician will want to know about the trauma that has disturbed you so, as well as the pattern of your symptoms. Your Empowerment Journal entries will be useful in describing how and when your symptoms developed.

If you do need professional help to get your symptoms under control, seek top-quality psychological treatment in concert with top-notch medical care. The ideal is for you to coordinate the two. Have both health-care professionals communicate with each other on a regular basis about your progress.

Many people wonder about how best to choose a professional who will offer sound psychological assistance for adjusting to a major trauma. How to identify a resource person will depend on your geographic area and the quality of health care there. But no matter where you reside, search until you find a psychologist with whom you *feel* comfortable. Find someone you trust and respect. Ask your physician or clergyman for references. Call your local psychological association for verification of the individual's credentials. If you choose to see a psychiatrist, counselor, social worker, or church-affiliated therapist, follow the same procedure. Choose someone who relates well to you and your needs, but by all means check up on their credentials and track record.

Transition Signal 2: Emotional Release and Recharge

Oddly enough, even though you can benefit from denying the full extent of your losses, during Stage II you will also find yourself desperate to release your negative feelings about how your life has changed. This is healthy, and your expression of rage over your circumstances is a sign that *you are fully ready to let go of your attachment to the past.*

If you are disappointed, angry, sad, lonely, or afraid because of your trauma, you must find a way to discharge those emotions. An excellent rule to remember is *emotions should be expressed, not depressed.*

Of course our culture and self-imposed restrictions often work against the natural and restorative expression of our emotions, especially our negative ones. Because of Western societal taboos, men in particular appear to have a learned tendency to inhibit emotions like fear and sadness. They report that they hold in fear and sadness because the culture considers men who cry or *quake in their boots* to be weak. Men's inhibition of some emotions may be at the root of such maladies as anxiety disorders, cardiovascular problems, and gastrointestinal symptoms.

On the other hand, the women in my classes and consultation sessions exhibit great hesitancy to directly express their *anger*. Our culture considers anger to be a less-than-feminine response in any situation. So what do most women do with their anger when they are adjusting to a tragedy, loss, or crisis of any kind? They hold it in, of course. In fact, many turn it in on themselves. If they can't abide expressing their anger, or if they can't or won't identify the culprit, they create an actual mental *depression* by getting mad at themselves. One of the most accurate clinical definitions of depression is "*anger turned inward.*"

The trap here for all of us is that fear and anger are the two most basic, automatic emotional reactions to severe threat. Remember, trauma almost always triggers one or both. And when our negative emotions escalate, we must find an outlet for our mounting feelings or they will strain and damage us.

Another line from Lee Iacocca's autobiographical account of a career catastrophe is pertinent to this discussion: "I was full of anger, and I had a simple choice: I could turn that anger against myself, with disastrous result. Or, I could take some of that energy and try to do something productive [p. xv]." This statement makes the point well that fear and anger, natural reactions to trauma, must be channeled so they can benefit us.

As men and women who have grown up in this culture, we would be smart to be aware of the problematic Western social taboos against expressing fear and anger. As adults, many of us must actually teach ourselves to overcome our inhibitions and express our emotions. We must relinquish our own strong admonitions against releasing negative feelings and find appropriate ways of acknowledging and venting them. Once you do, you will be able to detach yourself from a past that is no longer yours. Emotional release is also one of the first steps toward reclaiming your inner power. As long as you feel afraid or angry, the power to frighten you or to make you mad is *outside* of you. And, in that case, the situation—not you—is in control of your emotions.

RELEASING FEAR AND ANGER IN STAGE II

Many people find that as anger and fear build up during Stage II, so does their physical tension. You know that the original source of negative emotional reactions is your perception of the trauma as threatening and dangerous. When you feel threatened, you are naturally programmed to use your adrenaline charge either to attack or run. But because you cannot deal with trauma by fighting or fleeing, your tension builds and you need an outlet.

In Stage I you learned how to discharge some of your initial fear and anger by questioning yourself about what was disturbing you. What had disappointed you? What were you angry about? But you were so shocked by the impact of your trauma you could only reach a vague understanding of the source of your terror and rage. Because you then released only some of your fear and anger, it was not yet possible for you to heal fully.

Now, during Stage II, you will find yourself wanting to explore the sources of your disturbances even further. Don't be apprehensive about delving into your disappointments. It will benefit you. As you begin to appreciate your negative feelings more fully, you will be able to release them a bit more, and you will come to appreciate the deeper reasons you are so upset.

Let me be very clear with you that uprooting your anger and fear will complement your use of *positive denial*. When you use positive denial, you refuse to visualize the catastrophic consequences of your trauma. As we said earlier, it is healthy for you to deny the possibility that negative ramifications will occur. It is also good for you to avoid thinking about the minute details of those ramifications. But recognizing and releasing your anger and fear allow you to make room for more positive emotions that are part of finding the benefits in your new world.

Here's an example of how the process of releasing your fear and anger works to advance your empowerment.

RUNNING AWAY FROM HOME

I recently consulted with a top-ranking executive at a Fortune 500 corporation on the East Coast. The man lived on Long Island and worked in New York City. When I first met Joel, his company was in the process of being purchased by its strongest competitor. Joel had been next in line for the job of chief operating officer, but with the buy-out, the position was in question. The financial and organizational features of the buy-out process were scheduled to be completed in twelve months.

I suggested that in order for Joel to explore fully his new reality during the corporate buy-out process, he had to allow himself to relieve his pent-up anger, hostility, and anxiety. Joel was full of fear about his future and felt deep disappointment that he had failed to achieve his career aspirations. He was willing to release his negative emotions but was uncertain how to do it.

We discussed some alternatives and Joel came up with the technique that I now call *running away from home*. Here is how it worked.

Joel decided that every Sunday he would set aside at least six hours for doing whatever he felt like doing to release tension and to *get away* from the reality that his career was in limbo. Sometimes he would take a train into New York City and just wander around, or go to a baseball game, or browse through bookstores. At other times, he'd drive to the beach or to a small town he had never visited.

During those self-constructed periods of time out, Joel would often feel as if he were ready to cry or ready to hit something. Instead of trying to control those feelings, I asked him to be curious about them. After all, he could afford to shed a tear and to heave a stone into the water when he was alone, away from home. No one was there to watch him or make him feel embarrassed by his expressions of suffering.

Joel kept a journal of his experiences when he "ran away." We discussed them thoroughly in order to get to the *root* of his disturbance. As we found the deeper sources of Joel's anger and fear, he was able to face them and to free himself of their hold on him.

Gradually, Joel found that he was able to focus more of his attention and efforts on taking advantage of his current career situation, even with all of its uncertainty. His weekend releases helped him to recharge his energy for zeroing in on his job reality during the week.

RECORD YOUR EXPRESSIONS

You can also accomplish this healthy release of negative feelings by writing down your particular experiences of running away in the journal you keep.

You may want to do it for a portion of every day or every week. As you track your own feelings and find ways of releasing them, make a note of how you find ways of expression. If you have someone to talk to about what you feel and what you learn about yourself in the process, that self-disclosure will also be helpful.

Remember, releasing your negative feelings about your trauma and letting go of the disappointments and the expectations that fuel your anger and fear are signals of progress in Stage II.

Besides releasing emotions about the past, Stage II is the time you begin to recharge your emotional batteries. You can learn to engender excitement and enthusiasm and to capitalize on today. At least you will find that you are able to shift your attention away from the way things were and what might have been, and focus instead on opening yourself to the glory of the moment.

Make notes of that, too. Give yourself a permanent record of the times you wonder: What can I master? What can I learn? What can I gain by investing all my mental, physical, and emotional energy in the present? As you ask yourself these questions, your answers will be recharging your emotional batteries. You will confirm that you have more fully embraced your world, which has been turned upside down, as a partner and an ally. And those accomplishments are worth writing about.

DREAMS: THE ROYAL ROAD TO EMOTIONAL RELEASE

Several months ago, a man came to see me complaining about his dead-end career and his dead-end marriage. From our first conversation I realized that Richard had tremendous anger over his situation but had never felt comfortable acknowledging it. Richard grew up in a family with a mother who yelled and screamed at the slightest provocation. Richard vowed he would never behave that way.

So for years Richard intentionally swallowed his anger whenever he felt offended or disappointed by someone. He also made very few demands on the people in his family or at the office so that he could avoid any conflict. By Richard's forty-third birthday, he began to realize just how miserable he was. After several months of muddling around wondering if he were crazy, Richard finally sought help.

When he came to see me, he was well past the shock stage of his crises and into exploring his options. But he still had no idea how much anger he harbored deep inside. In the process of his work with me, Richard never was able to deal directly with his anger. The very thought of being angry at someone made him visibly anxious. Although Richard did not express his anger in a discussion, he was able to release it in his dreams. His dreams were full of shouting matches with business partners and stern exchanges with his spouse.

Many people who have undergone a trauma find that if they encourage themselves to release whatever is bothering them in a dream sequence, they benefit greatly. If you feel that you are unable to make enough contact with your emotions to release them fully while you are awake, give yourself permission to do so while you are asleep. As always, I recommend that you record what you remember of your dreams in your journal; reflect on them and decide what they might mean for your recovery.

A CASE OF PERMANENT EMOTIONAL SHUTDOWN

Unfortunately, people do not always continue to grow by releasing and recharging emotions. Review with me the following example of someone who allowed the threatening aspects of his trauma to take over and diminish his life while he was in Stage II of his adjustment.

Greg was referred to the Stress Center for stress management and biofeedback training by his cardiologist. Greg was forty-five years old and had just suffered a moderately severe heart attack.

The first time I met with Greg, he told me that he had been running his family carpet business for eight years, but since his heart problem, he'd felt incapable of doing it. Greg complained that the pressures of the job were grueling. He expressed doubt that he could ever learn to cope with them. He also stated that he was afraid to push himself too hard. In his parting comments that day, he said that his brother was better suited for dealing with the demands of the customers and employees.

As I listened to Greg explain his predicament, I became more

▲ DREAM BLUEPRINTS ▲

Even scientists who study dreams from a physiological perspective believe that dreams are more than just a collection of random neural activity. In *Dreaming Brain,* the author, J. Allan Hobson of Harvard, maintains that dream messages are transmitted from our brain stem, not from the outside world, to higher centers in the brain. Thus, it is the cortex that must make sense out of those chaotic signals.

Those high-level associations yield metaphors that are loaded with information and meaning.

---

and more concerned about his recovery. Although Greg had every reason to be cautious about putting himself right back into a pressure cooker at work, it was not in his best interest to close his mind to any options at so early a stage of exploration. It seemed to me that this bright and successful executive, who had survived a life-threatening illness, might be building an airtight case for taking himself out of the mainstream of life. I was afraid that his body was alive and mending but his spirit was dying a slow death.

As time passed, my original fears were borne out. Greg worked with a team of us at the Stress Center for eight months with no improvement in his outlook. In fact, his anxiety over returning to work—any type of work—increased rather than decreased over time.

On the last visit Greg made to my office, he was walking with a cane. He complained of weakness in his legs, despite the fact that no physical cause for his problem could be found. Greg reported to me that he had applied for disability payments from Social Security because it was obvious to him that he could never work again. He pleaded with me to write a letter of support because his cardiologist had refused to do so. His physician would not attest to Greg's disability either. His examinations revealed that Greg's cardiovascular system had made a good recovery from his heart attack, and therefore his claim for disability was not justified.

It was disheartening to watch this man, who had so much potential to restore his health and happiness, choose to drop out of life. Greg had succumbed to the threats of his trauma. And not only had he severely damaged himself in the process, but his wife and family suffered, too. They lost the vital husband and father they once had to the clutches of Greg's fear of living on and facing his heart problem.

What do you think of Greg's way of dealing with his trauma? Hopefully it is vastly different from your own. Greg never gave himself the chance to master Stage II. He remained trapped by the real and imagined problems his illness had triggered. As a result, Greg grew progressively weaker physically; he had lost his courage to live. He walked away from my office that day resigned and defeated.

Transition Signal 3: Paying Attention

As you know, our attention is one of our most precious commodities of exchange. Idiomatically, we even assign it to a kind of monetary value when we say, "Pay attention." Whenever we *pay attention*, we calculate the return on our investment. In the case of mastering Stage II of your adjustment, paying attention to the present provides the greatest yields. You will find yourself every now and then tempted to focus on a past or future that would have been possible "if only . . ." When you do slip into the past or the future, it will be easy for you to come back to the present moment. As William James wrote in an essay in 1890 on exceptional mental states:

> Everyone knows what attention is. It is the taking possession by the mind, in clear and vivid form, of one out of what seem several simultaneously possible objects or trains of thought. Focalization, concentration, of consciousness are of

its essence. It implies withdrawal from some things in order to deal effectively with others, and is a condition which has a real opposite in the confused, dazed, scatterbrained state. . . . The abolition of this condition is what we call the awakening of attention. One principal object comes then into the focus of consciousness; others are temporarily suppressed. [*Principles of Psychology*, vol. 1, p. 402]

You are free now of the confused, scatterbrained state that so characterized Stage I. And precisely because you are free of that chaos, you can *spend* your attention on the circumstances of the present and relegate other matters to dim awareness. You are now capable of disciplining your mind to focus on matters of your own choice.

"MORE THAN ENUFF"

If you would like to reinforce your capacity to focus your attention at will during Stage II, I suggest that you use the mental position of "just enuff" to train your concentration on the present moment. I coach my clients during Stage II of exploring to say, "I have *just enuff* courage to look at the here and now. I have *just enuff* concentration to dwell in the present. I have *just enuff* curiosity to find the benefits of the current situation." These encouraging phrases actually ratify what is happening automatically, and they help prevent your giving in to the temptation to dwell on the past. Many people find that in Stage II they actually have *more than enuff* interest in their new reality to spur them on toward a full recovery.

Transition Signal 4: Exchanging Questions for Comments

As long as you continue to ask "Why is this happening to me?" you are not living in the present. The search for *why* indicates you have not let go of the past. The search for *why* essentially is a philosophical question of no use to you during transition.

Reserve these kinds of inquiries for a later date, when you have the *big picture*. From the vantage point of a panoramic view, you can entertain the question *Why?* Later, if you want to, you can determine what the larger meaning and purpose were behind your trauma.

During transition Stage II, however, you will begin to wean yourself from the preoccupation with your past by asking a variety of versions of the question "Now that this has happened, what kind of world do I live in?" With a question such as this, you acknowledge that life will never be the same again. As you ask the question, you already have embraced your changed life as a partner, and you have made yourself ready to find the best ways of dealing with your new world.

In the next chapter you will learn ways of exploring your new reality thoroughly, so that you can answer the question "What now?"

This exploration is heroic work, no matter what the venture may entail. I believe that the following excerpt from Alfred, Lord Tennyson's "Ulysses" describes the inspiration and devastation a person feels in Stage II in searching for how to grow stronger and more alive through trauma.

> . . . Come, my friends,
> 'Tis not too late to seek a newer world.
> Push off, and sitting well in order smite
> The sounding furrows; for my purpose holds
> To sail beyond the sunset, and the baths
> Of all the western stars, until I die.
> It may be that the gulfs will wash us down;
> It may be we shall touch the Happy Isles,
> And see the great Achilles, whom we knew.
> Though much is taken, much abides; and though
> We are not now that strength which in old days
> Moved earth and heaven, that which we are, we are,
> One equal temper of heroic hearts,
> Made weak by time and fate, but strong in will
> To strive, to seek, to find, and not to yield.

PUSHING OFF TO STAGE II

As you push off now to learn several methods of exploring your newly wrought world and the impact it has had on you and your resources, remember that you have four transition signals that will fortify you to do this search that is always demanding and sometimes disheartening. Those readiness signals that you will be successful in making the necessary Stage II transitions are:

1. *Positive denial:* Your self-protective mental capacity to mask the extent of your loss and to channel your anger and fear into serving the opportunities that are part of your upheaval.

2. *Emotional release and recharge:* Your spontaneous and calculated methods for giving expression to negative emotions that stem from what is threatening you and for engendering the beginnings of positive emotions that you associate with your possibilities and opportunities.

3. *Paying attention:* As you realize that you are now focusing on the present moment and on your challenging opportunities more than on your losses, you can strengthen your ability to focus your attention at will while encouraging yourself that you do have *just enuff* of what you need to do so.

4. *Exchanging questions for comments:* Your tendency in Stage II is to stop demanding so many answers from life about why your trauma struck you down. Instead, you find yourself commenting on what you have left and how to use it to foster your health and happiness.

Armed with these Stage II signals of your gradual recovery and self-empowerment, you can be "strong in will / To strive, to seek, to find, and not to yield."

8

▲

Creating a New Mental Map

You have come to the threshold of the second stage of adjusting to stressful change and you are now ready to fully explore your world turned upside down. In this chapter you will learn how to examine the mental compartment you have created for your changed circumstances. I will show you how to make a *mental map* of your new reality so you can navigate through this period in your life.

The mental map you make will guide you in replenishing your vital resources. It will define for you how you must direct your thoughts, feelings, and actions to live successfully in your new reality. The mental map gives you an accurate picture of the paths now open to you for fully restoring your inner balance.

Your major objective in the second stage of adjustment to trauma is *to map out the channels of your new reality that lead to restoring your health and happiness.*

In order to accomplish this objective, which will make use of both your conscious and intuitive mental powers, you must be able to live and think totally in the present moment. I cannot emphasize this point too strongly. You must confine your attention to your mental compartment for the here and now to find your way to fulfillment.

SEIZE THE HERE-AND-NOW AS YOUR ALLY

The journals of Henry David Thoreau include two compelling essays about how important it is for anyone to *live* in the here and now. Their message is especially true and difficult for someone working through an adjustment to a life-changing trauma. Thoreau's message is reflective and intense. I hope it will inspire you to bring order to your chaos by *living in the moment* during Stage II.

> Live in each season as it passes; breathe the air; drink the drink; taste the fruit; and resign yourself to the influence of each. . . . Open all your pores and bathe in all the tides of nature, in all her streams and oceans, at all seasons. [Vol. 5, entry of August 23, 1853]
>
> Take time by the forelock. Now or never. You must live in the present, launch yourself on every wave, find your eternity in each moment. Fools stand on their island opportunities and look toward another land. There is no other land; there is no other life but this. [Vol. 12, entry of April 24, 1859]

This passage gives reassuring encouragement for diving fully into the reality of life as it is for you now. Thoreau shows excitement for "drinking the drink" and "tasting the fruit" that is available. By implication he advises you not to have passion for *what you wish you could have* or for *what you used to have*. Rather, he inspires you to consume fully and to savor the *rewards you do have*, NOW.

This savoring of *the way life is* will deepen your understanding and appreciation of your own existence. Accepting your circumstances as they are, as a reality full of challenges to be mastered and conditions to be explored, will make you wise about yourself and about life.

True wisdom requires a fully integrated knowledge, not just a surface understanding of issues and events. In fact, the Latin and Hebrew words for *wisdom* are closely related to their words for *tasting*. The ancient linguistic roots of the word *wisdom* can be another reminder to you that you must *consume* your reality to achieve a thorough understanding about your world turned upside down. You can take full advantage of its possibilities only by digesting it and savoring the new reality. You must absorb your world fully, if you want to discover how your life can best be lived. Please don't try to rush this process. Most people need three to four months to appreciate fully the open and closed channels of their new circumstances.

In this chapter you will learn the skills that will help you seize the here and now as your ally; they will encourage you to become wise about your new existence. The exercises take time and thought. You will want to read them more than once before undertaking each of the skill builders. Work with each until you are satisfied that you have mastered the technique.

MAKING YOUR NEW MENTAL MAP OF "REALITY"

Let's take a look at two systematic ways for you to evaluate what you need to make a map of how you can restore your well-being and top performance in the midst of traumatic upheaval. First, I have developed a simple yet comprehensive questionnaire for you to use to map the impact of your trauma. The questionnaire is a self-evaluation. It is based on my theory that there are three major categories of resources that contribute to your vitality and stress resistance and are disturbed or depleted by trauma. (See Chapter Three, page 35.)

My research shows that resources in the Personal, Productivity, and Partnership areas are conceptually distinct and contribute to a single factor that describes your vitality and resistance to stress. They can be depicted graphically, as you know by the following pyramid.

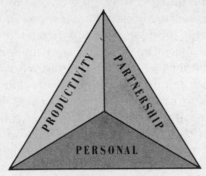

Model of resources that contribute to vitality and full functioning

With this model in mind, you can complete your Personal Balance Profile and use it to assess the extent to which you are currently meeting your needs in each of these resource areas. If you have just experienced a major life change, you will find that many resources have been depleted.

The questionnaire that you are about to fill out will yield a profile of the resources that are a priority for you to replenish at this time. It will suggest what you should do to empower yourself to meet other challenges.

Let me emphasize that this is not a scientifically validated test for diagnosing psychological problems or distress. It is a sound educational self-help tool designed to give you information about yourself and your reaction to stress.

PERSONAL BALANCE PROFILE

Complete the following questionnaire by circling the number that corresponds to how well each phrase describes you currently. The rating system is devised to estimate how often each phrase applies to you:

Creating a New Mental Map

0 = Never
1 = Rarely
2 = Sometimes
3 = Frequently
4 = Almost always

Self-description	*Frequency*
1. I have stamina	0 1 2 3 4
2. I think creatively	0 1 2 3 4
3. My friends are a source of comfort	0 1 2 3 4
4. I have a clear sense of direction	0 1 2 3 4
5. I make progress toward my goals	0 1 2 3 4
6. My family is on my side	0 1 2 3 4
7. My co-workers support me	0 1 2 3 4
8. I am emotionally on an even keel	0 1 2 3 4
9. I concentrate well	0 1 2 3 4
10. I have clear priorities	0 1 2 3 4
11. I have high energy	0 1 2 3 4
12. I am decisive	0 1 2 3 4
13. I can confide in someone	0 1 2 3 4
14. I feel healthy	0 1 2 3 4
15. My principles and beliefs sustain me	0 1 2 3 4
16. I feel in control	0 1 2 3 4
17. I am self-confident	0 1 2 3 4
18. My work is meaningful to me	0 1 2 3 4
19. I feel recognized for my contributions	0 1 2 3 4
20. I show others empathy	0 1 2 3 4
21. My work is satisfying to me	0 1 2 3 4
22. I have people I can count on	0 1 2 3 4
23. My closest family members respect me	0 1 2 3 4
24. I have important work to do	0 1 2 3 4
25. I reach out to others for help when I need it	0 1 2 3 4
26. When I have trouble, I am optimistic about how things will turn out	0 1 2 3 4
27. I believe that bad things happened due to chance	0 1 2 3 4
28. I have someone who backs me up	0 1 2 3 4
29. I am well loved	0 1 2 3 4
30. I am proud of myself	0 1 2 3 4

31. My work is challenging 0 1 2 3 4
32. I manage my responsibilities well 0 1 2 3 4
33. I coach rather than criticize myself 0 1 2 3 4
34. I am proud of my work 0 1 2 3 4
35. I can let go of my anger easily 0 1 2 3 4
36. I can reassure myself that things turn out for
    the best 0 1 2 3 4
37. I can stop worrying when I want to 0 1 2 3 4
38. I enjoy taking a risk 0 1 2 3 4
39. I feel a strong sense of commitment 0 1 2 3 4
40. I am happy 0 1 2 3 4

Scoring: Add up your ratings for the numbered items listed
under each of the categories below:

I. *Personal Resources* _____
                              Score
    1, 2, 8, 9, 11, 12, 14, 15, 16, 17,
    26, 27, 30, 33, 35, 36, 37, 38, 39,
    40

II. *Productivity Resources* _____
                              Score
    4, 5, 10, 18, 19, 21, 24, 31, 32,
    34

III. *Partnership Resources* _____
                              Score
     3, 6, 7, 13, 20, 22, 23, 25, 28, 29

INTERPRETING YOUR PERSONAL BALANCE PROFILE

Now that you have calculated your scores, you will be able to
interpret them. Your first step in the interpreting process is to
determine what percentage of your resources in each category
is present and what percentage has been depleted by the trauma.
Use the accompanying tables to calculate these percentages.
Circle your scores and corresponding percentages for each
area.

Creating a New Mental Map

Scores for Personal Category	Percentage of Resources Present	Percentage of Resources Depleted
0	0%	100%
8	10%	90%
16	20%	80%
24	30%	70%
32	40%	60%
40	50%	50%
48	60%	40%
56	70%	30%
64	80%	20%
72	90%	10%
80	100%	0%

Scores for Productivity Category	Percentage of Resources Present	Percentage of Resources Depleted
0	0%	100%
4	10%	90%
8	20%	80%
12	30%	70$
16	40%	60%
20	50%	50%
24	60%	40%
28	70%	30%
32	80%	20%
36	90%	10%
40	100%	0%

Scores for Partnership Category	Percentage of Resources Present	Percentage of Resources Depleted
0	0%	100%
4	10%	90%
8	20%	80%
12	30%	70%
16	40%	60%
20	50%	50%
24	60%	40%
28	70%	30%
32	80%	20%
36	90%	10%
40	100%	0%

CALCULATING YOUR PERSONAL BALANCE

The most useful way to analyze your questionnaire results is to assess your overall balance by comparing the total scores in each resource category (Personal, Productivity, and Partnership) to one another. Ask yourself comparison questions such as these:

▲▲ Do I score higher in any one of the categories—i.e., Personal, Productivity or Partnership—with respect to the resources that are *present or depleted?*

▲▲ How much of my effort and time do I spend in each category? Do I need to focus more on the category of resources that is most depleted?

▲▲ Am I getting a good return on my investment of effort and time, as evidenced by the presence of many resources in each category? Or am I spinning my wheels, as evidenced by my lack of resources? If so, do I need to devise some new strategies for replenishing those lost resources?

Your broad comparative analysis of your three categories will give you a picture of your strengths and weaknesses in one or all of them. It provides you with clear direction for which resources you need to replenish in order to recover from your trauma. This information is crucial for setting your empowerment objectives.

EXAMINE YOUR PATTERN

Most of my students find this part of the evaluation extremely helpful for goal setting. For example, I just recently consulted with a group of women, each of whom was going through a different type of traumatic stress: one had just undergone a serious operation; several had recently divorced; and two had children in drug-abuse treatment programs. Although the sources of their trauma differed, the women were surprised to find out that the patterns of negative impact were similar.

The women all scored high in their percentage of resources in the category of Partnership; but they scored poorly in levels of Productivity and Personal resources. In those two important aspects of vitality, the women reported that almost all of their resources had been depleted. They experienced fatigue, inability to concentrate, emotional outbursts, and bouts of despair; and they had difficulty setting goals and having a sense of mastery.

After analyzing their results, the women realized they were severely out of balance. And they were able to pinpoint their exact trouble spots in the areas of Personal Resources and Productivity Resources. The profile helped them to understand which resources within those two categories would require the most work.

▲ ACCEPT YOURSELF ▲

. . . If I can accept that I am who I am, that I feel what I feel, that I have done what I have done—if I can accept it whether I like all of it or not—then I can accept myself. I can accept my shortcomings, my self-doubts, my poor self-esteem. And when I can accept all that, I have put myself on the side of reality rather than attempting to fight reality. I am no longer twisting my consciousness in knots to maintain delusions about my present condition. And so I clear the road for the first steps of strengthening my self-esteem.

So long as we cannot accept the fact of what we are at any given moment of our existence, so long as we cannot permit ourselves fully to be aware of the nature of our choices and actions, cannot admit the truth into our consciousness, we cannot change. [Nathaniel Branden, *Honoring the Self*, pp. 64–65]

This type of analysis will help you gain a direction, too. You can benefit from the results of your Personal Balance Profile by directing your coping efforts toward the components of your well-being that need the most attention.

Once you have compared the relative strengths and weaknesses *between* categories of resources, you can further your self-analysis by examining your specific pattern of strengths and weaknesses *within* each. To accomplish this introspection, it is important to go back and reread the individual questions for each category. (The scoring key tells you which questions belong to each category of resources.)

As you reread each question, you will get a clearer picture of the resources you need to replace to achieve better balance. For instance, in the category of Personal Resources, you may find that most of your physical energy and stamina have been depleted. Your item-by-item analysis might reveal that because you lack energy, stamina, and resilience you often become sick. But your analysis also could indicate that you are stronger mentally because you do clear, logical, and creative thinking and your self-confidence is high.

Make notes about your particular pluses and minuses within each category in your Empowerment Journal.

YOUR ANALYTICAL VIEW

Now that you have completed this section of your self-evaluation, you have a much better conscious understanding of the impact of your trauma or crisis. You know which major category or categories of resources are in good supply and which are most lacking at this time. You also have examined in detail the specific resources within each category that need to be replenished. This completes your interpretation of your Personal Balance Profile.

This analytical view makes it possible for you to set clear goals and priorities for restoring your inner resources while you adjust to the aftermath of your trauma. Finding new ways to meet your needs is exactly what empowering yourself to master trauma is all about.

The Personal Balance Profile reflects your analytical and logical thought process. Another tool for evaluating the new rules of your changed reality relies more on your intuition than your logic.

YOUR CURIOSITY QUOTIENT

The second fundamental tool for making yourself a new and accurate mental map of your upside-down world is your *reflective and intuitive curiosity*. Your reflective and intuitive curiosity will yield information about your current state of inner balance that the questionnaire method could not. With this approach you tap into your own deepest subconscious understanding of the impact a trauma has had on you. You reveal to yourself information your conscious logical mind is unable to realize.

You may at first have difficulty learning how to explore the depths of your intuitive knowledge about your lost resources. You have already come through a lot of emotional turmoil and may be hesitant to churn up the waters again. Or, you may not trust your intuitive judgment.

Let me assure you that in Stage II you are ready to know more thoroughly the true ramifications of your trauma. You have made enough progress to afford to have a more accurate picture of your reality, even if that picture is not a pleasant one.

If you are apprehensive about squarely facing your trauma-induced world and looking for the number of ways it has affected your health and happiness, remember that your mind will automatically protect you from anything you cannot yet handle emotionally.

Discovering what channels are now open to you for restoring your lost resources as well as which paths are now dead ends is the well-earned reward for delving into the dark aspects of your trauma.

CURIOSITY QUESTIONING

To be sure you have a good feel for what I mean by using your reflective and intuitive curiosity for evaluating negative stress impacts, I will describe a man who is a prime example of someone who unleashes his intuition and curiosity to get to know a person in depth.

One Saturday morning my friend Julie was seated on the sidelines watching her son play soccer. All of a sudden that loyal mother's concentration was interrupted by the booming voice of a tall, portly man, the father of another player. "How ya doin', ma'am? Nice to meet ya! The name is Clump." My friend was startled and found herself looking up at a ruddy face that framed a mouth in perpetual motion. Julie extended her hand as Mr. Clump's eyes met hers with a stare. He sat down and slapped his right knee. "I've been seein' ya' here for the longest time—and I been wond'rin' what kind of life belongs to such a fine-mannered woman. Would ya mind tellin' me about yourself?"

▲ MUSIC TO REFLECT BY ▲

You don't have to be a devotee to be influenced by music. Most people rate high-pitched music as happy and exhilarating and low-pitched music as sad and serious.

When you are working your way through the process of recovering from trauma, surround yourself with auditory environments that are calming and reassuring. You can aid your relaxation through music. Although people do react differently, soft, melodic, nonvocal music usually has a calming effect. Review the selections given in Chapter Six and make the ones that relax you best part of the background for your Reflective Focus exercise.

He paused ever so slightly—enough for my friend to nod yes. Her nonverbal assent given, Clump darted out of the starting gate with a full, friendly gallop of questions:

"Where'd ya grow up? . . . In Oregon. Oh, I see. Isn't that somethin', Oregon. What's the ocean like there? . . . It's cold and wet, eh? You must of done some sailin' or fishin' . . . You did? Isn't that somethin'? And did ya ever win a fishin' contest? . . . Me neither. I sure like signin' up for 'em, don't you? The tryin's what gives me a charge. How 'bout your family? Any brothers or sisters? . . . Six! That's great. Well, isn't that somethin'? Are they all still alive?"

"One sister dead! What happened? . . . Did the car accident kill anybody else?" . . . Clump paused and stared out over the playing field. It was three or four minutes before he spoke again. "Thank goodness no one else died. How'd ya get over it? . . . Oh, you still miss her. I know how that is. I miss my wife that way, too. Sometimes when I walk into our kitchen, I can still smell her perfume and I can almost see her standin' at the window toward the lake. There's somethin' real important about bein' able to miss somebody that much even after they've been gone for years. It kinda makes ya a better person, don't ya think? . . . Do ya have your Mom and Dad still with ya? . . . Oh, just your Mom, and she's your best friend. Well, isn't that somethin'? For heaven's sake, have you always had that beautiful smile? I'll bet you've got a sense of humor, too . . . That's great! Laughin's the best medicine, I always say. I'll bet you're a handful when you're mad . . . Say, where's your husband? . . . Oh, too bad he's gotta work on the weekend, too. I drive a cab seven days a week. Workin's just like playin' for me, though." Then Clump's questions took an unusual turn. He asked, "Do you believe in God? . . . A Christian. Isn't that somethin'? What made you settle on bein' a Christian? . . . Has religion always been important to ya? . . . Well, I'll be darned. Isn't that great."

On and on Clump questioned and Julie answered. He was spontaneous and unabashed, and he had no pretensions. He was never flustered by the topic or the response Julie gave. For him, her life was an unending, intricate spiral meant to be explored and understood.

Clump had no reservations about finding the truth about Julie's experiences. No matter how terrible the facts might be, he had no inhibitions about uncovering them. He pursued any line of questioning that might be valuable. Every answer was satisfying. He showed no need to have the story unfold in any particular way. He needed only to know what happened and what my friend experienced. He liked her and his desire to know her seemed insatiable.

That Saturday morning, Julie felt that she had had an encounter with a special person—someone who wanted to know her as she really was.

If you are somewhat put off by Mr. Clump's apparent brashness, I can only tell you that my friend found his free-spirited and courageous curiosity most engaging. And I believe that Mr. Clump's unorthodox style can help you remember that in Stage II you must ask questions—even questions that may lead to answers you would just as soon not face.

I will show you how to probe deeply, without reservation, into your mind and heart. You will come away with a deep, accurate wisdom about your world. And this newfound wisdom will help you to better take care of yourself.

▲ CURIOSITY QUESTIONING ▲

Step 1: Reflective Focus

Now it's time for you to prepare yourself for plunging in and intuitively exploring how your trauma has changed your reality. I believe that you can do the best job of exploring your subconscious if you are relaxed but feeling energetic. One way you can achieve high energy and deep relaxation simultaneously I call Reflective Focus. Read the guidelines and then practice the method.

GUIDELINES FOR REFLECTIVE FOCUS

The goal of Reflective Focus is to reach a light trance state, sometimes called the alpha state because it primarily produces alpha brain waves which have very low frequencies of only 8 to 12 cycles per second. This light trance state can be achieved through many methods of relaxation.

Find a quiet spot that is as distraction-free as possible. Lower the lights so that the room's illumination is soft. Sit upright in a chair with your feet on the floor and your arms resting comfortably in your lap. Be sure you're comfortable. Now take a few deep breaths and think the word *relax*.

Inhale and exhale slowly, feeling more and more relaxed. Close your eyes and use your imagination to see, in your mind's eye, the triangle I used to represent the three components of inner balance. You can make the triangle any size and color that appeals to you.

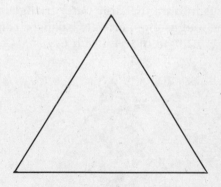

Next, outline the three inner triangles and label them Personal Resources, Productivity Resources, and Partnership Resources. See the labels clearly. Notice the center point in the triangle, the point at which the three inner triangles meet. This is the center of the figure, and it represents the concept of your inner balance.

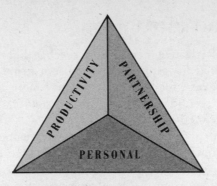

Focus on that center point and breathe very deeply and slowly. Let your image of that point glow with radiant warmth and light. Realize that this center point signifies what you are going toward. It's a magnet that can pull you toward your goal of inner balance, where all your needs are being met.

Feel how relaxed, and at the same time how energized, you are as you focus fully on the large outer triangle, with its three inner triangles, and its one perfectly balanced center point.

Now you are ready to proceed with *Curiosity Questioning*.

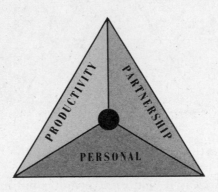

Note: Please reread the guidelines until you have mastered the sequence of visualized images. Then practice the sequence until it becomes easy for you. This is a prerequisite for moving to the next step of Curiosity Questioning. You can tape-record the directions or have someone read them to you, if you think that would be helpful.

Step 2: Impact Assessment

Now that you are in an energized and relaxed internal state, it is time for you to consider the impact of your trauma in each of your three key areas of need: Personal, Productivity, and Partnership resources. Imagine the whole triangle again, but this time zero in on the Personal Resource area.

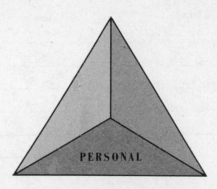

Watch yourself mentally walk into that portion of the triangle to explore it. As you enter that space of Personal Resources, ask and answer the following sorts of questions.

PERSONAL RESOURCE ASSESSMENT

Mental: Can you think logically and clearly? Can you control your thoughts, your attention, your imagination, and what you say? Are you creative and self-confident?

Physical: Do you have high energy, resistance to disease, stamina, and strength?

Emotional: Can you experience your emotions, express them appropriately, and relax when necessary? Can you laugh and find humor in situations?

Spiritual: Do you have a belief in a power greater than your own, a power that operates for good? Do you have strong values, ethics, and spiritual beliefs that support you?

Write your answers in your journal on a chart such as the one that is shown here. Cross-reference your notes with the results from your Personal Balance Profile. Add any resources that you feel you might be missing from this list.

PERSONAL

Resources Present	*Resources Depleted*
_____	_____
_____	_____
_____	_____
_____	_____
_____	_____
_____	_____
_____	_____

Next, look at the whole triangle again, but this time focus on the area of Productivity Resources.

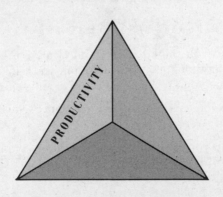

Creating a New Mental Map

See yourself mentally entering that portion of the triangle to explore it. As you enter the space of Productivity Resources, ask and answer the following sorts of questions:

PRODUCTIVITY RESOURCE ASSESSMENT

Purpose: Do you have a sense of meaning and value from the work you do?

Achievement: Are you able to accomplish important goals and objectives? Do you feel a sense of progress?

Contribution: Have your efforts advanced the progress of causes greater than your own? Are you a quality contributor?

Recognition: Do you appreciate the effort you put forth to be productive? Do others recognize your achievements?

Again, write your answers in your journal on a chart such as the one that is shown here. Cross-reference your notes with the results from your Personal Balance Profile. Add any resources that you feel might be missing from this list.

PRODUCTIVITY

Resources Present   *Resources Depleted*

_____   _____

_____   _____

_____   _____

_____   _____

_____   _____

_____   _____

Finally, complete your exploration of the impact of your trauma by focusing intensely in the area of your Partnership Needs.

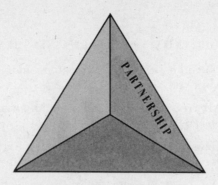

Mentally step inside this portion of the triangle and ask and answer the following sorts of questions for yourself:

PARTNERSHIP RESOURCE ASSESSMENT

Intimacies: Are you involved in mutual self-disclosure and nurturing relationships?

Friendships: Do you have camaraderie with co-workers, neighbors, and associates?

Family Bonds: Are you supported by family members?

Affiliations: Do you feel you are a valued member of important groups, communities, and societies?

Continuity: Do you sense a connection to history, nature, and the universe?

Write your answers in your journal on a chart such as the one that is shown here. Cross-reference your notes with the results from your Personal Balance Profile. Add any additional resources you feel might be missing from this list.

PARTNERSHIP

Resources Present	Resources Depleted
_____	_____
_____	_____
_____	_____
_____	_____
_____	_____
_____	_____
_____	_____

COMBINE YOUR RESULTS

Take a few minutes now to review each chart in your journal and make a Summary List of the major resources you must restore to be healthy again. Only list the resources in each area that have been depleted for this portion of the exercise, as shown in this sample chart.

Resource Category	Resources Depleted
	_____
	_____
	_____
	_____
Personal Area	_____
	_____
	_____
	_____
	_____

Resource Category   Resources Depleted

Productivity Area

Partnership Area

Now you must find an avenue or channel of support for restoring each of the depleted resources on your list. This is how you will achieve inner balance once again. Step 3 will help you to find channels for satisfying your unmet needs.

Step 3: Identifying Channels of Satisfaction

When you review your list of depleted resources, you can readily identify which channels of satisfaction have been closed to you by your trauma.

Creating a New Mental Map

You can search for your new wells of support and avenues or channels of satisfaction by asking *yourself* what kind of help you need to restore your lost resources. You can also consult with friends, experts, and others who know your situation or who have recovered from a similar trauma to help you think of possibilities.

The main ideas to consider are *how your world now works and how to search for sources of available support.*

A structure like this one may be helpful. Transfer your summary list of depleted resources from your reflective focus activity and from your questionnaire results onto the following chart. Do this work in your Empowerment Journal. For each lost resource ask yourself, "What channels can I now tap into to restore this resource?"

Resource Category	Summary List of Depleted Resources	Possible Channels to Restore Resources
Personal	_____	_____
	_____	_____
	_____	_____
	_____	_____
	_____	_____
Productivity	_____	_____
	_____	_____
	_____	_____
	_____	_____
	_____	_____
Partnership	_____	_____
	_____	_____
	_____	_____

Generating your own possibilities for new channels of satisfaction is critically important to your overall progress and growth. Concentrate on doing your work thoroughly here. The results of this step will prepare you for Stage III. If you can identify multiple channels of satisfaction, you will be motivated highly enough to invent and test strategies for taking advantage of them. That is the work of Stage III.

Before you go back to complete your charts, take a look at an example of how a middle-aged executive who was stagnating in his career and his marriage learned to unleash his *reflective and intuitive curiosity*. Review carefully how he set himself up to restore his inner balance and achieve a better life for himself by using the Curiosity Questioning three-step process:

1. Reflective Focus

2. Impact Assessment

3. Identification of Channels of Support

THE PLATEAUED EXECUTIVE

A forty-five-year-old executive came to see me because he was bored at work, restless at night, and had an extremely short fuse with his wife. Darrel felt numb and lifeless. He felt he was trapped by a life that was boring. He was shocked by this unexplainable downturn in his usual motivation and zest for life. I suggested we begin to explore his situation by using Reflective Focus. He agreed to learn the process, but at first he was uncomfortable with the method. He had never before prepared himself for analytical work by relaxing. He believed he could only solve his crisis by being charged up. Eventually, through practice, Darrel learned that he was far more creative if he followed the guidelines of Reflective Focus before he did any precise evaluation or planning.

In his Stage II exploration of the negative impacts of his stagnated career and marriage, Darrel rehearsed the Reflective

Focus guidelines. He then reviewed each resource area, one by one, to complete this summary list of his depleted resources. He noted the following results:

Resources Category	Resources Depleted
Personal	▲ Restful sleep ▲ Motivation ▲ Energy ▲ Happiness ▲ Knowing the value of life
Productivity	▲ Enthusiasm for going to work ▲ Drive to achieve
Partnership	▲ Intimate exchanges ▲ Excitement about going home ▲ Sexual intimacy

As you can see, Darrel had a long list of depleted resources after the onset of his mid-life trauma. The day Darrel and I began to discuss his new sources of support, he recalled a dream he'd had the night before. In it he was driving a car through lush, hilly terrain in what he thought was the European countryside. He was on his way to pick up some valuable packages from various locations. It was his business to collect those packages and to keep them for himself. Darrel recalled a pleasant feeling about the journey.

I mention his dream because it represents the themes in the dreams of many people during Stage II. Darrel's dream symbolized his readiness to take an important journey that would yield him something of value. He felt good about the journey, and he saw himself in the *driver's seat* and *collecting rewards* all the way.

You, too, may have dreams that signal your readiness at an unconscious level to find new channels of reward or paths to satisfy your needs. (Be sure to record any dreams you may have in your Empowerment Journal.)

With his dream for added encouragement, Darrel struggled to identify which new ways were available to him for restoring his life to a rewarding, even keel. He came up with the following possibilities in a later session:

1. *Depleted Personal Resources*
   Energy, motivation, rest, happiness, value

   Possible Channels of Restoration
   ▲ Exercising four times per week
   ▲ Visualizing success in productivity and partnership areas
   ▲ Following a plan of action
   ▲ Coaching vs. criticizing self-talk

2. *Depleted Productivity Resources*
   Enthusiasm, drive to achieve

   ▲ Restructuring my current role at the office
   ▲ Considering other career options

3. *Depleted Partnership Resources*
   Intimacy, excitement, sexuality

   ▲ Involving my spouse in the rebuilding process
   ▲ Spending more quality time at home
   ▲ Conducting an inner search to identify my personal desires

Notice that Darrel defines avenues where he might find some help and reward. He has not specified the actions he will take to exploit those channels—those wells of support. In this phase of his adjustment he only needed to identify the channels. The exact goals and action steps he will create in order to take advantage of those channels are the work of Stage III. It took Darrel four weeks to complete this part of his process.

YOUR EXPLORATION PROCESS

Now that you understand how to complete the three steps of Curiosity Questioning, it is your turn to follow those steps. Don't forget to combine the results of your questionnaire with those that you obtain from your reflective-intuitive process. The combined results will give you the best map of your new reality, a real sense of what is in it for you if you continue the process.

After you have completed the exercises and have answers that satisfy your active curiosity, the following signals will tell you that you are ready for Stage III, *Inventing* your strategies.

READINESS SIGNALS

☐1. Motivation to continue to gain from the trauma.

☐2. Interest and involvement in everyday activities, such as shopping, reading newspapers, watching television, working, and socializing.

☐3. A reduction in alarm reaction symptoms: better concentration, fewer mood swings, more restful sleep, and less cognitive and emotional numbness.

☐4. Self-confidence and a sense of being grounded.

☐5. A keener appreciation of your values, your strengths, your weaknesses, and your options in light of your changed reality.

Remember, the demands on your adaptive energy are still moderately high in Stage II, and only slightly less intense than in Stage I. You will benefit substantially if you take adequate nutrition, exercise, relaxation, and rest to give you stamina.

Proceed to Stage III and take with you the mental map of your newly formed world. You can use this map to guide the direction of your actions. Remember what Thoreau says, "Take time by the forelock. . . ."

▲ EVEN COLOR CALMS ▲

Research on the psychological impact of color reveals deep purple to be the most soothing. This may be why reducing the illumination in a room to create a kind of twilight darkness has such a positive impact on relaxation. [Faber Birren, *Color: A Survey in Words and Pictures*]

9

▲

Masterminding
Your Success

Some people say that *time heals everything*. It is true that the passage of time helps in the recovery from a major trauma. Several months after your trauma, its devastation and upheaval will have diminished. But without your active participation in adjusting to new conditions, the chances for your healing and growth will be slim. Time passing is not equivalent to personal growth. You are the major factor in your progress. Before you enter Stage III, I'd like you to think about that for just a moment.

You have not only survived the first stage of adjustment, you emerged from it with a set of challenges you established for yourself. Then you entered Stage II, where you constructed a mental map for operating effectively in your new world in order to restore your lost resources. Now, at the threshold of Stage

III, you are preparing to *act* in your own best interest again. You have come a long way.

During this period you will personally commit yourself to a set of goals, take control of your resources, and restore yourself to top working order. In Stage III your task is to *invent* ways of living your life fully again.

In addition to appreciating your progress to this point, I recommend that before you study the skills for mastering the goals of Stage III you take some well-earned time out. Tune in to what is happening inside you right now. At the threshold of this new stage of adjustment, you have an opportunity to appreciate the internal assets that will assist you in Stage III. Your thoughts, feelings, and circumstances are very different from what they were in Stages I and II.

Review your scorecard of progress for a view of Stage III benchmarks. (See page 66 for the complete Self-Empowerment Scorecard.)

During Stage III you will be very active on your own behalf. Notice from the scorecard that this is the first time in the process of your adjustment that your mental and emotional reactions are uniformly positive. You can expect to experience surges of creative ideas and a high energy level for pursuing rewarding and enjoyable tasks. You will be spending less and less energy on managing painful emotions during Stage III than you did during the previous two stages.

You will feel self-confident and settled enough in your new reality to take some risks. You will find yourself experimenting with the new attitudes and life-styles you believe will make you healthy and happy again. A willingness to try again is crucial.

Of course experimenting is risky. Sometimes your strategies will work and sometimes they won't. But now that you are in Stage III you have experienced enough progress that if you should fail at something it will not overwhelm you.

There is a certain sense of relief that comes with the ability to *roll with the punches*. That resilience will increase your self-respect. Many people are surprised at their renewed enthusiasm

			Stage III Invention	
Mental and Emotional Reactions			Creativity, Experiment- ing, Progress, Achievement	
Goals			To verify success strategies	
Sample Time Frame for Mastery			12–16 Weeks	
Demands on Adaptive Energy			Moderate	
Primary Adjustment Assets			Creativity	

SELF-EMPOWERMENT SCORECARD

for life, once they have begun to bounce back from trauma. You too will be proud of your ability to stay in the game.

Stage III is not all coasting downhill, however. For several weeks, even months, you will need sustained effort to establish fully your best success strategies. But you will have more patience to accomplish the work of Stage III because you reaped the benefits of gradual growth during Stages I and II. Your own experience now tells you that your life is becoming more and more rewarding and less and less disappointing.

THE STRESS-RESISTANT PERSON

Your increased willingness during Stage III to be responsible for your life and for mastering trauma is conditioning you to be a more stress-resistant person. None of us can avoid stress-filled experiences. Recent studies reported in a Harvard Medical School newsletter by psychologist Raymond B. Flannery confirm that people who are willing to *solve* their problems through trial and error are much more likely to be healthy during stressful periods than people who react passively to life-altering events. The studies also revealed that people with clear goals were far more resistant than those who had none.

There is no question that your progressive healing and growth during Stage III depend on your setting goals and on your willingness to pursue them. You must shape your own destiny and place emphasis on actively inventing and testing out your goals through directed strategies.

▲ STRESS INOCULATIONS ▲

When a chain of events entails multiple loss experiences, it produces stress; when it entails multiple challenges successfully met, it produces stress inoculation. These are the findings of David Meichenbaum and Michael Jaremko, co-authors of *Stress Reduction and Prevention*.

Remember that every time you challenge yourself to master a tough situation, or even a minor hassle, you are building up your resistance to stress of any kind.

As you move into Stage III, you will—possibly for the first time—sense that you are *actively* participating in revitalizing your own existence. As you continue to feel more vital, you will be engaged in the major, unrelenting task of the universe— that of creating the best that is possible in life. With your strategies aimed at reclaiming your life, you will be participating in nature's never-ending process of renewal. The universal significance of your acts of self-creation is embodied in a line from Goethe's *Faust*: "shaping, reshaping the Eternal Spirit's eternal pastime."

YOUR CREATIVE SURGES

Let's focus now on your *creative energy,* which is the well from which you invent the clear goals that will promote further growth and development. You will discover that your goals actually emerge from the creative surges that will be such a frequent part of your Stage III experience. Up until this point you have had very few spontaneous, inspiring moments. But in Stage III you can count on having effortless insights about how to take advantage of your trauma. These ideas will simply occur to you as you move through your daily routines. It is important that you seize the opportunity these creative moments will offer. Jot down your thoughts in your journal; tell a friend about them; discuss your brainstorms with a professional counselor.

As long as you take advantage of the creativity that is welling up inside you, your goals will define themselves easily and precisely. You will not have to engage in any painstaking work to draft your objectives. During Stage III the conditions that spawn the urge to create in human beings are present.

▲

CREATIVE CONDITION 1:
THE NEED TO CONNECT INNER WORLD WITH OUTER WORLD

The research of psychologist Vera John-Steiner has identified *intensity of preoccupation* as a prerequisite for any type of creativity. In her recent book *Notebooks of the Mind: Explorations of Thinking*, John-Steiner links our creative surges to our search for meaning. She says that we are most likely to be creative when we need to connect our inner world with some aspect of the outer world. For instance, many people hold the healthy belief that things happen in their best interest. This belief is part of the inner world of those individuals. If the outer world changes and causes a person traumatic loss, then that person's inner and outer worlds are at odds.

Robin, one of my clients, is someone who believes strongly that life turns out for the best. When Robin was fired from her sales management position, she found her inner world (optimism) was in conflict with her outer world of reality (losing her job). The outer-world reality did not match her inner sense that life is good and just. It is precisely the continuation of that conflict between Robin's inner and outer realities that spawns creative energy, but only when we are ready for Stage III.

Like everyone else, Robin had to find a way of reconciling her innermost positive beliefs about life with the outer reality of loss. She chose—and it was her key choice—to keep alive her belief that things happen in her own best interest. She began to think deeply about her options, talents, and experiences, and she outlined some possibilities. As a result, she spawned a rush of new career goals, ones she never would have created had she not been fired. She reacted with a strong will and allowed her creative energy to emerge. In essence, what Robin did was to reconcile her inner and outer reality by letting her beliefs, not her trauma, dictate the ultimate outcome.

This act of reconciliation, through the bonding of ourselves to the way life is, helps us find meaning and breeds in us a sense of control over our own existence.

There is no question that one of the forces that drive you

during Stage III is your need to incorporate what you have learned about your new reality (the results of your exploration during Stage II) into the fabric of your thoughts, feelings, and actions.

You want to connect with your new reality and make it mean something positive. During Stage III you will find yourself following an internal imperative that compels you to learn how to be happy and healthy in your upside-down world. And it is your striving for renewed vitality that is your "intense preoccupation" and one of the instigators of your creativity.

CREATIVE CONDITION 2:   UNCERTAINTY

Another condition that makes your creative energy so abundant during Stage III is the uncertainty you feel about how things will turn out. Believe it or not, uncertainty is a true asset. It makes you more *mindful* of yourself and how your world works.

For example, if you attend a party with people you don't know, the uncertainty of that social situation may make you much more self-conscious than usual. As a result, you may monitor your speech or your appearance more intensely than you would at a party full of your friends.

This dynamic of becoming more mindful or self-conscious during uncertainty is magnified many times when the uncertainty you must cope with is the result of a traumatic life event. This is so because the uncertainty of the trauma situation is much more crucial to your health and happiness than the uncertainty of a social gathering. Therefore, you become more mindful of significant aspects of your life such as your life-style, your philosophies, and the values that shape your attitudes and behaviors.

I've had students of my system tell me that if it hadn't been for their crisis, they would never have realized that they had their priorities all mixed up. For some it takes a heart attack or a divorce to wake them up to the fact that they have been living their lives out of balance with what's important to them.

There is great uncertainty about life after a trauma such as a heart attack or a divorce. And it is uncertainty that strips us of our standard ways of operating, propelling us to come up with new ways of acting and being in response to our new circumstances.

Harvard professor of psychology Ellen Langer, in her book *Mindfulness*, cites acute awareness as the foundation of an intuitive, improvisational response to life. Her research over the past fifteen years suggests that when people face uncertainty they notice the world around them and act more in accordance with their own feelings. In essence, they come up with more creative and less routinized responses to what goes on around them because their environment feels strange and unpredictable.

These two factors—an intense preoccupation with connecting your inner and outer worlds, and the mindfulness caused by uncertainty—are what unleash your creativity. Use them to invent the goals that will give clear direction to your growth.

OF POSSIBILITIES AND OPPORTUNITIES

Spark your creativity and goal setting by turning back to Chapter Six (p. 128) and looking over the list of opportunities and possibilities that you generated in Step 2 of Turning Threats to Challenges. While you are reviewing your work from Stage I, add to that list any other rewarding aspects of your traumatic situation that became evident as you moved through the subsequent stages. For example, as a consequence of living through your trauma you may have developed more patience or you may have deeper insight into your priorities. Be sure to reflect on the opportunities and possibilities that exist in each of the three areas of vital resources: Personal, Productivity, and Partnership.

What I have just suggested that you do purposely and systematically—review your notes on the possibilities and opportunities of your trauma—you will find yourself doing automatically during Stage III. Most people who learn this process report that their thoughts and imagination are flooded with ideas and images of whatever may be of ultimate value in their traumatic circumstances.

It could be that while you are daydreaming about your particular trauma, you will unearth valuable lessons about what never to do again; or you may be surprised, during a telephone conversation, perhaps, by feelings of support and love from an unlikely source; or one night while you are taking a shower, you may suddenly sense an unforeseen career opportunity or some strength within yourself that is a result of your trauma.

Whatever the pearls from your misfortune may turn out to be, they will emerge in full force from conscious and unconscious thought during Stage III. To paraphrase a passage in an essay on creative writing by Honoré de Balzac, quoted in André Maurois's biography of the novelist, "ideas will pour out like a battalion of soldiers marching down the battlefield. Wise philosophies will come charging in with their standards flying! *And flashes of possibilities will pop up like sharpshooters.*"

Whatever you do, don't miss the opportunity to capture the mighty forces that come parading forth from your mind. During any mundane, mindless activity you, too, may have a creative burst.

This is where your journal and your discussions with trusted confidants or a therapist become invaluable. You can capture your thoughts and images by recording them in your journal and by talking about them. Giving them spoken and written form makes them more memorable and a potent force.

DEPLETED RESOURCES

Your creative energy will help you to remind yourself of the resources you have lost or that have been severely disturbed by the impact of your trauma. Once again your past work in identifying which of your resources were damaged or lost will encourage spurts of creative illumination. You made notes about which of your resources were depleted as you mastered Stage II. Refresh your memory by reviewing the list you made in Chapter Eight (see p. 185). As you reflect on this list, make any additions or deletions that are appropriate, given your progressively deeper understanding of the negative impact of your trauma.

My clients usually identify most of the negative impact on their Personal, Productivity, and Partnership resources by the time they are ready to begin to master the goals of Stage III. In fact they know their losses so well they are tired of dwelling on them. Enough bad news is more than "enuff" by Stage III. You, too, will find it so. For example, if in Stage II you identified your depleted Personal Resource as loss of energy and enthusiasm, your depleted Productivity Resource as insufficient income, and your depleted Partnership Resource as companionship, you will now be able to think of those losses as focal points for improvement and replenishment. In Stage III, your losses become your goals.

I want you to review the following two examples so you will have a clear picture of how your ultimate goals should emerge clearly during Stage III.

SHAPING GOALS IN STAGE III OF A BUSINESS TRAUMA

Here's an example of my own adjustment to the traumatic business failure I introduced in Chapter Four. Remember I lost seventy-five percent of my projected revenue down the drain. During Stage III of my adjustment to the canceled business contract, I listed depleted resources and then forced myself to examine my opportunities. My notes looked like this:

▲

TRAUMATIC BUSINESS LOSS

Resource Category	Opportunities/Possibilities	Resources Depleted
Personal	▲ To grow in self-confidence ▲ To improve my problem solving	▲ Enthusiasm ▲ High energy
Productivity	▲ To evaluate my ability to be an entrepreneur ▲ To develop new products	▲ Sufficient income for business operation ▲ Sufficient vendor requests
Partnership	▲ To build a stronger work team	▲ Viable client base

After reflecting on my situation, I noted the goals that emerged by aligning them on a list that corresponded to each opportunity and each depleted resource I had identified. You can review the final results of my six-week period of goal shaping by examining the following chart.

As you acquaint yourself with this example of my determined efforts, you will realize that you have either fewer or many more issues than I identified. Remember also that trauma rarely has the same degree of impact in each of the three areas critical to inner balance. This means that it is unlikely that you will have an equal number of issues emerge in each category. Expect to have a pattern of goals that is unique to you and to your particular trauma.

Let me give you one more example of how this goal-shaping process works before you begin to fill out your own chart. The most important concept for you to grasp at this moment is that goal shaping is a refinement of your earlier work—a kind of *shaping and reshaping!* It will come to you automatically in the

TRAUMATIC BUSINESS LOSS

Resource Category	Opportunities/ Possibilities	Resources Depleted	Goals
Personal	▲ To grow in self-confidence ▲ To improve my problem solving	▲ Enthusiasm ▲ High energy	To increase: ▲ self-confidence ▲ enthusiasm ▲ energy level To improve: ▲ problem solving skills
Productivity	▲ To evaluate my ability to be an entrepreneur ▲ To develop new products	▲ Sufficient income for business operation ▲ Sufficient vendor requests	▲ To earn more income ▲ To recruit more vendors ▲ To develop new products ▲ To evaluate business skills
Partnership	▲ To build stronger teamwork		▲ To increase teamwork and shared vision
		▲ Viable client base	▲ To develop a more diverse client base

midst of surges of creative energy. You have no skills to learn. You have only to listen closely to your inner self as you set your course. The charts are meant to capture and record what comes to you spontaneously.

SHAPING GOALS DURING DIVORCE

Before I met Susan she had lived through months of confusion and struggle. She had waited until after graduate school to get married. While studying for her doctoral degree, she met Jerry. He sold advertising for a popular radio station in Chicago. Susan and Jerry dated, moved into her home together for almost a year, and then married when Susan completed her doctorate. Their firstborn came during the first year of marriage and their second baby eighteen months later.

Within just a few months after their wedding, Susan realized that Jerry had become extremely critical and demanding. He insisted that they buy a radio station with Susan's savings. She agreed. During the four years of their marriage, Susan acquiesced time and again to Jerry's demands for financial support. She allowed his demands on her time to separate her from her family and friends. Susan let Jerry's demeaning comments about her begin to erode her self-image.

Her two children were Susan's only source of pleasure. She found that they helped to dull the emotional pain she felt from her husband's rejections. Susan then found out that Jerry had begun an affair with another woman during the third year of their marriage.

The truly traumatic information came when Susan discovered that Jerry had been married six times and that each marriage had lasted about three years. Jerry had children from those marriages scattered throughout the Midwest. As Susan later found out, Jerry's pattern in those marriages was the same. He mishandled the couple's finances and then would sue for divorce. By the time Jerry was finished spending all of Susan's savings, he had moved out of the house and filed for divorce.

Jerry reneged on child-support payments and then for a year or longer fought for custody of the children. He failed to get custody because he had been convicted of child abuse and molestation during visitation periods with his other children.

When Susan came to my office she had already received

▲ DREAMS REALLY CAN COME TRUE ▲

You can choose the subject of your nighttime dreaming by giving yourself a suggestion. Just before you fall asleep, think of a one-sentence description of what you would like to dream about. For example, in Stage II and Stage III of your adjustment to trauma, you may want to give yourself dream assignments in the form of questions such as:

1. How will I resolve my loneliness?

2. How will I recover my energy?

3. How will I restore my enthusiasm for work?

Before you go to sleep, write down a question in your journal. Repeat it over and over again until you fall asleep.

---

extensive psychotherapy during Stages I and II of her adjustment. As a result, she had insights into the blind spots that had led her into her situation. She also had a good grasp on how she could benefit from what was a tragic series of events.

Susan was ready to shift her focus from personal loss to the long-term financial struggle she faced of supporting a family as a single mother. She needed to establish long-range goals, but she was stumped. That was where our work together began. Susan's creative energy was flowing full force. "I think of myself as a teacher. I've taught junior high. But I can't imagine that I would make enough money teaching," she said.

She was clearly in the process of shaping her goals. The notes that she kept in her journal are in the chart below.

Susan eventually was hired as a well-paid program manager in a corporate training center. The strategies she used in securing this type of job flowed directly from her well-formulated goals.

Resource Category	Opportunities/ Possibilities	Resources Depleted	Goals
Personal	▲ To learn about myself and and how I contributed to my own tragedy	▲ Self-confidence ▲ Self-respect	▲ To engage in self-development ▲ To learn how to forgive myself
Productivity	▲ To establish a rewarding career ▲ To become financially independent	▲ Financial security ▲ Interesting work	▲ To establish a career plan that satisfies financial and personal needs
Partnership	▲ To make my family strong ▲ To find a trustworthy mate	▲ Companionship ▲ Intimacy	▲ To learn about relationships ▲ To reach out for support

SHAPING YOUR OWN GOALS

Now it is your turn. Remember that goal shaping is very important to your overall process of growing stronger and healthier and of making your life rewarding again. Your goals set your direction. They also make you more stress-resistant by putting you—not your trauma—in charge.

Give this goal shaping your full attention. Assume the mental position of Reflective Focus to allow your creative energy to do its work. Some people find that the goals they adopt have emerged independently of their thoughts. Feel confident about whatever goals occur to you at this stage. You can always refine them as you go along. This is *your* growth process. Go ahead now and make a chart like this one in your journal to record your goals as they emerge.

Trauma _____

Resource Category	Opportunities/ Possibilities	Resources Depleted	Goals
Personal			
Productivity			
Partnership			

FROM DREAMS TO DISCOVERY

This is an excellent point at which to look at the subject of dreams again, and how your dreams can assist not only your goal shaping but your success in the stage of Invention. Up until now, your dreams have encouraged you to grow by helping you sense your deepest fears (Stage I dreams) and by telling you that you are ready to explore your traumatized world (Stage II dreams).

▲ DREAMS: YOUR PATHWAY TO ▲
UNDERSTANDING YOURSELF

Sigmund Freud's belief that our dreams are the "royal road to the unconscious" is still held by many psychoanalysts and psychotherapists. Dreams provide the quickest entree to the elusive realm of our mind beyond our conscious awareness. That part of the mind often holds answers to our most urgent concerns, which is why we can benefit from tapping into the messages of dreams.

The language of dreams is often symbolic. Most dream specialists believe that there is a special usefulness in a person's associations to the metaphors and surface structure of a dream. But because the language of dreams can often be confusing and unacceptable to our conscious minds, professional assistance can be helpful for interpretation.

As you move farther and farther through Stage III, you may notice that your dreams are giving you clues about goals and the best strategies to use to reach them. Here is an example of how dreams can lead to important discoveries.

Jack, at forty-seven, had no history of health problems when he suddenly began having trouble walking. Only eleven months after his first fall, the right side of his body became paralyzed from the shoulder down. Repeated tests yielded no firm diagnosis. Jack's condition five years later remains a mystery. He continues to search for causes and medical therapies to help regain his mobility.

When he arrived for his first session with me, Jack's despair had taken its toll. His body looked defeated as he leaned on a cane and shuffled into my office. His head was bent down, his speech slow, and his manner very passive. Yet there was still spunk left in his attitude. "It's very important to me not to give in to this thing," he said. "I don't know what's happened, but I want to beat it." Jack worked diligently to learn the process for growing through adversity.

After two months of hard work, just as he entered Stage III, Jack reported that he had begun to dream very graphically about sailing. The dreams confused and amazed Jack because he had *never* been on a sailboat in his life. In his dream he had a breathtaking, exhilarating feeling as he maneuvered the sails and tacked across a large freshwater lake. When he would tell me about his dream experiences, his voice became enthusiastic— like a child describing what he got for Christmas. His language was filled with metaphors for physical movement when he described making *tremendous strides* across the expanse of shimmering water.

It was apparent that the thrill and excitement in Jack's mind's-eye images came from the potent, effortless movements that he enjoyed by *sailing*. He came to realize how important it was for him to compensate for his lost ability to move freely. Jack learned that he could regain some sense of graceful, independent movement with the help of a sailing vessel.

Jack enrolled in classes to learn how to design and build a variety of sails and the sailing craft itself. Just attending these courses gave him a sense of independence and self-esteem. Later he entered a local boating competition as further incentive to master his newly adopted skill. He became more virile as he became more mobile. He pushed his outer limits of movement beyond their bodily confines into the great expanse of lakes and seas.

There's no telling whether Jack would have thought of taking up sailing without paying attention to his dreams. Students of my system have found that they often become more inspired about empowering goals and strategies through their dream images than they do through conscious, analytical thinking.

The lesson to be learned here is that it is probably wise to encourage yourself to pay attention to any images that pop into your mind—especially those that come to you while you are asleep.

Another type of dream that you may experience during Stage III, Inventing, is the recurring dream. One of my executive clients who was going through the traumas of a new job, a new marriage, and the loss of his best friend to cancer had this recurring dream. Immediately following Stage II and just before he began his Stage III Inventing, the executive dreamed about a house.

In the dream he would sometimes give a tour of the house to a small group of guests. First they would survey the daily living quarters of his small, but nicely decorated ranch house. Then, suddenly, he would realize that there was a new, completely separate wing of the structure, with multiple floors, gigantic rooms, and many extra features. All those spaces looked particularly stunning in color and design, and the executive's guests were always duly impressed with their beauty and expanse. The executive was shocked because he didn't know the wing existed!

As the dream continued, he would guide them through the new wing and wonder if he'd ever been there before. The wing felt both familiar and foreign to him—as though he were exploring that part of his house for the hundredth time and the first time, simultaneously. He was always surprised, but pleased, to have discovered, or rediscovered, that vast but hidden extension of his home.

The recurring dream always signaled the beginning of a particularly creative period for the executive. It announced to him that he was ready to try different ways of redefining his life. It told him that he was about to invent some new ways of acting and being that would benefit his progress.

You can learn to trust your intuition and subconscious thought, too. Remember, your inner resources for beginning the creative work of inventing goals and strategies are to be found at many levels—even in your dreams. At this stage, many people I work with report having dreams with *construction* or *building* themes.

Spontaneous dreams are relatively easy to interpret. Often you can best understand what a dream may mean for your growth process by returning to the dream experience to re-live it.

In his book *At a Journal Workshop*, psychologist Ira Progoff suggests how to approach learning from dreams. His first recommendation is what *not* to do. Progoff tells us at first not to analyze the meaning of dreams logically or intellectually. He feels this is premature and that we will learn more if we

> return to the place in our experience where our dreaming occurred so that we can reenter our dreams and enable them to continue themselves. All our dreams are part of the moving flow of imagery that is continuously present at the depth level of the psyche. Each dream is an excerpt of that large and ongoing movement. It is a bucket of water sent up to us from the underground stream of imagery within us. In order to extend the movement of our dreams, therefore, it is not necessary for us to return to the condition of sleep in which the dreams occurred, but only to place ourselves back in the flow of imagery that is moving within us beneath our conscious minds. This is the flow from which our dreams were drawn. . . . We do this in a spontaneous and unguided way, not specifying in advance which of our dreams are to be called back to our attention. Rather, we let our minds go back over our dreaming as a whole. We wish to see which of our dreams will recall themselves to us when we place no restraints upon ourselves but merely let our minds roam over the generality of our dreaming. [pp. 234–235]

Trust your own interpretation. Many dream images are self-explanatory, as Jack's sailing adventures were to him. And, as you begin to keep track of your dreams, you will find that you will "just know" the meaning of many of your dream adventures. Your understanding of them can assist you greatly in shaping your goals.

It's often said that "dreams are windows to the soul." I believe they are. Logical reasoning can be of great value in leading you to invent appropriate goals for improving your life, but there is equal value in tapping into your innermost feelings through dreams to make certain your goals reflect your best direction.

A quotation from the seventeenth-century French philosopher Blaise Pascal emphasizes the contribution your innermost feelings can make to any endeavor:

Le coeur a ses raisons que la raison ne connaît point. (The heart has its reasons that know nothing of reason.)

STAGE III: EXPERIENCES

So, here you are, involved in the initial work of Stage III, Creating Goals. What is your experience? You are likely feeling stronger than you did in Stage II. Most people can't believe how strong their surges of creative energy are. And along with the shaping of goals come vivid images of the future—some positive, some not.

Like many other people who have worked through this process, you may have a tendency initially in Stage III to worry about how things will turn out. It is neither the panicked concern of Stage I nor the seductive lure of the past you felt in Stage II. In this period you may find yourself haunted by an uncertain future.

It is true that no one in Stage III can be certain yet of how good life will be at the conclusion of their adjustment. But despite the uncertainty, you are able to telegraph positive results for yourself by envisioning the final results you *want.*

One definition of *worry* is "envisioning the final results that you don't want." Why would anyone want to telegraph doom or gloom? I don't believe that anyone actually *wants* to promote disastrous outcomes for themselves, but many people fall into the bad habit of worrying instead of envisioning success.

We develop the habit of worrying, with genuine concern for how things will turn out. Unfortunately, the outcome of many events in life is outside our direct control. This lack of control frightens us and our fear can trigger anxiety and worrisome thoughts.

During the goal-shaping process of Stage III you need to eliminate *worry* and to facilitate *glory*. It is of critical importance that you imagine ultimate success—not failure—when you attempt to thrive under adverse circumstances. So take this opportunity to *unlearn* your worry habit and replace it with positive mental prophecies. As the Caribbean folk song suggests: "*Don't worry—be happy!*"

One strategy for eliminating worry and other negative thoughts is to understand the unnecessary credit worry is given. People often credit worry for their success. Have you ever been in a situation in which you didn't know the outcome, so you worried about it beforehand? Then, when everything went fine, you credited the positive outcome to the fact that you had worried? And if everything did not go fine, you promised to worry twice as hard the next time? Obviously, the reason things didn't go well is that you didn't worry enough!

Either way, worry wins. Worry gets credit for success and, if it fails, it gets relied on even more the next time. But if you think about it, the reason you did well was not really because you worried, it was because you were good at what you were doing and you rose to the occasion. You took action. And, if you didn't do so well, all the worrying in the world wouldn't have helped you, anyway.

Worry is useless. The next time you find yourself worrying about

▲ the car not starting
▲ being late to work
▲ not having enough money
▲ smoking too much
▲ how your hair looks
▲ getting your work done on time
▲ or anything else . . .

ask yourself, will worrying

▲ make my car start?

▲ get me to work on time?

▲ earn me more money?

▲ help me quit smoking?

▲ make me look better?

▲ get my work done sooner?

▲ solve any other problems I may have?

If worry is useless in situations of small concern, it is equally useless in circumstances of great concern. This insight should help you eliminate worrisome thoughts.

If you need more help shutting off the worry cycle, try worrying *better* than you ever have before. Here's how:

1. Realize that worry is a vivid misuse of your imagination. You show yourself mental movies of a catastrophe that might happen, could happen, will happen.

2. Extend your mental movie *beyond* the dreaded moment, see the worst happen, then watch yourself cope well with the worst possible case. This is a positive use of your imagination.

3. This will give you confidence that you can deal with whatever happens. And, your confidence defuses your worry for good.

And remember, you will do yourself the most good by vividly envisioning success. Spend your mental energy on your path to growth, not your path to setback.

MOVING AHEAD

Armed with your Personal, Productivity, and Partnership goals, you are ready now for your second series of inventions in Stage III. You will learn next how to invent strategies for accomplishing the goals you have shaped. Your visions of what you want will help motivate and encourage you in this next part of your growing process.

You are in charge, so charge on!

10

▲

How to Achieve
Your Possibilities

It is one thing for you to create goals but quite another to take the action necessary to make them happen. Each of the goals you have shaped spontaneously and consciously is meant to achieve this overriding objective: to help you grow stronger through adversity by restoring your inner balance of resources. In the Invention stage, your creativity inspired your goals. Now you will learn the skills to get you there.

In this chapter you will take the next critical step in your progress. You will learn strategies to change your thoughts, feelings, and behavior so that you will begin to experience a healthier, happier you.

I want to make one final point before we turn to how to reach goals. Many people who advance through Stage III change their objectives several times in the process. That is nothing to worry about. The process you are following is fluid and meant to respond to and yield new results as you yourself change.

Although your goals have already emerged, you can, and should, modify them if you feel they do not represent your best interest anymore.

For example, in the last chapter I spoke of Susan, a woman who wanted to establish career and relationship goals after a traumatic divorce. Remember that she also had as a goal learning about the "blind spots" that had allowed her to be attracted to a dangerous partner. In the course of her work with me, during Stage III, Susan modified that self-knowledge goal. Instead of striving to find ways of examining her shortcomings exclusively, she committed herself to discovering her inner strengths and to using them to regain her self-confidence.

That was a very wise revision of her goals because examining her strengths brought Susan self-confidence, and having self-confidence was a key to reaching her other goals. You may be interested to know that Susan did not make this revision until she was almost finished with her Stage III work. I hope Susan's shift in objectives will inspire you to change your mind about your priority goals any time you feel it is desirable. It will be a true signal that your creative process is hard at work. As Goethe said, "*Shaping—reshaping, the Eternal Spirit's eternal pastime.*"

PUTTING YOUR CREATIVITY TO WORK

Once again your creativity will be the most valuable resource as you invent strategies you want to lead you to your goals. Think of the stage of *Invention* as a great research experiment. You are a scientist conducting the research, and you are about to make breakthrough discoveries. As with any major research project, your experiments will teach you as much when your strategies fail as when they succeed.

Flexibility Gets Results

For example, after the death of Barbara's son in a tragic car wreck, Barbara's grief was still so intense by Stage III of her adjustment that she decided to avoid groups of people who might mention his loss. She refused to attend church and dropped out of her bridge club and weekly tennis game. For six weeks she was virtually a recluse.

During her dropout strategy, Barbara found to her surprise that her grief became worse. She faced that fact and changed her strategy. She became active in MADD (Mothers Against Drunk Driving). That strategy allowed her to process her grief and to use her rage constructively. Barbara used her own will to change strategies and was courageous enough to realize her first strategy wasn't working.

When a strategy succeeds, you will integrate it into your lifestyle and overall approach. When a strategy fails, you will exclude it from your behavior. In this process of dealing with adversity, if you don't take chances, you may never survive your ordeal and once again have a fulfilling life. The parable of "The Two Frogs," recounted by Roger Von Oech, a creativity consultant to corporations, in his book, *A Whack on the Side of the Head*, makes this point for us.

THE TWO FROGS

Once upon a time, two frogs fell into a bucket of cream. The first frog, seeing that there was no way to get any footing in the white liquid, accepted his fate and drowned. The second frog didn't like that approach. He started thrashing around in the cream and doing whatever he could to stay afloat. After a while, all of his churning turned the cream into butter, and he was able to hop out. [p. 123]

When it comes to dealing with trauma, you must learn by trial and error which strategies will help you to "hop out"— and strategy testing takes time and effort. Of course, thrashing about like a tenacious frog in cream is not enough. The name of this game—growing strong through adversity—requires that you calculate your best approaches to restoring your lost resources, that you take a risk, and that you fail sometimes. Most important, it requires that you *try again*. You must actively struggle to find your best approaches to reaching your goals. In a recent *Psychology Today* review article, Dean Simonton, professor of psychology at the University of California at Berkeley and the author of *Genius, Creativity and Leadership*, stated that he believes genius is inseparable from failure.

"Great geniuses make tons of mistakes," he said. "They generate lots of ideas and they accept being wrong. They have a kind of internal fortress that allows them to fail and just keep going."

In your process of strategically inventing new attitudes, feelings, and behavior that will work to your advantage in your traumatized world, you can unleash this type of genius in yourself. First, generate alternative actions; next, try out some of those options; and then, evaluate their success. You cannot be certain if a strategy is effective until after you test it.

It is a sure thing that some of your strategies will test out well and others poorly. After all, you are striving to achieve new goals in a world turned upside down, using many strategies you've never tried before. That is a formula that welcomes failure along the way to ultimate success. It is the call to struggle, the call to creativity, the call to genius.

Rollo May, a distinguished psychologist who has made a lifelong study of creativity, believes that we must indeed stretch—even struggle—to be creative. In his book *The Courage to Create*, he said, "The creative act arises out of the struggle of human beings with and against that which limits them." In a way, Rollo May tells us that creativity is the marriage of spontaneity to limits. With complete freedom in our experimentation, we can generate a *wish list* of goal-directed strategies, tempered by what our circumstances and our capacities allow.

It is true that all growth in life springs from the tension of creativity, the tension between limits and drive. The river, the plant, the embryo, the stars—all these gain their form and momentum from such fundamental tension. And so you, too, will encounter tension and struggle, especially when you take action to make your life better. For this reason, it is important that you become as comfortable as you can be with mistakes, errors, and all forms of *failing* that occur because you have been creative and have taken a risk. Let your creative genius go to work for you.

YOUR FAILURE FOCUS

I always ask people who are at the point of inventing their success strategies to consider three axioms about the value of failure before they begin the formal process of Invention. I ask the same of you now. Consider the following points and remind yourself of them whenever you are disenchanted or depressed because a strategy of yours has bombed. And remember always, the struggle of trial and error is essential to all creation and growth.

CONTRIBUTIONS OF FAILURE

▲ Failure tells you what doesn't work and when to change direction.
▲ Failure leads to new ideas.
▲ Failure provides you with an opportunity to try something new.

I am sure that you remember the old adage:

"To Err Is Human
To Forgive Is Divine."

It points out that it is the forgiving of ourselves that makes the process of failing a redemptive one. I would like you to take the adage one step further. Modify the first line to read:

"To Err Is Divine."

After all, without the mistake, the error, the failure as it were, there is no risk taking, no opportunity for advancement. Repeat the phrase "To Err Is Divine" as your first reaction whenever you discover that one of your success strategies has *failed*. Saying this phrase to yourself can make you proud that you have tried to restore your vitality. It will also help to keep you from self-recrimination and second-guessing your decisions. It compliments you for taking a risk, and it sets you up to learn and to be motivated by *failing*.

OUT OF STRUGGLE: HARMONY

Overall, you will find that the strategy-building part of Stage III is quite exhilarating and rewarding—even with its inherent creative tension. You can now breathe a little easier because the major hurdles of the journey to grow are over. You have arrived at the threshold of reinventing your life, and you have given yourself the promise of success. As you invent your strategies, you will find out how to fulfill that promise. This is a precarious but exciting point. You have moved from the alarming shock of your trauma, through the turmoil of accepting your new world of loss and gain, to this awkwardness of beginning to succeed in that world. You now are about to taste the fruits of your labor. You can be certain that you will regain your confidence and a strong sense of balance by the end of Stage III.

There is one sure indicator that you are ready to invent and experiment with different approaches to reach your goals, and that is that your perception is now sharper than it was earlier. Many people report that just before they come up with new ideas and strategies in this stage, a sort of mental fog dissipates.

It is as if a heavy mantle of confusion has been lifted from their shoulders. They actually feel lighter, less dense, and not so weighted down. They say things like "I feel as though I am emerging from a cool, dark cave into a clearing with warm, bright sunlight. Suddenly I feel alive and fully awake for the first time since my ordeal began."

Be glad that the darkness of confusion is behind you, and welcome the fact that you can see where you are going. You will derive great satisfaction from your clarity. Being clear will assist you in the Invention process of generating, selecting, and testing success strategies. Your clarity will help you bring true order to the chaos brought on by your trauma. Now you will feel your life draw together instead of pull itself apart.

As you test out how to go about restoring your resources given the possibilities of the moment, some of your strategies will fail. Some approaches will collide with the limits of your new reality. But don't worry, that combination of opposing forces will give rise to an inner harmony and balance by clarifying what will and will not work. Harmony is always born of opposing forces. As the Greek philosopher Heraclitus observed 2,500 years ago, "Unwise people don't understand how that which differs from itself is in agreement. Harmony consists of opposing tension, like that of the lyre and the bow."

Get ready now to struggle, to come into full agreement with your world, and to achieve the maximum benefits possible. Invent your strategies for restoring your health and happiness.

▲ DESIRES HELP US GROW ▲

In 1968 Abraham Maslow published his landmark text on how human beings develop and grow, *Toward a Psychology of Being*. Maslow became a major proponent of the theory that people grow in pursuit of such positive desires as safety, belonging, respect, prestige, and love. He contended that the realization of this hierarchy of desires results in self-actualization, a state of high satisfaction, autonomy, and mastery.

INVENTING STRATEGIES FOR SUCCESS

HOW TO "INVENT"

The process of Inventing that I teach in my consultations and workshop classes is the one I recommend to you here. It has four parts:

INVENTION PROCESS

> Part 1: Generate
> Part 2: Initiate
> Part 3: Evaluate
> Part 4: Integrate

This particular procedure for Inventing success strategies is generic to any creative process where the end result is a core change of adaptive and useful attitudes and behaviors.

Let's take a look at what each of the parts involves and how they fit together by reviewing them briefly. Then we will examine each step in depth.

OVERVIEW OF THE INVENTION PROCESS

Part 1: Generate

To start the Invention process, you will *generate* a whole set of alternative strategies that might lead you to your goals. The generation process is best served by brainstorming techniques. You get the most out of brainstorming by devoting short periods—about thirty minutes—to the task.

Part 2: Initiate

Next, select certain strategies from the set you have generated and try them out. Trying-out periods vary in length according to the complexity of the strategy and the amount of time it takes to get results.

Part 3: Evaluate

After you have given your selected strategies a chance to work, you will evaluate the results. You may want to evaluate at several points during the tryout period. Usually it is clear within two weeks after you have initiated it whether a strategy is yielding the desired benefits.

Part 4: Integrate

Finally, you will incorporate into your routine those strategies that have succeeded in bringing you closer to your goal of restoring vital resources. You will emerge with a composite set of new ways of thinking, feeling, and acting that yield health and happiness. You will eliminate those strategies that have not worked.

This integration process can take up to six months or even a year before complex habit changes become a permanent part of your routine. It is not until Stage IV of your adjustment to trauma that these newly integrated strategies will become automatic and be beyond your conscious effort and awareness. During Stage III you will have to discipline yourself and make certain that you maintain the strategies that bring you success.

Note: Apply this process of inventing and testing strategies to each of your Empowerment goals in the areas of Personal, Productivity, and Partnership resources. Now, let's delve into each part of the process of Inventing so that you will be able to proceed easily.

Part 1: Generating

Looking at possible action strategies that lead you to rewards is not a new task for you. As far back as Stage I, you learned how to turn threats into challenges, ending the process of shifting with a series of challenging "What if I were to ——————" statements.

During your crisis stage, Stage I, you envisioned actions you might take so that you could eventually seize the opportunities and possibilities of your changed world. You were then too overwhelmed to act. During Stage II you explored how your world and your inner resources were impacted by your trauma, still not a time to take definitive action. It is now time for you to act. You will need a set of options from which to choose, so your first task is to generate alternative strategies.

You can generate success strategies by drawing from your work in the previous stages. Start by going back to the goals you shaped for yourself in Chapter Nine and in your journal. Then revisit Stage II in Chapter Eight and your journal notes to review the channels of support you identified. Finally, go all the way back to Stage I in Chapter Six to what you identified as challenging about your trauma. Constructing a chart such as the one on page 225 will help you organize this material. I have made some sample entries for your clarification I drew from the Stage III work done by a client of mine who is the president of a large insurance company.

Ed came to see me because he was forty-two and bored with his life. He complained that he had peaked early. As incredible as it might seem, Ed was suffering from premature success. He felt listless and agitated at the same time. He had no enthusiasm and was deathly afraid that life had nothing more to offer. He had earned status, responsibility, and financial goals—much more and much faster than he ever guessed he could. Ed felt he was ahead of schedule by ten years! That was so disconcerting for him, he began to question whether he was shallow and to wonder if life would ever be exciting again.

During Stage I of his mid-life upheaval, Ed experienced a rash of symptoms. He was severely depressed and absent in spirit from home and work. He realized during the early stage of adjustment that he had to go into himself to ever be productive and satisfied with his life again. The notes on the third column of Ed's chart describe what he identified as his challenges.

In Stage II Ed had been able to explore his deflated world and to come up with channels of support while he pursued his challenges. As you can see from the notes in the second column, Ed identified a variety of support channels that ranged from reading to psychotherapy, to marriage counseling, to spending more time at home.

I have listed some of the goals that emerged for Ed during Stage III, Inventing. Examine them and see how he developed a clear direction out of his challenges and his channels of support.

Ed went on to revitalize his life on the career and marriage fronts by testing out an excellent list of success strategies over a period of six months. I will show you a segment of Ed's success strategies. But first I would like you to begin working on your entries in a summary chart like the sample displayed here. Make your notes in your journal.

As always, make additions and deletions to your notes according to what is currently appropriate. When you have completed this compilation and have studied it, you will automatically think of strategies to accomplish your goals. The strategies will be based on

1. exactly what you want to accomplish.

2. the supportive channels you can access to restore lost resources.

3. what challenges you about your trauma.

Now you are ready to generate your set of success strategies using a brainstorming technique. Remember, the rules of brainstorming are that you accept all the options that occur to you without evaluating them. All ideas—no matter how outlandish or ineffective—must be included. This approach permits you to step back and study an array of suggestions, each of which has a value simply because you generated it. A suggestion

SAMPLE ENTRIES FROM CLIENT NOTES

Resource Category	My Goals (Chap. 9)	Channels of Support (Chap. 8)	Challenging "What Ifs" (Chap. 6)
Personal	▲ To be in good physical condition ▲ To feel at peace and proud of myself	▲ Spiritual readings ▲ Psychotherapy	▲ What if I were to delve into my feelings and get to know myself?
Productivity	▲ Handle the stress and make the best of current job ▲ Rewarding career path	▲ Colleagues ▲ Career consultant ▲ Professional development reading	▲ What if I were to find out what I want to accomplish?
Partnership	▲ More communication and warmth in my marriage	▲ Marriage ▲ More time and attention at home	▲ What if I I were to make my marriage a priority?

might not be *the* answer, but its presence may lead you in the right direction.

Here's a sample list generated by Ed, the insurance executive who was in a mid-life career crisis. One of his goals under Personal Resources was staying in good physical condition. Ed had to maintain a hectic travel schedule through many peak periods of demand. His brainstorming for this Personal Resource goal yielded these strategies for success:

▲ Select hotels with exercise facilities.
▲ Use airport concourses for conditioning walks.

▲ Drink four extra glasses of water a day to counteract dehydration from long flights.
▲ Eat three balanced meals a day.
▲ Walk to lunch and breakfast.
▲ Use stairwells for exercise in hotels without exercise facilities.
▲ Avoid excess alcohol, sugar, and fat.
▲ Learn to juggle.

"Learn to juggle"? How unusual, how illogical. How much promise could juggling hold for improving physical conditioning? Did you already guess that juggling turned out to be a major factor in promoting the conditioning of this plateaued executive client? Juggling *was* a new skill that held Ed's attention. He could pull out his bean bags in his hotel room, in an airport waiting lounge—almost anywhere—and become completely absorbed in mastering this tricky feat of eye-hand coordination. When he was juggling, Ed was totally absorbed, he thought of nothing else—not even the endless requirements of his business.

Juggling provided this harried executive a much-needed diversion and became a prerequisite for engaging in much more vigorous exercise because it helped him make the transition from mental to physical activity.

USE STRATEGIC CONSULTANTS IN BRAINSTORMING

Another aid to brainstorming is to generate strategies with someone who is qualified to help you reach your goals. It is amazing how a narrow perspective on your part can lead to failure. Sometimes you need someone else's objective, creative point of view to unclog your blocked creativity. I call this type of assistance strategic consulting.

Peers who have survived and turned around traumas similar to the one you are dealing with may be able to offer you good suggestions, but they are not your most objective consultants. Sometimes peers feel their way is the *only* way. Therapists, counselors, and ministers are trained to give you guidance in generating strategies that are your own best approach. They can encourage "possibility thinking"—how to stretch your creative boundaries, break through the limits constructed by habit and routine. When you suspend your normal frames of reference, you will be able to create new and better success strategies.

This is a good time for you to line up your strategic consultants. (You may want more than one.) Schedule at least an hour's worth of time to begin brainstorming strategies. You will know at once whether you and your consultant work well together. If the relationship is working, you will come away enthusiastic about at least some of the consultant's ideas and feel well supported emotionally.

Keep in mind that outside help can be a great boost during Stage III because you may be weary by then. Even if you did not seek outside assistance during the first two stages, you may benefit from this impartial caring and guidance in the third phase. An outsider who is full of energy, viewing your situation with a fresh mind, will be able to encourage you to keep up the fight. Just as a water station can bolster the stamina of a marathon runner at the thirteen-mile marker, a strategic consultant can keep you going. You'll know that you're not alone.

▲ A LITTLE HELP FROM YOUR FRIENDS ▲

Stevan Hobfoll at Kent State University has evaluated the role of social support in reducing the negative impact of stress. His evaluation shows that you can benefit from the help of others if

- ▲ support is mobilized quickly;
- ▲ the supporter has the desire and capacity to help you;
- ▲ you believe that a network is ready to provide aid; and
- ▲ the support fits the demands of the stressful circumstances.

No matter how much support and how many indispensable suggestions you may receive, you are the ultimate decision maker. You alone generate your final set of success strategies. Begin to brainstorm now, and after you have developed your set of success strategies, enter them in your Empowerment Journal on a chart like the one shown here.

BRAINSTORMING WITH YOURSELF

Resource Category	My Goals	Optional Success Strategies
Personal	_____ _____ _____ _____	_____ _____ _____ _____
Productivity	_____ _____ _____	_____ _____ _____
Partnership	_____ _____ _____	_____ _____ _____

Part 2: Initiating

Now that you have your set of options, it is time to initiate some of them. How do you know which ones to try? My suggestion is to let your intuition be your guide. After you have gotten all the expert advice and input you need, trust your own intuitive judgment about what will work best for you in your upside-down world.

This process of giving priority to your own judgment produces the highest quality transformations in Stage IV, a kind of *metanoia*—from the Greek, meaning profound change of mind or spiritual conversion. Metanoia is possible only when you go with your inner hunches about what will work best. Often logical, or even expert, advice alone simply won't work because it does not strike the right chord inside you. That is why your subjective judgment is the final word in this process. You are the authority that counts.

THERE ARE NO "RIGHT" STRATEGIES

Let's look now at Donald's case. When Donald arrived for his first interview, I learned that before his coronary bypass surgery, he had built a successful career as a chemical engineer. The diagnosis of extensive heart disease had come as a complete surprise to him, his family, and his colleagues. One day he was robust and physically healthy, the next day fragile and gravely ill. He gradually had come to terms with his condition. Donald had done his homework about the ramifications of his disease and the impact that his surgery would have on his life-style and longevity.

Donald received excellent education and training about the do's and don'ts of nutrition, exercise, and stress. He'd learned biofeedback to calm his body; his wife prepared meals low in sodium and animal fat. He walked the requisite number of minutes at his assigned exertion level, and so on. But he was still anxious, depressed, tired, unproductive, and difficult to live with. What was wrong?

Donald was initiating sound strategies, but he was following a prescription someone else had laid out for him. He'd adopted the strategies he was given without taking into account his own solutions. He was like a smoker who knows he ought to quit to avoid the risks of emphysema and lung cancer but who never has the internal motivation to follow through. Donald's strategies were failing because he had not yet become his own authority on how to recover. You will learn on page 232 how Donald eventually created strategies that brought him true and lasting success in restoring his Personal, Productivity and Partnership resources as you read on.

ACTING "AS IF"

Don't make the mistake that Donald made and you will stay on course. As you initiate the strategies that can strike a harmonious chord within you, realize that the step will be time-consuming and tough. You cannot afford to make snap judgments on what will make you successful; and you often have multiple goals and many strategies you are testing and evaluating simultaneously. It may help you to deal with the complexity of your Inventing task to think of yourself as being in the middle of your experiment. Many roads do lead forward at this point, but you must travel each one at least part of the way to see whether it leads to your destination or is a dead-end trail.

Don't hesitate to give each strategy any extra advantage for success that you can. Let me demonstrate the value a positive mental attitude can play in breeding success by recounting a personal story about a famous psychologist to whom I have already referred. William James lived and wrote prolifically at the turn of this century. In his work and in his private life, he used a process of experimentation to generate productive new behaviors and attitudes he called "acting as if."

When William James was a young adult, his life amounted to little more than total failure. He was unemployed, unhealthy, and severely depressed. Yet, he pulled himself together and became productive and healthy by acting *as if* what he did would make a difference. By assuming and believing that certain behavior, thoughts, and feelings would make him successful, they did.

Science is full of cases that verify the positive effects of self-fulfilling attitudes and prophecies. Cancerous tumors can be eliminated with the aid of positive imaging. Sports figures can improve their records by visualizing success. Businesses thrive on confident investment speculations.

The fact is that whenever we believe that we can accomplish something, we increase the odds that we will reach our goal. So don't be surprised if many of your strategies succeed. The important thing to remember is that they will have a better chance of making life better for you if you have *faith* that they will.

Part 3: Evaluating

I have two points of caution for you to consider as you evaluate your strategies: *don't give up too soon on any one strategy, and don't assume too quickly that a particular strategy is successful.*

▲ LIFE SHALL FLOURISH ▲

Psalm 92, verses 5–9, assures us that despite iniquity and wickedness, God's work is just and life shall prevail.

> How great are thy works, O Lord!
>   Thy thoughts are very deep!
> The dull man cannot know,
>   the stupid cannot understand this:
> that, though the wicked sprout like grass
>   and all evildoers flourish,
> they are doomed to destruction for ever . . .
>   for, lo, thy enemies shall perish;
>   all evildoers shall be scattered.

Here are some examples of what can happen if you ignore these precautions.

If you are getting results, stick with the strategy for a while to confirm its value. Do not assume it will work forever. That assumption may backfire on you as it did for Donald when he initiated his first set of externally imposed strategies. He found that some activities worked for a while and then lost their rewarding features. The actions that fizzled out in the long run for him were those listed here:

Donald's Goals	Success Strategies
Increased energy	▲ working at the office for six hours per day
	▲ walking outside for one hour per day
Continue career as a chemical engineer	▲ transfer out of his position into one with less pressure
Be more open with family and friends	▲ discuss his angry feelings at least once a week

Eventually Donald had to modify those strategies to promote his progress. As it turned out for Donald, in order

▲ to increase his energy level, he needed to work eight, not six hours; to exercise only forty-five minutes; and to rest twenty minutes after lunch.

▲ to continue his career, Donald transferred jobs three times before he found the right fit.

▲ to be more open in his relationships, Donald found he had to learn how to listen.

Beware also of the tendency to *overdo* putting each strategy to the test. Out of overzealousness and impatience, you may stretch your testing to ridiculous lengths just as a friend of mine did after adjusting to the trauma of a disappointing romance.

After breaking up a long-term romantic relationship, Terry decided that one of her goals would be to become physically strong and energetic. She needed to build her stamina. Terry chose long-distance running as a success strategy. She believed that running an average of sixty miles per week would make her tougher and build her resilience. Terry increased her mileage gradually and sustained a sixty-mile strategy for two months.

One day she twisted her ankle while on a twelve-mile run. Instead of giving in to the pain of the injury, Terry persisted in her strategy of running the distance that day and for twelve consecutive days thereafter. She was stuck in her strategy—so much so that she failed to take good care of herself, even when her body sent her a clear signal to change.

Two weeks later Terry had an X ray and found out that she had fractured her leg. It was healing, but she was shocked to learn that her activities had retarded her progress, not advanced it. You can learn from Terry's mistake that you can extend a good strategy too far. Pay close attention to your signals of success and failure to be sure you *are* on the road to progress.

SIGNALS OF SUCCESS

Evaluate your success in terms of how you feel inside as well as in terms of how much progress you have made. This internal evaluation is particularly important when you have shaped a goal that has no real measure of internal fit. For example, a goal such as regaining financial security can be achieved by using a wide variety of strategies. Some strategies might produce internal tension and dissatisfaction, even though they effectively produce financial success. They would not be truly successful strategies.

You may want to evaluate your internal success signals by using the *Self-Evaluation of Adrenaline Impact* questionnaire in Chapter Six (p. 124). This assessment tool will help you to make certain that during the challenging process of pursuing your success strategies you are generating *adrenaline assets* for yourself instead of *adrenaline liabilities*.

COACH, DON'T CRITICIZE YOURSELF

In the evaluation process you may wonder if even successful strategies will ever lead you to your ultimate goals. Your strategies may be working, but the path to your goal may be long and arduous.

In pursuing long-range goals—such as building a new career or developing an intimate relationship—you need to be your own best coach, not your own best critic. Unfortunately, most of us have far more practice being our own "best critic" rather than our own "best coach."

One way to be a coach is to be careful about what you say to yourself (Self-talk), and what you say out loud in conversation about your progress. You need to be careful because what you say dictates, to a large extent, how you will react emotionally to your long-term growth. Consider the following example:

▲ BUFFERS AGAINST THE TRAUMA OF WAR ▲

A rare study of *immediate* stress resistance during a massive crisis was carried out by Stevan E. Hobfoll of Kent State University and Perry London of Harvard University on Israeli women whose loved ones were being mobilized for combat. The researchers reported that women who possessed the coping resources of self-esteem and a sense of mastery had less anxiety and depression during that traumatic first week of uncertainty in the Israel-Lebanon war, which began in June 1982.

Situation: Work overload—Deadlines—Lack of cooperation

Critical Self-talk: I'll never finish.

How do these people expect me to ever get this done all by myself?

You'd have to be Superman to be able to do this.

These negative statements about a stressful work situation promote such feelings as resentment, being overwhelmed, frustration, anger, and the like. With negative emotions come pessimism and low motivation. Now, take the same situation and consider the impact of positive Self-talk.

Coaching Self-talk: Let's see how much I can get finished.

Working intensely makes the day go quickly.

If I do the best job I can in this tight situation . . .

I'll get a lot of self-satisfaction.

Even though the situation is admittedly tough, with positive, coaching Self-talk, you can encourage rather than discourage yourself. This self-coaching mentality will lead to enthusiasm and feeling in charge of yourself. Self-confidence and determination will follow.

With coaching Self-talk you save your energy and maintain a good mood during situations that would feel stressful if you let your *critic* talk you into it.

PART 4: INTEGRATING

When you reach Part 4, you have chosen a series of success strategies that are best suited to help you achieve your agenda for personal growth. The value and merit of those options have begun to take hold. You are thinking, feeling, and acting in ways that improve your life. You are on a solid course and it is time to integrate your action strategies into your permanent repertoire of approaches to living.

Practice integrating those attitudes and skills often so that they become your automatic responses. We will examine how this happens in the next two chapters. This process of Integration will lead you directly into the self-transformation that takes place in the fourth and final stage of your growth.

In fact, it is your ability to integrate the best of your success strategies into your day-by-day routine that produces your *Readiness Signals* for progressing on to Stage IV.

Your Stage III *Readiness Signals* include

☐1. a strong sense of confidence in your capacity to cope.

☐2. feelings of mastery over adversity.

☐3. applying success strategies to everyday living, without thinking.

☐4. a strong sense of control over your life.

☐5. high energy and stamina.

☐6. restful sleep.

Thanks to your creative energy and your willingness to believe in yourself enough to take chances, your success strategies have worked. You have made your world of thoughts and feelings overlap with your world of actions. Some actions that you imagined and hoped would help you change your life for the better have proven successful. You are achieving your possibilities and are ready to become a new person living a better-than-ever life.

Congratulations! You are a champion who has paid the price, and your final victory is near at hand.

11

▲

Do-It-Yourself
Life Living

AMOR FATI

Amor fati is a Latin phrase that means "the love of one's fate." If you are able to act in your own best interest, despite stressful trauma, you will actually come to *love* your fate. This happens because you have been able to triumph over adversity by embracing it.

Because of the self-empowering process, your future is not solely determined by chance or some force outside you that you cannot control. Your ultimate fate is partially your own choice, the result of your active partnership with adversity. You have chosen the champion's adventure: to be challenged by trauma and to restore yourself and your life to what you have

---

▲ A SENSE OF CONTROL ▲

People who see themselves as having a moderate to high degree of control over events show less anxiety and depression in response to negatively stressful changes than people who see themselves as having little if any control over environmental events.

Researcher Irwin Sarason and his colleagues at the University of Washington discovered the stress-buffering effects of "a sense of control" over a decade ago.

---

chosen for yourself. You have chosen to be ultimately responsible for how your life turns out. You have claimed your own destiny.

Following this kind of tough and demanding course of personal growth in response to adversity is what I term "Do-it-yourself living."

YOUR STAGE IV EXPERIENCE

For everyone who enters Stage IV, the pressures and hurdles of a *traumatized* life are *transformed* into the natural pressures of everyday, ongoing reality. The demands on your adaptive energy are mild. You use less energy in this stage of transformation because you are capitalizing on your momentum rather than initiating something new. Your efforts are spent in *doing* rather than in *analyzing,* in *expressing* rather than *interpreting,* in *releasing* rather than in *building.* As you stabilize, you know that you have produced a lasting and beneficial transformation for yourself.

What you experience as you enter this phase of stability is the relief you feel whenever you get positive results from a well-conceived and well-executed project. When your upside-down world turns right side up, you feel safe and sure of yourself in the center of your new reality. You have engaged challenges and embraced demanding conditions. You generated goals and you experimented with action. Now the *new you* emerges, a metamorphosis. You have adapted, in the best way possible, to the way life is.

Let's look now at your Scorecard of Progress and focus on the experience and goals of Stage IV. (See page 66 for the complete Self-Empowerment Scorecard.)

SELF-EMPOWERMENT SCORECARD				
				Stage IV Transformation
Mental and Emotional Reactions				Satisfaction, Mastery, Meaning, Growth
Goals				To stabilize new achieve-ments
Sample Time Frame for Mastery				12–20 Weeks
Demands on Adaptive Energy				Mild
Primary Ad-justment Assets				Commit-ment

This portion of the Self-Empowerment Scorecard emphasizes that you have arrived at your destination of personal growth and fulfillment. You may be surprised at your arrival, but you have great cause for celebration. As you move through Stage IV, your goal will be to complete your personal transformation. Two of your new attitudes tell you that you are ready to make your gains permanent and positive: *commitment to sustained growth* and *an appreciation of the value of crisis and trauma.*

COMMITMENT TO SUSTAINED GROWTH

The case of Doreen, a manager in a fast-paced, high-turnover newspaper operation, was referred to me by the paper's executive vice-president. Doreen had not adapted well enough to her new responsibilities as editor of the daily life-style section. Her rough exterior and toughness—qualities that had made her a top-flight political reporter—were hindering her ability to manage in a less driven division.

When we first met, Doreen made it clear that she had no time for warmth or light conversation. She was attractive, but her fine facial features were overshadowed by her severe, closely cropped hairdo. She wore a conservative business suit and sat very erect and motionless. While I found her façade to be very serious, it struck me that she had a gentle quality, a real note of curiosity about herself and a genuine interest in eliminating her limitations as a manager.

I recall in particular one moment during our first interview that showed Doreen's tender side. She was nervous and tense about giving me a full description of her shortcomings, but she acknowledged that her career was on the line. She said, "I will lose this job or take a demotion if I don't change." Her eyes welled with tears as she continued, "I just have no idea how to begin."

As her story unfolded, I learned that Doreen had always relied on hard work and savvy to get ahead. Overnight those skills were no longer enough. She now had to emphasize and fine-tune her leadership skills and abilities to get along with people.

Her peers found her irritable and a loner. Her co-workers were turned off and angered by her abrupt responses. And, most significantly, her subordinates complained that they were highly dissatisfied with their jobs and the quality of Doreen's supervision. Doreen's career was in great jeopardy.

We decided to explore her new reality by asking people how they thought she ought to change in order to be more effective. With some coaching, Doreen surveyed her employees comprehensively about their perceptions, attitudes, and concerns regarding the way the section operated. She asked them to evaluate her personal strengths and weaknesses. Remarkably, she got one hundred percent participation in the survey, with reporters and clerks making lengthy written comments.

The results showed that her staff had a love-hate relationship with Doreen. They praised her impeccable confidence, drive, and hard work and indicated that she inspired them. But her personal inaccessibility intimidated them. They said she had an air of distance. They were reluctant to approach her.

Doreen took the important step of publicly announcing the results of the survey and what she intended to do to improve her performance. She established open-door hours so that any worker could talk informally with her about ideas for the section. She scheduled more team meetings and instituted a new performance-incentive system. She personally recognized top performance on a weekly basis by taking those who earned it out to lunch and sending a memo about their accomplishments to her boss.

Although this approach was totally new for Doreen, she came to believe it was her only way of turning around a bad situation. Doreen struggled to follow those success strategies and made a major effort to transform herself.

It was only in Stage IV of her adjustment that Doreen discovered she had to keep Inventing new strategies to maintain her solid position as a leader. She had to commit herself to developing new ways of bringing out her personal effectiveness as a communicator. She had to release once and for all her outmoded notion that leaders were not closely involved with their staff. Constantly revamping her strategies made it possible for Doreen to see herself as an astute and conscientious manager of people. She now could inspire and guide them. Her flexibility became an automatic part of her leadership skills.

As it turned out, Doreen's adjustment to her trauma was accompanied by a long-term commitment to doing whatever it took to be a successful leader. She made a commitment to thrive, no matter how often she had to change her behavior to do so.

You may find that your traumatic event requires that you continuously invent new success strategies, as Doreen had to do. Inventing and reinventing ways to meet your own needs in a given situation is a mark of commitment to thriving. When you sense this in yourself, you will be sure you are in Stage IV.

ANOTHER FORM OF COMMITMENT

There is another true mark of commitment to ongoing success that involves repeating the same success strategies over and over again, in order to deal with a traumatic situation that does not subside. Let me tell you about someone who must repeat her primary success strategy *countless times,* every day of her life, in order to remain strong and healthy under her traumatic circumstances. You may detect this type of commitment in your own behavior.

One steaming day in July, at the end of my first visit to Israel, I took a hot, crowded taxi to the airport. The four of us who were jammed into the back seat of that *sherute* got to know each other well during the hour-long trip.

One passenger was a woman who had taught art at a local university. She had lived in the Jewish Quarter of the Old City of Jerusalem all her life. She told me how her heart ached over Israel's internal tragedies—its history of war and terrorism and the death of young men and women soldiers. Yet, she was completely at ease with living her life there. She had evolved a strategy for thriving under daily living conditions that were often tense and even dangerous.

While teaching art at the university, she had been struck by how art is a powerful tool for expressing hidden feelings. She decided that families in war-torn Israel could benefit from expressing their experiences through art. From this idea she developed a new type of family portrait, a tableau she makes out of clay. Each family member appears in the tableau, in a three-dimensional, familiar background that has some special meaning. She places family members in positions that show how they relate to each other. She adds pets, or dishes, or other paraphernalia that reflect the family's life-style and history.

She only makes use of *positive* family dynamics and symbols. Thus, her creations possess a healing quality, for each family member is able to see, through art, his or her importance to the others. The tableau is a permanent clay record of family affection and esteem.

Amid the violence in the Old City of Jerusalem and in the West Bank, this woman is fulfilling herself and giving others support and relief by living out her commitment. The artist in her makes her life rewarding, despite dire living conditions that may last a long time. You may need this type of unrelenting commitment to sustain your success.

APPRECIATING CRISIS AND TRAUMA

How many times have you looked back at how much your life has changed, and how much you have grown since your trauma, and said to yourself, "I can't believe how different I am now and how different my life is!"

It was Heraclitus who, 2,500 years ago, said: "Nothing endures but change." And although we know this ancient adage is true, more today than ever, we are often surprised at the speed and substance of our own growth. We seem particularly surprised when we grow by adjusting to crisis and trauma.

No one seeks out traumas that bring grave setbacks and

profound loss. All of us recoil from events that turn our world upside down. But you now have no doubt that you can use those periods to become stronger and healthier and to enrich your life. Because you are no longer in a state of upheaval, you are more able to be objective about what the whole experience has meant to you.

In psychological terms, crises and traumas of any sort represent novelty in our lives: a break from the familiar routines. They are powerful, novel circumstances. It may be of some interest to you to note that our modern psychological approach to dealing with adversity has its ancient religious and mythological counterparts. For centuries people have been trying to come to terms with how to deal effectively with adversity. Cultures and religions generated many of their myths and stories, which contain wisdom about how to capitalize on crises, as resources for their adherents. You may find it valuable to supplement the system you have learned here with the wisdom of your favorite religious passage.

ANCIENT FORMULAS

Take the Old Testament story of Noah and the Flood, for example. This biblical wisdom reinforces the notion that you must be challenged by trauma and move through progressive stages to realize the trauma's potential benefits.

The story of Noah begins as he accepts God's challenge to prepare for an event that will devastate the world. Noah builds an ark for the tumultuous times ahead.

You also have built an ark to sustain you through trauma. It is your self-empowerment system and your inner balance of vital resources.

In the Noah story the initial catastrophe lasted forty days and forty nights, a time frame remarkably similar to Stage I, the challenging period of many traumas, which you know typically lasts from four to eight weeks. Most translations of the Hebrew Bible then tell of the water rising until the 150th day, when the established order of things disappeared from the face of the earth. This time calculation corresponds to the realization of profound loss during Stage II, exploring a new reality. This segment of the biblical metaphor illustrates the drawn-out nature of the second stage of adjustment, as well as its tumultuous character. You can surely appreciate Noah's devastation when the flood wiped out the world as he knew it. It is how you felt during Stage II.

Then the waters subsided and became calm. The flow of water from the fountains of the deep and the windows of heaven came to a halt, and the ark rested on Mount Ararat. Then Noah began testing and experimenting, which is, as you know, the work of Stage III.

By one account a raven, by another a dove, was sent from the ark to test conditions in the world. The bird returned immediately because the lowlands still were inundated. A second dove was released after seven more days. It returned with an olive branch, which told Noah that the valley was dry. After another seven days, a third dove was sent. It never returned, indicating to Noah that the earth was again safe to inhabit. Noah gained security from the risks of experimenting with new ways in his new and foreign reality.

Finally God sent a rainbow and a message to Noah: Go forth, be fruitful, and multiply. Noah, out of appreciation for his journey and his salvation, built an altar to God. Noah's burnt offerings were a tangible sign of his inner reconciliation to the disastrous flood.

At that moment of reconciliation, Noah completed Stage IV. He was transformed, blessed by growth and survival. The Lord is said to have smelled the sweet savor of Noah's commemoration of his willing sacrifice, and He seems to have been so deeply touched, He vows never again to destroy all life. The lesson here is that your life will never again be destroyed in the same way either. You have moved to new ground.

Like Noah, you must agree to promote your own growth rather than bemoan your new existence. Once you grasp that your personal growth is closely linked to your having dealt effectively with trauma, you position yourself to capitalize on traumas in the future, to enter into partnership with whatever devastates you.

You may want to ponder other cultural myths and religious stories so that you can deepen your appreciation that crisis and trauma are truly vehicles for your own growth. The work of Carl Jung is a rich reservoir for the study of myth and religion. Originally a follower of Freud and the founder of his own psychoanalytic school, Carl Jung wrote volumes of provocative overviews and in-depth studies of how human beings express struggle and transformation in secular and religious art, literature, and music. Most of the representations Jung studied belong to what he termed the *collective unconscious*, that element of mind that unites all of us to each other and to the cosmos.

According to Jung, each of us must become aware of the rich contents of our collective unconscious process in order to achieve true awareness of ourselves. He called this process of becoming oneself *individuation*. For Jung, individuation is the goal of life: "Everything living dreams of individuation, for everything strives towards its own wholeness, and the greatest possible actualization of the self is the aim of life." (Letter, April 23, 1949, *Word and Image*, p. 78)

Our struggle toward individuation is fraught with crises and

▲ MEANING OVERCOMES MISERY ▲

Psychiatrist Viktor Frankl, in his seven-year observational study of survivors of Hitler's death camps, reported that some people emerged from their concentration camp experience with a heightened sense of self.

In his book *Man's Search for Meaning*, Frankl suggests that people who are able to find a purpose in their suffering and death are able to resist hopelessness and despair. He proposes that when the cherished meanings of one's life lose their validity due to a trauma, the healthy person creates new meaning that takes the trauma into account.

traumas because images from our collective unconscious often overwhelm our conscious mind. For this reason individuation is understood as a heroic adventure, a battle against the awesome might of dragon (the unconscious) for the sake of fully realizing selfhood.

In *Mysterium Coniunctionis* (The Mysterious, Mystical Union), Jung explains the motif of this heroic exploit. See how it resembles the path you took to master adversity.

> In myths the hero is the one who conquers the dragon, not the one who is devoured by it. And yet both have to deal with the same dragon. Also, he is no hero who never met the dragon, or who, if he once saw it, declared afterwards that he saw nothing. Equally, only one who has risked the fight with the dragon and is not overcome by it wins the hoard, the "treasure hard to attain." He alone has a genuine claim to self-confidence, for he has faced the dark ground of his self and thereby has gained himself. . . . He has *arrived at an inner certainty which makes him capable of self-reliance, and attained what the alchemists called the unio mentalis* [the unity of mind]. As a rule this state is represented pictorially by a mandala. [emphasis added]

Mandalas are circular designs that are symbols of the universe. They are characteristically found in Chinese art and religion. Jung believed that mandalas also appear to people in their dreams as archetypal images of transformation.

MANDALA

PERSONAL SYMBOLS OF TRANSFORMATION

Because of your heroic adventure mastering trauma, you too have arrived at inner certainty and achieved self-reliance. It is time now in Stage IV for you to look for the symbols of your own personal transformation and growth.

As with every other stage, your dreams offer you a rich source of information about your current state of well-being. In Stage IV dreams usually are full of symbols that reflect newly achieved health and happiness. Sometimes these symbols give the first clue that an inner transformation has occurred. In fact, some people don't even realize they have reached Stage IV until their dreams tell them so.

Donna Spencer, a psychotherapist who is an expert in Jungian dream analysis, recounts a Stage IV dream of one of her clients in her article *The Playful Use of Words in Therapy*. Dr. Spencer's client dreamt about her own transformation before she was *consciously* aware of her own growth. With her permission, I include Dr. Spencer's case description and her personal communications to me about that Stage IV dream. As you read them, notice how the logical waking mind can be pessimistic, while the subconscious mind is extremely optimistic.

▲ DREAM RECALL ▲

How often does a man say as he wakes in the morning, "I had a wonderful dream last night," and relate how Mercury or this or that philosopher appeared to him in person and taught him this or that art. But then the dream escapes him and he cannot remember it. However, anyone to whom this happens should not leave his room upon awakening, should speak to no one; but remain alone and sober until everything comes back to him, and he recalls his dream. [*Paracelsus: Selected Writings*, p. 134]

Another client defied all methods of traditional treatment to deal with her guilt and anxiety about a marriage outside the church. This woman was withdrawn sexually, was extremely religious, and was anxious to the point of severe depression. After several methods of treatment were unsuccessful, she commented, "I guess nobody can help me but myself, and I certainly don't know what to do." I decided to let her help herself and simply suggested that she stay open to whatever method her unconscious would use to solve the problem.

Within a few days she called me frantically saying that she had a dream that must mean bad luck. She said all she could remember was a series of numbers that added up to *13*—an unlucky number. I asked her to come in for an appointment. She began telling me the dream. She had a wonderful glow on her face as she recounted the dream, but she insisted the numbers added to *13* and must mean something unlucky. I asked her if the number *13* appeared in the dream. She said it did not. This led me to suspect that her recall of the number *13* and her feeling of bad luck were her conscious interpretation, not the deepest meaning of the dream for her. So we probed further. I asked her what numbers had occurred unconsciously in the dream. She exclaimed with a smile on her face:

"6 4 2 1"

They were exactly in that order. We played with the sounds of this sequence of numbers, repeating them often out loud. Soon the client lit up and said: "God's given me a Christmas present. The message of the dream is

6 4 2 1
Sex for two, won!"

Dr. Spencer's client was able to discover through her dream that she had won the right to have sex with her husband after all of her struggles. Her insight was so affirming for her that Dr. Spencer reports that the client left her guilt and anxiety behind and actually went home to prepare for a second honeymoon with her husband.

As farfetched as this dream interpretation may sound, it is

the insights from dreams like this that help people break through their heartache to see a way out of pointless suffering. Dreams can be the most reliable guide to a person's psychological growth. That is why I have asked you to record your dreams and to reflect on what they might mean. Trust your unconscious dream processes as an accurate signaling system confirming your Stage IV transformations.

In some cases working with a professional who can help you to re-experience your dreams is beneficial. Sometimes your logical conscious mind is incapable of thorough insights into your dream symbols.

In addition to your dream life, your waking life offers you signals that you are in Stage IV of your adjustment. You have watched for readiness signals at the end of each stage of progress that told you you were ready to move on to the next phase. What signals should you look for to assure yourself that you are ready to complete this final phase of transformation?

Here is another set of signs to verify that you have, indeed, restored your inner balance. These *Signals of Inner Balance* come with my congratulations for your accomplishments.

SIGNALS OF INNER BALANCE

Watch for these signs of being *centered* in yourself, as you complete the work of transforming in Stage IV.

☐ 1. Tendency to think and act spontaneously.

☐ 2. Enjoyment of simple pleasures.

☐ 3. Reluctance to be judgmental.

☐ 4. Loss of interest in dominating or in escaping stress-ful situations.

☐ 5. Inability to worry (a very serious symptom).

☐ 6. Frequent overwhelming episodes of appreciation of your vital resources.

☐ 7. Contented feelings of connectedness with others and nature.

☐ 8. Frequent attacks of self-confidence.

☐ 9. Increasing capacity to accept what happens rather than to make something happen.

☐ 10. Susceptibility to accepting care and kindness from others, as well as the controllable urge to reciprocate.

12

▲

Becoming a Champion of Change

The culmination of your adventures in coping with adversity is the realization that your life is filled with rewards again and you are back in balance as you go about your daily business. It may seem almost magical that your inner world and outer world are in harmony and synchrony. Yet at the same time you know how hard you have struggled to recover your health and happiness.

As you enter Stage IV, you feel alive and vital. You experience a glorious kind of renewal that puts you in touch with nature's life cycle. As an ancient Chinese proverb states, "In time the mulberry leaf becomes silk." Just as the mulberry leaf is destroyed by the caterpillar and then transformed into something better, the trauma that consumed you provoked your profound transformation. By virtue of your inner strength and skills, you transformed your life for the better.

During Stage IV will come the moment that you realize you now are *silk* instead of a *mulberry leaf*. This is time for joy, reflection, and storytelling.

THE IMPORTANCE OF TELLING YOUR STORY

At the culmination of a complex process, such as the one you learned in thriving during adversity, it is important for you to reflect on what actually happened and be able to tell the story. Reflecting and storytelling reinforce your gains and, as you will see in just a moment, are also a boon to health.

When you relive your growth process by recalling what happened and then expressing your reflections in the words to a story, you internalize your recollections and make them part of you forever. This is how you learn what went well and what turned out poorly. Your reflections reveal to you your own inner strengths that promoted your accomplishments.

You may, in Stage IV, for the first time during your adjustment to your trauma, want to tell your story. In some ways internalizing your growth experience is analogous to learning lines for a part in a play. First you read over the lines; then you rehearse them over and over again mentally; and then you are ready to speak them. The mental rehearsal allows you to integrate the lines fully into your memory bank and then to recall them at will.

That's what I would like you to be able to do with your growth experience. I would like you to retrace mentally the sequential steps of your progress often enough so that you can recall them at will, integrated to form a story.

When you learn how to reflect on your experiences and use those reflections to solidify your transformation, you will be meeting your Stage IV goal.

STAGE IV GOAL

To fully transform yourself by integrating your new ways of acting and being a healthier and happier person.

I always remind people who are entering Stage IV about the tremendous power of reflective storytelling for personal transformation and healing the deep wounds of trauma.

An unhealed trauma is like a loaded gun in your mind that could go off at the slightest provocation. We've all met people who mull over the traumatic events in their life and who become emotional invalids as the result of their pent-up anguish.

Telling and retelling your story, as often as necessary to fully release your negatively charged feelings, is one medicine that heals. And, when your story emphasizes the positive aspects of how you mastered the trauma, you automatically will reinforce the success of your newly formed strategies. Consider the following research findings made by James Pennebaker and his colleagues:

▲ Men and women who have suddenly lost their spouse in an accident or due to suicide remained healthier if they talked to other people about their tragedies than if they did not.

▲ People who kept a journal of their feelings about a life event that affected them very deeply, in a traumatic and upsetting way, had fewer trips to the doctor, fewer health complaints, and fewer drugs prescribed in a six-month follow-up period than other people who kept a journal about neutral life events such as going to the ball game.

▲ People who disclosed their feelings about a trauma showed improved immune-system functioning six weeks after the end of the research study.

Apparently we can boost our immunity and keep ourselves healthier if we unload our troubled feelings and remind ourselves of what we have managed to accomplish despite our stressful adversity. We can do it through our private Empowerment Journal and in conversations with friends and professionals.

▲ CONFESSION IS NOT ONLY GOOD FOR THE SOUL ▲

In their newest book, *Healthy Pleasures,* researchers Robert Ornstein and David Sobel cite myriad evidence that telling your own story can help you heal. The following example is perhaps their most compelling.

Thirty-three survivors of the Holocaust gave videotaped interviews about their experiences during World War II while skin conductance and heart rate were monitored.

Virtually all these survivors had suffered, many of them in silence, for decades. They had been displaced from their homes and forcibly relocated in ghettos. Many endured random beatings. Most witnessed the deaths of children, close friends, and family members.

Was it better for their health to disclose the most private aspects of their experiences? Those who more freely describe their powerful trauma reported fewer health problems. Expressing *both* the facts of the trauma and the emotions seems to be critical for health improvement. [p. 186]

Here is one story of trauma that celebrated the success and promoted the health of the person who told it.

ELLEN'S STORY

Ellen couldn't wait to tell me about the transformations she had achieved as the result of almost two years of hard work. Ellen had needed to adjust to the trauma of her father's grave illness, which had put Ellen in charge of the floundering family business.

At her six-month follow-up interview, this business executive walked into my office, sat down, looked me in the eye, and said proudly: "You won't believe how much I've changed. I'm always on time now. My reading stack is always cleared within a week. All of my phone calls are returned within one day. I'm still working nine- and ten-hour days, but I have tremendous energy in the evenings. I feel like I'm back in control. I believe in myself again. I know I can handle anything that's important enough for me to tackle."

She leaned back in her chair and smiled. I noticed how pleased with herself and confident she appeared. Just eighteen months before, Ellen was a near casualty of a little-understood trauma in life—a change in power in a family business. Through political connections and a raw brand of charisma, Ellen's father had built a thriving investment-brokerage business. But he had become ill, forcing Ellen to shoulder more and more of the burden of the business before she felt ready to do so.

When she began her work with me Ellen was twenty-eight. She felt anxious, confused, and overwhelmed by the prospect of taking over her family's company. She knew that she lacked her father's charm and political allies. To make her anxiety worse, Ellen's mother was constantly reminding her of her shortcomings. She told Ellen that she saw no chance of her being capable of keeping the business profitable and of making a financially comfortable retirement possible.

Ellen also sensed resentment from the staff of the firm, where she had worked as a salesperson for six years before her father became ill. Ellen was torn between following her dream to take over the firm, as her father wished, and simply walking away from the hassles and entering another career altogether.

After a painstaking examination of her options, Ellen decided in favor of the family business. She established her goals and invented success strategies, and engaged this change *as if* she would become the company president, knowing full well that at any time she could opt out of the situation if necessary. Not only did she believe that she had the skills for heading the company from her training as a master's-level business graduate, but she was enthralled by the idea of making her mark at such a young age.

So Ellen chose the path she wanted to follow, but it was fraught with roadblocks and pitfalls. She had to accept the attitudes of staff people who resented her father's absence and missed his inspirational leadership. She had to confront the jealousies of those who believed she inherited the presidency by birthright and not by hard work and ambition. She had to bolster her self-confidence to deal with the remnants of a weakened organization—one that had been fueled by her father's popularity and held together by his strong personality, rather than by sound business practices.

Finally, Ellen had to face the fact that she was all alone in this task. Her greatest supporter, her father, was little help because of his illness. And Ellen's mother was never her ally. She continued to strike out at Ellen with harsh barbs and criticism.

In spite of those obstacles, Ellen established herself as the company leader. And in the midst of her challenges she maintained a sacred schedule of exercise and good eating habits. She made sure to exercise in the places and at the times when she was most likely to make contacts for the business. Ellen, a long-time renter, bought a house to make a statement to her staff about her independence and stability.

She made dramatic changes in the business, too. Ellen appointed an office manager and formed a task force that was responsible for developing policies on a wide range of issues from marketing, to personnel, to the status of subsidiary firms. Ellen fired several deadwood employees her father had tolerated, and she sold two subsidiary companies. As these structural changes made a positive impact, she gained confidence that her academic training would yield her approaches to her business that worked as well as career experience.

Ellen also took a symbolic step. She redecorated the office, turning her father's area into a conference room and re-establishing the president's suite elsewhere. One of the biggest changes in company morale occurred when Ellen learned to accept and appreciate the employees' natural grieving for her by then deceased father.

None of this happened easily. Many times when Ellen talked to me she choked up about the unearned criticism and abuse she took from the staff, who persisted in comparing her performance to her father's. She resented the fact that, as president, she had to re-earn the faith and trust of staff who had been her peers when she was on the sales staff.

In her herculean personal and professional effort, Ellen often was exhausted from fighting unmet deadlines, overwork, and overextension. She fell into periods of confusion and uncertainty. She had trouble setting priorities, whether they concerned new hiring practices or restructuring divisions of the company.

But Ellen persisted and worked diligently for more than a year. Gradually she saw her efforts come together. When she remarked that I wouldn't believe how much she'd changed, I responded, "You've changed because of how much you've grown." Her success stemmed from her decision to marshal her own resources rather than try to re-create her father's strategies. That would have been counterproductive. She invented her own solutions, just as you have done.

By Stage IV, Ellen knew that she had succeeded in mastering her upside-down world. What she needed to accomplish next was a fuller appreciation of *how* she had been able to grow stronger and more skillful. Telling her story to me was Ellen's first step toward fully internalizing her successful experiences.

MY OWN STORY RETOLD

My own progress after the death of my brother detailed in Chapter One took a major positive turn in Stage IV of my recovery and growth. It was in December, exactly one year after Jim's devastating death, that I first became aware that I might be plodding through all of the heartache and confusion to a better mindset. I found myself with extra energy and even some creative ideas. I noticed that my mind raced ahead, but my activity level could not begin to keep pace with my thought processes. Creative solutions to what appeared to be disastrous business problems popped up out of nowhere. Something mysterious was happening to me on the inside, bubbling up to the surface, to my conscious level—the results of all my struggle to make sense out of tragedy.

Before long my energy level was up and I had reserves to go the extra miles of effort to accomplish important tasks. Suddenly many things seemed important, in stark contrast to my earlier confusion and malaise.

During this phase of Stage IV, I became captivated by my immediate work. I felt intrigued again by the possibilities of new projects. My vision of the past with all of its pain was just as intense and real, but now so was my appreciation for what that pain had taught me.

As I advanced to Stage IV, I could almost feel myself undergo a metamorphosis. I felt happy again and rewarded by the work I was doing at the Stress Center. My knowledge of my strengths, as well as of my shortcomings, was far superior to what it had been. I was more at ease with the prospect of living, or of dying—whichever condition would prevail. Even my relation-ships with other people seemed more honest, less tense. I had matured.

I sensed that part of the beauty of this life is due to paradox. When opposites clash, our consciousness is raised, our awareness is heightened, our capacity to grow is expanded. My final stage of adjustment taught me this power of contrasting elements. It was in the juxtaposition of Jim's death and my personal growth that I was able to glimpse answers to the eternal questions of WHY? Why death? Why tragedy? Why crisis? Why loss? Why disappointment? I had been forced to face it.

The WHY answers were hidden deep within the power of paradox. My brother's death turned out to be a vital force that provoked me to live better. Real tragedy had forced me to become a deeper person. It nurtured my urge to create. The senseless waste of a young life instilled in me a longing to become more alive.

Although death had smashed with one blow all the previous bridges of communication between Jim and me, my struggle gave me one more chance to make our personal connection worthwhile. By letting the meaning of Jim's death fully infiltrate me, I would be able to be more aware and more full of passion for being alive. And that is precisely what happened.

As Jim's death taught me to see life more clearly it seemed to me that my former perceptions of things, life, and injustice had been terribly distorted. I look back now at the emotional roller coaster I rode that first year following my brother's death, and I know for certain that that event was the most important teacher of my life. I still find myself slipping backward sometimes into a mental fog where I can't seem to see the meaning of adversity. I am still looking for answers to WHY and still learning from Jim.

Let your trauma become a teacher by learning to express your story and to retell and reflect on it as often as you are inclined to do so.

HOW TO TELL YOUR STORY

STEPPING-STONES TO SUCCESS

The stories of Ellen's mastery over her trauma and tough business challenges and my own Stage IV experiences are examples of how to trace the benchmarks of success.

The recounting of one's stepping-stones to Empowerment is vital to the structure of therapeutic storytelling. As you engage in the process of Stage IV, I would like you to chart the structure of your own stepping-stones to success in your Empowerment Journal.

The best way to start is to clear your mind of extraneous

thoughts so you can review your success. Do this by using Reflective Focus, as you did for exercises in Stages II and III. This time, while you are in this calm but energized mental state, you will remind yourself of your benchmarks of progress during each stage of growth.

Begin recording and charting in your journal the successful steps you took during Stage I.

"When the crisis occurred in Stage I, to eliminate my threats and to create my *challenges* . . ." Think back to that time and say to yourself:

First I _____ ;

and then I _____ ;

and next I _____ .

Remind yourself what you did to advance your progress until the point at which your actions crossed over to the threshold of Stage II. Record your thoughts in your journal.

"In Stage II, as I *explored* my world turned upside down . . ." Think back to that time and say to yourself:

First I _____ ;

and then I _____ ;

and next I _____ .

Remind yourself what you did to advance your progress until the point at which your actions crossed over to the threshold of Stage III. Record your thoughts in your journal.

"In Stage III, as I *invented* goals and strategies to make my life rewarding and fulfilled . . ." Think back to that time and say to yourself:

First I _____ ;

and then I _____ ;

and next I _____ .

Remind yourself what you did to advance your progress until you reach the point at which your actions crossed over to the threshold of Stage IV. Record your thoughts in your journal.

"In Stage IV, as I restored my health and happiness and transformed my life . . ."

First I ———————————————————————— ;

and then I ————————————————————— ;

and next I ————————————————————— .

This completes your historical chronicle of how you grew stronger and healthier through adversity.

Was this a difficult process for you? Which benchmarks of success did you recall easily? Ask yourself how you felt as you reviewed each benchmark. Go back and note your feelings alongside each benchmark. Many people find that until they systematically review the history of their successive steps to growth, they have only a dim awareness of what actually led to their success and how they felt along the way.

After generating your stepping-stones to success, you will not only see what happened more clearly, you will feel proud and excited about your accomplishments.

Because you have reflected on and recalled the highlights of your progress from Stage I through Stage IV, you now are ready to discover exactly what inner strengths you called on to achieve those benchmarks. This next step in evaluating your inner strengths will help you to deepen your insight into your self-empowering growth process.

STRENGTH BOMBARDMENT

Go back now, and in your mental position of Reflective Focus, examine which of your inner strengths you drew upon so that you could achieve each successful stepping-stone. Make notes of your inner strengths.

Becoming a Champion of Change

Stage I: My Inner Strengths Were

Stage II: My Inner Strengths Were

Stage III: My Inner Strengths Were

Stage IV: My Inner Strengths Were

Please do not hesitate to give yourself credit and to pat yourself on the back. Most likely you are not accustomed to taking an inventory of your inner strengths. But when you evaluate which of your Personal resources helped you succeed, give yourself the recognition you deserve. It will bolster your confidence that you will effectively handle any possible future traumas by tapping into those same strengths.

Here are some examples of inner strengths that my clients have discovered helped them to cope with trauma, to grow stronger, and to make their lives better. As you consider these common-denominator inner strengths, supplement your list with those you see operating in yourself.

Common Inner Strengths During Stage I

▲ determination to prevail over adversity
▲ openness to being challenged
▲ willingness to struggle
▲ faith in the support of other people and a higher power

Common Inner Strengths During Stage II

▲ interest and curiosity about the trauma
▲ courge to know reality
▲ sense of responsibility to meet one's own needs

Common Inner Strengths During Stage III

▲ creative goal setting and strategic planning
▲ willingness to fail
▲ visions of how to restore inner balance

Common Inner Strengths During Stage IV

▲ honest appraisal of personal accomplishments
▲ self-appreciation
▲ capacity to feel negatively and positively towards trauma
▲ increased stress resilience

When you complete your list of inner strengths, you may be surprised to find out what profoundly valuable personal resources you have had at your disposal. Remember, these insights into yourself can be tremendously encouraging and motivational.

Most likely you had to muster your inner strengths during periods of suffering and struggle. As you are coming to realize, it is those difficult periods that bring you enlightenment and rewards. What you are doing now, by reflecting on and expressing how your inner strengths contributed to winning those struggles, will help you to discover your best essential ingredients for being a *champion of change*.

DISCOVERING YOUR TRANSFORMATIONS

This last portion of the storytelling process will help you more than any other to make a commitment to your original goal: to learn to thrive through adversity. This is the part in which you will have an internal dialogue about the positive transformations you were able to make at each stage of progress, and about the ultimate transformation for the better that has occurred in you and in your life as the result of your struggle to grow.

The prospect of having a *conversation* with yourself about how you have changed your thoughts, feelings, and actions might seem strange to you at first. But you will see how easy and valuable this type of internal dialogue can be.

To have an internal dialogue about each of your successful transformations:

1. Assume your Reflective Focus position. And then review your journal notes and trace your progress through each stage of Empowerment, so that you refresh your memory of those details.

2. Close your eyes and imagine our large triangular symbol of inner balance with the three interlocking triangles that meet in the center.

3. Recall the label of each category of resources
   a. Personal
   b. Productivity
   c. Partnership

4. Begin your internal dialogue about your transformations, remembering to reflect upon each component of inner balance as you proceed:

a. In Stage I of my crisis, I felt threatened by my trauma in many ways, so I had to shift from a perspective of threat into a position of challenge. I found that I could encourage myself by focusing on the following opportunities and challenges that were made possible by my trauma. (Refer to the work of Chapter 6 in your journal.)

b. In Stage II I explored myself and my world more closely. I found out which resources had been depleted and which channels of support and reward were open to me. (Refer to the work of Chapter 8 in your journal.)

c. In Stage III, through my combined focus on depleted resources, opportunities, and channels of support, goals emerged to guide my actions. (Refer to the work of Chapter 9 in your journal.)

In Stage III I also invented my success strategies. (Refer to the work of Chapter 10 in your journal.)

d. Now, in Stage IV, my success strategies have helped me to satisfy my needs and restore my vital resources. They have *also* created unforeseen positive spin-off effects. I have transformed my life for the better in the following ways (reflect on these benefits and then record them in your journal in a chart like the one shown here):

POSITIVE TRANSFORMATIONS IN MY LIFE

Personal Transformations?

Productivity Transformations?

Partnership Transformations?

This last step completes your internal dialogue about your transformations.

Now take a moment to review your path of progress and the positive transformations in your life in a more analytical way. Use the Self-Empowerment Summary Chart to guide your review (see p. 268). Your Reflective Focus thoughts and images will provide input to this summary, along with your notes from previous exercises. You may want to put this chart into your journal. It is a capsule statement of your story.

TRANSFORMATION HIGHLIGHTS

Through the process of reflection and analysis you have reached the pinnacle of your journey. From atop this perspective you can see how your transformed thoughts, feelings, and behaviors actually restored your whole range of depleted resources. You witness once again how these transformations, in turn, created other benefits that have transformed your life in ways that make it worthwhile to go on living.

At this final juncture of storytelling, you realize that your inner transformations were brought about through the power to seek health and fulfillment.

In some very favorable ways, you were able to change your own thinking, emotions, and actions so you could take advantage of the opportunities available to you in your traumatized upside-down world. You rewarded yourself by restoring your inner balance to become a stronger, more productive and loving person.

STAYING ON TOP

SELF-EMPOWERMENT SUMMARY CHART

Stage I	Eliminate Threats	Illuminate Possibilities	Brainstorm "What Ifs"
Challenge (decrease threats) (increase possibilities)	What is troubling me?	What are my possibilities?	What if I . . . ?
Stage II	*Personal*	*Productivity*	*Partnership*
Exploration (depleted resources and channels of support)	Resources: ----------------- Channels:	Resources: ----------------- Channels:	Resources: ----------------- Channels:
Stage III	*Personal*	*Productivity*	*Partnership*
Invention (goals and strategies)	Goals: ----------------- Strategies:	Goals: ----------------- Strategies:	Goals: ----------------- Strategies:
Stage IV	*Personal*	*Productivity*	*Partnership*
Transformation (vision to reality)	How are my personal resources strengthened?	How has my productivity improved?	How have my partnerships been strengthened?

Think about the amazing recovery you have made. Realize that these transformations will be with you as long as they remain useful to you. Know that whenever you need to, you can transform yourself again, so that you remain a *champion of change*, a person who stays on top whenever the world turns upside down.

THE JOURNEY'S END

As you have seen, this story you have told about your own struggle to master adversity is a major tool of self-affirmation. It also gives you a sense of completion. In Stage IV, after you have recounted your story to yourself, you will notice that your attitude toward past, present, and future has shifted.

You will feel tender, not devastated, when you think about the past and what your trauma caused you to lose. You will be fulfilled in the present moment and happy to be alive, instead of empty and resentful about living. The future is promising after you have reflected and recalled your struggle to grow, because you know that your life is better and it is you who have made it that way.

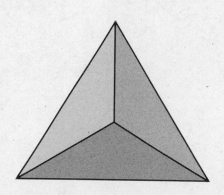

PART

III

▲

13

▲

Four Easy Steps
to Self-Sabotage

There is a great deal of pain in life, and perhaps the only pain that can be avoided is the pain that comes from trying to avoid pain.

—R. D. Laing

I quote psychotherapist and author R. D. Laing here to remind people that suffering and struggle are multiplied when we try to avoid coming to grips with the heartaches and disappointments in life. To resist the pain and challenge of trauma is to travel a dangerous and harmful path. If left unchecked, the resistance to deal with trauma can lead to a full-blown mental and physical breakdown; can rob you of a meaningful life; and can sever your ties to people you love.

Hans Selye, the father of stress research, described the potentially catastrophic effects of unresolved stress in his theory, the General Adaptation Syndrome, which he proposed in 1936. In it Selye suggests that the body defends itself physiologically against a dangerous stressor in three successive stages: Stage I,

At the 1978 St. Louis University conference on New Perspectives on Stress, Dr. Hans Selye told the audience: "If anyone tells you that they can eliminate your stress, run in the other direction because what they are really saying is that they want to kill you. The absence of stress is death."

Alarm; Stage II, Resistance; Stage III, Exhaustion. Selye's theory implied a fourth stage of harm following physiological exhaustion. That stage, of course, is death.

Dr. Selye's stages of physiological defense against the demands of a stressor are depicted in the following graph:

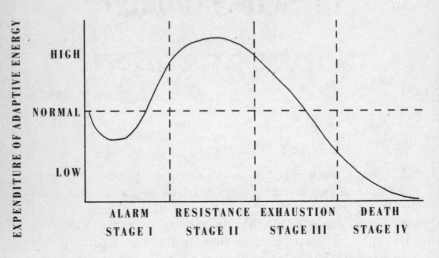

Expenditure of adaptive energy in the stages of the General Adaptation Syndrome

According to Dr. Selye, the supply of your adaptive energy surges during the Alarm Stage to meet the emergency. If the threat continues, your adaptive energy maintains itself through Stage II, Resistance, but begins to drop off rapidly if the stressful demand cannot be resolved. In Stage III, if the stressor has not been eliminated, you will eventually run out of adaptive energy and become exhausted physiologically. I have added a fourth stage to the chart to emphasize that physiological exhaustion can lead to death.

Dr. Selye was primarily concerned with describing what happens to the body when it fights off a physical invader such as a toxic substance or fatal germ. We are concerned with describing what happens to a person who tries to ward off an emotionally traumatic event.

When someone tries to combat a psychologically stressful life event, a debilitating process similar to Selye's General Adaptation Syndrome can occur. This collision course is what I call the *Diversion process*. I use the term *diversion* because when you mentally resist dealing with stressful life events, you take a detour from a course that produces health and happiness to one that *seems* less difficult and less painful. This diversion jeopardizes your Personal, Productivity, and Partnership resources.

▲ DISTURBING NEWS ▲

Again the danger is one of futility through too much evasion of problems rather than of positive damage.

And, if a person does work through to some insight deeply disturbing to him, I believe there are several considerations that we can rely upon. One is that hitting upon some truth is not only disturbing but is also, and simultaneously, of a liberating quality. This liberating force inherent in any truth may supersede the disturbing effect from the beginning. If so, a feeling of relief will ensue immediately. But even if the disturbing effect prevails, the discovery of a truth about oneself still implies a dawning recognition of a way out; even if this is not seen clearly it will be felt intuitively and thus will engender strength to proceed further. [Karen Horney, *Self-analysis,* p. 32]

THE STAGES OF DIVERSION

There are four progressive stages of deterioration in the Diversion process that lead up to damaging setbacks. Think of these stages as parallel and opposite to the four progressive stages of growth in the Empowerment process. The following chart describes this relationship.

Diversion Course			*Empowerment Course*	
Stage I:	Resistance	opposes	Stage I:	Challenge
Stage II:	Rejection	opposes	Stage II:	Exploration
Stage III:	Retreat	opposes	Stage III:	Invention
Stage IV:	Regression	opposes	Stage IV:	Transformation

The first phase of Diversion occurs when you resist being challenged by your possibilities to benefit and grow stronger through adversity. Opportunities are always hidden in trauma. But if you resist looking at them, concentrating instead on the threatening aspects of events, pondering your real and potential losses, you will intensify negative alarm signals such as anxiety, confused thinking, sleeplessness, forgetfulness, and depression.

In the second phase of Diversion, you surpass the resistance stage and begin actively rejecting. You subconsciously and often consciously *reject* all that is responsible for trauma. Often, people in Stage II of Diversion lose their faith and trust in the fairness and goodness in life. They reject their own responsibility for making the best of trauma to restore their health and happiness.

Generally this rejection of life and its benevolence, and one's self-responsibility, increases negative alarm reactions. As those reactions build, they take on the course of much more serious breakdowns, such as depression, cancerous tumors, and even heart attacks.

If left unchecked, rejecting one's trust in life and in oneself can lead to a full-blown retreat from coping. If you enter this *retreat* in Stage III of Diversion, you will box yourself into a no-win corner where you feel hopeless, resentful, and trapped. These negative perspectives trigger addictive behavior in many people. In order to endure the pain of avoiding the painful lessons of how to live a full life in spite of its disappointments, people turn to drinking, overeating, and overwork to numb their escalating suffering.

The very last stage of Diversion culminates in a major regression of mind, body, and spirit. The person who gives up the struggle, does not cope, does not grow, ends up taking one giant step backward. I have found that people who proceed to Stage IV of Diversion have permanently damaged some major aspect of their life such as their health, their career, or their friendships.

Across all stages of Diversion, emotional responses are frozen in avoiding reality and pain. Anyone on a Diversion course becomes preoccupied with how to retaliate against or cover up what really is happening. Attempts at Diversion may even be

---

▲ CUTTING OFF EMOTION CUTS YOU OFF FROM LIFE ▲

Feelings such as anger, sadness, fear, and disappointment are not a problem if we relate to them directly and let them inform us about life. John Welwood, in *Awakening the Heart*, describes how negative emotions grow into damaging and explosive forces in our lives.

Suppose I wake up feeling sad. Instead of *letting this sadness touch me and put me in contact with what is happening in my life,* I may concentrate on how it punctures my self-image of being a together, successful person. In that it seems to undermine the self-image I would like to maintain, I stand back from it and judge it as bad. But when I judge sadness negatively and cut myself off from it, it becomes frozen, losing its tender quality that connects me to life. [p. 82; emphasis added]

extended into attempts to convince oneself, and others, that extreme negative reactions are justified. With every stage of Diversion, bear in mind that you lose self-respect, become increasingly dissatisfied with your own lack of effectiveness, and face a gnawing insecurity that life is a complete disaster.

Although we can reverse this process, some people never do. Diversion, for example, can become a problem for people whose life-long spouses die.

THE DIVERSION PROCESS DESTROYS HOPE

It is natural for widows or widowers to resist a healthy recovery from their loss. Because they are lonely and confused, they resist the possibility of restoring the love they've lost, and even the possibility of friendly companionship. They often assume they can never meet their needs for intimacy through a new partner. They refuse to compensate themselves for what they lost through their mate's death by making other relationships stronger or by finding meaningful work to do. To resist is natural and understandable, but it is never healthy.

Although it is very difficult to find a way to be happy without someone you have loved and depended on, some survivors not only resist their fate, but also enter Stage II of Diversion, which is Rejection. In this phase they may become emotionally depressed, physically ill, or both. Their mental and physical breakdown at this stage often stems from their lost trust in life and their refusal to be responsible for restoring their health and happiness.

If they move on to Stage III of Diversion (Retreat), and continue to recoil from dealing with their loss, some will rely on alcohol, television, and/or self-pity or sink deeply into the past to avoid the pain of learning to live a full life alone. By retreating into addiction or depression, they naturally endanger their health, productivity, and partnerships. The odds in reversing this downward spiral are overwhelming. In the face of this type of adversity, most who are left alone simply give up hope, and many others die.

Diversion Is More Common Than You May Think

How often do people actually suffer the downward spiral of diversion in response to a traumatic event such as loss of a partner? Statistics show that people who are separated, divorced, or widowed are two to three times more likely to die prematurely than their married peers. They are also admitted to hospitals for mental disorders at five to ten times the rate of people who have a mate.

Young people who lose a mate or a child unexpectedly seem to fare even worse. In a study of the long-term effects of losing a loved one in an automobile crash, researchers Darrin Lehman and Camille Wortman of the University of Michigan found that the bereaved survivors were less optimistic about life, had fewer social interactions, had more job difficulties, and had significantly more psychotic symptoms. In fact, this research team found that bereaved spouses were indistinguishable from psychiatric outpatients on six of nine indicators of mental disorder, four to seven years after their tragedy.

Recovery from the traumatic loss of a loved one is difficult, and the chances for the survivor's suffering long-term damaging effects are significant. But the prospect of recovering from this type of tragic loss is significant also, if the survivor is willing to learn how to restore losses and accept help in the process.

Look now at the general path of damage to your vital resources as the result of following the course of Diversion.

Diversion's Impact on Personal Resources

If you follow the Diversion process, you will suffer major setbacks.

You may register damage to your body through chronic illness or physical exhaustion. Or you may experience a mental setback from lowered self-esteem or negative attitudes that feed your resentment or sense of injustice.

The emotional damage of Diversion often creates an unrelenting cycle of anxiety or depression, or both, with hostility as a frequent characteristic of emotional decline. Finally, spiritual difficulties may emerge because Diversion can cause you to lose your hope in the future or to abandon your faith in a higher power and a benevolent universe.

▲ DISEASES OF STRESS ▲

The American Academy of Family Physicians reports that two-thirds of office visits to family physicians are the result of stress-related problems.

Unresolved stress contributes, directly or indirectly, to six of the leading causes of death in the United States: coronary heart disease, cancer, lung ailments, accidental injuries, cirrhosis of the liver, and suicide. ["Stress: Can We Cope?" *Time*, June 6, 1983, p. 48]

Diversion's Impact on Partnership Resources

Whenever you fail to meet your own needs and restore the resources vital to your inner balance, an almost inevitable consequence is that you will either *withdraw* or *become excessively* dependent on others.

We have all known people who have withdrawn so much into themselves that they rarely initiate social interaction. This happens frequently when someone is overcome with grief or guilt. When grief or guilt captures you, either one isolates you from people who could make a positive difference in your life. You don't feel like being with other people and other people don't want to be with you.

We all know people who become extremely needy when they cannot face the pain of their trauma. Their excessive dependency is a form of helplessness; it indicates that the individual does not feel competent to solve his or her problems. Naturally, others often feel overburdened by the demands of those who divert themselves from coping.

Tension mounts if you become consumed with avoiding the impact of your trauma. Remember that this tension can come between friends, sever family ties, and disrupt working teams. The cost of broken relationships is exacted in divorce, disenchantment, and even suicide as the final statement of disconnection.

▲ NEEDING OTHERS TOO MUCH CAN CAUSE PROBLEMS ▲

The subject of excessive dependency on other people and its damaging effects on health and happiness is addressed extensively in Melody Beattie's newest book, *Codependent No More*. She helps the reader understand why needing too much help, love, and approval is harmful:

> Needing people too much can cause problems. Other people become the key to our happiness. I believe much of the other-centeredness, orbiting our lives around other people, goes hand-in-hand with codependency and springs out of our emotional insecurity. I believe much of this incessant approval seeking we indulge in also comes from insecurity. The magic is in others, not us, we believe. The good feelings are in them, not us. The less good stuff we find in ourselves, the more we seek it in others. *They* have it all; we have nothing. *Our* existence is not important. We have been abandoned and neglected so often that we also abandon ourselves. [p. 91]

Diversion's Impact on Productivity Resources

In the most basic disruption of our productivity, Diversion erodes our sense of purpose by sending a person on a wild-goose chase to attain the impossible goal of avoiding change. This senseless effort and search chip away at our perception of what is worth working for in life. Diversion can occupy so much attention and energy that even moderate productivity demands aren't met.

Organizations in transition often find that their employees spend so much energy trying to fight the changes or dealing with the uncertainty of their economic and career future, they have very little energy left for work.

Resisting change and worry over uncertainty are two of the primary reasons that productivity declines during corporate mergers, acquisitions, spin-offs, and reorganizations. It is a case of *Collective Diversion* in which large numbers of people follow an unhealthy and unproductive course instead of a course of Empowerment. The unspoken tragedy is the damage that Collective Diversion causes individuals—not a company.

For many, Diversion leads to inactivity and dropping out of the work force. Not only does the individual lose, but organizations, families, and communities suffer from those setbacks. Some direct indications of those setbacks are financial reversals, premature retirement, job loss, and career burn-out.

CONDITIONS THAT PROMOTE DIVERSION

Some people slip into Diversion without realizing it. Their trauma has robbed them of their resources and left them feeling defenseless and overwhelmed by threat. These unsuspecting victims of trauma have some inner characteristics or conditions that promote the path of Diversion.

There are three conditions that make Diversion more likely:

▲ low reserves of vital resources (Personal, Productivity, Partnership).
▲ idealized expectations.
▲ earlier unresolved traumas.

Each one of these conditions encourages us to view trauma only as a threat and to see ourselves as powerless to cope. Let's examine how these forces operate so you can learn to neutralize their effects when they are present for you.

LOW RESERVES OF COPING RESOURCES PROMOTE DIVERSION

Diversion comes easiest when you're dragged down and the demands on your system have exceeded your ability to cope for a long period of time. Remember that any trauma may exert extensive pressure on your vital resources, and the repercussions may last for long periods.

If you already are at the end of your coping *rope* when another trauma occurs, you are more likely to slip into Diversion because you have severely depleted your resources to master adversity. Although this reason for following the course of Diversion is understandable, it doesn't reduce the damage.

In a study conducted in 1978, stress researcher Barbara Snell Dohrenwend found that people who lacked Personal, Productivity, and Partnership resources were more vulnerable to additional losses. A kind of loss spiral develops in people who don't have the resources to offset their most recent traumatic loss.

So for example, if a woman's husband dies and she has been economically dependent on him—i.e., without her own financial resources—her economic disadvantage is likely to interfere with her getting more education to upgrade her job skills. Her lack of job training will then precipitate economic stress on top of the stress of bereavement. This is one way that loss spirals can occur.

In another study battered women who lacked such resources as education, financial self-sufficiency, and occupational security were more likely to react passively to mental and physical abuse. They simply did not possess the resources necessary to cope

---

▲ LOSS SPIRALS ▲

The Diversion process produces a chain of multiple loss events in addition to the initial losses directly precipitated by a trauma. For this reason, a person who follows the consecutive stages of Diversion actually creates more and more stress that must be dealt with. The catch-22 is that as Diversion increases stress, it decreases vital resources. This condition makes it more and more difficult for a person to recover.

---

with their abusive husbands and to remove themselves from danger.

If you see that you are losing ground in Personal, Productivity, and Partnership resources and your losses are spiraling, here's what you can do. First, admit that you just are not up to meeting the demands of the trauma, and give yourself a specified time-out from responding. Recognize that you want to take charge of your reactions and you want to master the challenges of your situation, but put your strategy on hold until you can *replenish your reserves.*

Waiting and *placing your challenges on the back burner* very often are legitimate and healthy steps. They give you time to *seek the help you need.* And if you are faced with multiple traumas, you actually may benefit from playing down the severity of their combined losses and tackling one crisis at a time.

This delayed response is not classic psychological denial. Damaging denial occurs when you neither recognize nor do what eventually must be done. Resistance spirals out of control when you blind yourself to the fact that you are not coping.

Those who use healthy time out increase the likelihood of growing stronger and healthier and making their lives more worthwhile. The following example illustrates the value of doing whatever it takes to replenish your coping reserves before you set out to recover fully from trauma.

STOPGAP MEASURES WORK

In a strange sequence of tragic events, Carla's home burned to the ground one week and the next week she was held hostage in a bank robbery. Carla's husband was out of work and their financial resources were severely strained by the loss of their possessions in the fire.

After those traumas, Carla had difficulty sleeping, eating, and concentrating on her job as a bank teller. There was no way Carla could handle all of her problems simultaneously, so when she came in for help we paid attention to her most immediate needs. Carla took time out from some of her problems to *avoid* Diversion. If she had tried to deal with her flashbacks to the robbery, or her nightmares, or her low productivity prior to taking care of her more basic needs, her efforts would have been futile because her more basic needs were not yet met.

Carla and I put together a team of resources that would alleviate her financial pressure and need for shelter. Her church and the local social-service agency cooperated. Next we concentrated on helping her husband find employment.

Carla's success in restoring her most basic resources gave her a sense of progress and a strong foundation for tackling her full recovery. This unusual story illustrates how important it can be to prioritize efforts. Professional guidance and support are essential to the well-being of anyone who experiences a loss spiral of multiple traumas.

TIME OUT FOR ADVANCEMENT

David, age thirty-eight, a successful actor, suddenly became depressed and distant from his family and friends. His depression was intense, even though he remained successful in his television career.

David and I worked for four sessions. After many hours of reflection on his own, he concluded that he had reached all of his acting goals and had peaked years before he ever thought possible and, therefore, was hopelessly bored with his chosen profession.

Before our work together, David never dared to admit to himself that at his age he could be bored, burned out, and detest his work. His choice of *Diversion* away from this truth, by resisting, rejecting, and retreating, had led to his serious doubt and depression. But after pinpointing the source of his disorientation, David set out to reverse the *Diversion* and build a new career path. During that rebuilding period he discarded his previous definition of what success meant for him. He replaced it with different aspirations less financially dominated. David decided to dedicate himself to fund-raising and public education to preserve the environment. This work held great value for him.

When the realization of this new goal came, David was excited. However, when he reached the juncture of testing out strategies (Stage III, Invention), he discovered that he was not yet ready to launch into a totally new career. Instead, he wanted to gradually wind down his acting and accelerate his fund-raising activities. He wanted to buy himself some time for more planning, exploring, and thinking.

David's change in attitude, from *Diversion* to *Empowerment,* had an immediate, positive effect on his life. He returned to a fifty-hour work week and his mood was enthusiastic. He re-established himself as an affable and responsive colleague, friend, father, and husband. From the outside it appeared that David's life was going on as usual, but in fact he was simply recharging his batteries in preparation for a major life change and challenge, *and* using his familiar work environment to do so.

David intended to experiment with new ways of pursuing his new career goals as soon as he had restored his energy. Even though his choice was to remain in his acting profession for a time, his long-range outlook was dramatically different and relieved him from his burn-out and despair.

Now let's examine another condition that fosters *Diversion*.

IDEALIZED EXPECTATIONS PROMOTE DIVERSION

Do you harbor idealized expectations such as

▲ I should live pain-free.
▲ I should be able to be in control of what happens.
▲ I should strive to be perfect.

The preceding notions are typically ingrained in late-twentieth-century Americans. But they are distortions, and unless you are able to correct such distorted ideals, you will probably try to avoid struggling through crises.

If you expect life to be pain-free, you will resist the natural discomfort of growing through events that are sad, tragic, or disappointing. If you believe you must be in control, you will try to avoid feelings of devastation, bewilderment, anger, and loneliness because they tend to make you feel out of control. If you believe that you should be perfect, you will make yourself excessively vulnerable to failure.

One of today's most prevalent adult emotional distress signals is depression. I believe our misguided disdain for ourselves when we experience negative emotions contributes greatly to this pervasive problem. Somehow when we feel painful emotions, we think we have failed. We rage at this insult to our self-image, and the rage feeds upon itself. We try desperately to squelch and depress feelings that lead to self-criticism. The devastation of depression is often described as *anger turned inward.*

To dispel the expectation that life should be pain-free, it is crucial to accept negative emotions and to become eager to express your fears, your hostilities, and your frustrations in nondestructive ways. Whatever occurs, you will have an advantage in turning trauma into a tool for positive change if you *express* rather than *depress* the full range of your emotional responses—from hope to despair, enthusiasm to disenchantment, love to hate. For anyone interested in further training on how to deal with anger, I recommend Harriet Goldnor Lerner's book, *The Dance of Anger*. This text is particularly helpful for learning how to manage your anger in intimate relationships.

When you dispel the myth that you can live free of pain, you will stop searching solely for relief from your discomfort. Instead, you will be able to respect its presence, become curious about it, and relish it for what it might be able to teach you. This approach paradoxically reduces the pain of tension and struggling, and will help you to make use of your legitimate suffering.

No one has to relish trauma, but those who succeed in facing it as part of life will recognize its importance and value. Those who face it allow themselves to experience it so they can continue to grow.

There is another idealized expectation that makes people *Diversion*-prone.

SEEKING PERFECTION

Do you strive to be perfect? Do you glorify the results rather than the process of struggling to achieve something important? If your answer to either of these questions is *yes*, you have a barrier to sustaining your personal growth.

When you pursue superlatives such as the *best* job, the *most* money, the *perfect* mate, or the *perfect* you, you court disaster. And disaster surely is imminent if you settle for nothing less than perfect. To strive for perfection shows no respect for limitations.

I am not building a case for laziness or mediocrity. I am encouraging you to have a healthy respect for your own limits and life's limits. Why set yourself up for disappointment by harboring unrealistically inflated expectations?

If you approach your own growth and your own life in such a way that you strive to become the best person you can be, who is living the best life possible, you will feel fulfilled, but you will also fail. Failing is inevitable. You will fall short of your mark as you grow. Failure is valuable because it tells us what won't work; in other words, it reveals the limits of ourselves and our situation. When you fail, you have determined a boundary within which you can work to reach goals that help meet your need for inner balance.

The myth that we can achieve an ideal of success that is externally imposed perpetuates our hard-driving, self-centered, superlative-seeking selves. The myth divorces us from our humanity and our most critical accomplishments—personal growth and transformation.

GIVING UP BEING PERFECT

Many people who struggle through a major setback such as a divorce never are able to give up their need to be *perfect*. And their perfectionism turns out to be responsible for their damaged lives.

Let's look at the case of Gary, whose marriage to the woman he fell in love with in college had been in serious turmoil for eight years before it ended. Just as Gary turned forty, he and his wife decided to divorce. During my work with Gary, the major issue in his struggles with his new role as a single was to forgive himself for not being perfect.

When I first saw Gary he had already reconciled his feelings of disappointment toward his wife. He saw the divorce as a reasonable solution to their dilemma. During his adjustment to the divorce, Gary had achieved some degree of inner peace by experimenting with new ways of improving his capacity to relate to others on a deeper level. But he had not been able to achieve fully his personal growth goals. He was unable to focus fully on the present and immerse himself in his life as a single person. He spent time reminiscing about the past—even the hollow and painful times—and wishing for a magical cure for his mistake.

Although Gary and his wife both were convinced that their

marriage could never succeed, he agonized constantly over letting go of it in his mind. His resistance to going on with his life drained him of the energy that he needed to become fully functioning again.

Gary, like many others in his situation, was inhibited from beginning the rest of his life because of his need to punish himself for his mistakes. He had fallen short in his own eyes. He held himself totally responsible for getting into the marriage in the first place, for the lack of intimacy, and for the eventual demise of the relationship. His attitude went well beyond the healthy acknowledgment of one's contributions to a failed marriage.

Gary's self-recrimination grew out of the myth of superlatives. He kept saying things like "I should have been smart enough to see through this sham . . . I should have seen it when we were dating . . . If I had only known what love really is . . ." His need to punish himself for his imperfection clearly demonstrated his inflated expectations of himself.

I suggested to Gary that if he wanted to grow and become healthier, he had to welcome himself to the human race. He had to see himself as a well-meaning, highly principled person who could fail; learn important lessons from his mistakes throughout his lifetime; and most of all, forgive himself for his less-than-perfect track record. Others, including his family and even his church, had come to terms with the marital mismatch and had forgiven him. Gary, however, had not forgiven himself.

As far as I know, Gary never has tackled the tall order of forgiving himself and has never risked having another intimate relationship. He has lived alone, immersed in his teaching and his church activities. When Gary came for his last session, he told me that it was too much to ask that he give up the search for perfection in himself. He was a man who chose the permanent burden of searching for perfection.

No matter what adaptation is required by a trauma, you often are challenged to adjust your self-image and philosophy of life to more closely mirror reality. You may need to modify beliefs or attitudes that *promise too much*. Although you must guard against undue pessimism, if you are a high achiever you are more likely to expect too much rather than too little of yourself. You may even adopt the standards of outside authorities rather than set your own.

Be careful not to look back too often on what you have lost and cause yourself further defeat. Instead of ruminating over the shortcomings of your life, remind yourself of your successes. Give up seeking perfection and enjoy the journey!

And now for an examination of one more factor that facilitates *Diversion*.

EARLIER TRAUMATIC EXPERIENCES PROMOTE DIVERSION

History may repeat itself in our personal lives just as it does in the world at large. Trauma in life may mimic earlier childhood experiences from which you have not fully recovered. When this occurs, you may attempt Diversion because you were once hurt by a similar situation and want to protect yourself. Your previous experience with this kind of trauma tells you to beware because you probably will fail to cope again.

However, there is good news. As an adult you are far more capable of succeeding in most of life's demands than you were as a helpless child. As an adult you can heal your personal history of trauma if it repeats itself. You will be able to heal the injured child within you because successful coping will erase the failures of the past.

This healing can occur even in the depths of crisis. Larry, a friend of mine, had followed a fast track of achievement through journalism, politics, and advertising. One day he ran square into a stone wall. A series of corporate maneuvers suddenly left him in a dead-end advertising job, without much warning. Larry found himself in a small town, reporting to incompetent superiors who ruled the roost with verbal abuse. At the same time, he was involved in a waning romantic relationship.

At the end of his rope, Larry quit the job. He quickly picked up some consulting jobs, but his health began to deteriorate rapidly. His self-esteem plummeted, too. He walked around in a daze. He began avoiding old friends and colleagues and had haunting thoughts of suicide. He couldn't sleep and, when he did, he could barely wake up. He had crying spells, and as they built, he started to drink. The more he drank, the more Larry saw his life as a *prison*.

It was clear to everyone who knew Larry that his intense reaction to the corporate merger went well beyond what was called for in the situation. Larry started to work with an alcohol recovery program. He discovered that his career traumas had triggered insecurities developed during childhood. When Larry was three, his mother unexpectedly became critically ill. Her illness left Larry in the care of an adult who punished him harshly as a means of discipline.

Once Larry saw the similarities between his adult career trauma and his childhood crisis, he was able to begin to heal both wounds. The realization that traumas can trigger reactions from unresolved traumas gave Larry the reassurance that he needed to plan his recovery.

One night after Larry had completed his treatment program for alcoholism, he said to me, "I've read almost everything ever written, it seems, on this illness. I don't suppose I'll ever be certain whether my alcoholism was triggered by stress. What I do know is that during the worst period of my life, I somehow came to grips with my past and exorcised the demons that had haunted me. It didn't cure the illness, but it will make me a better person for the rest of my life. I don't have to set the whole world on fire anymore. I just set the fires I choose to."

If your initial reaction to a traumatic event in your adult life surpasses the demand, you also may be suffering from past hurt that needs special care and attention. Be sure to examine what problem in your past may be repeating itself and pushing you toward Diversion. As you confront past traumas and repair their damage, you will become freer to engage your current tasks with confidence and ability, just as Larry did.

▲ **BLAMING OTHERS CAN HURT YOUR RECOVERY** ▲

In 1977 R. J. Bulman of the University of Massachusetts and Camille Wortman of Northwestern University reported their findings on which personal characteristics of victims of severe accidents were associated with good coping.

The researchers found that people who accepted responsibility for their accident were able to cope well with their tragedy, whereas people who blamed someone else showed difficulty in coping. Accident victims who believed that life is fair reported themselves to be happier after their trauma then those victims who had more negative philosophies of life.

THE DANGERS OF SELF-SABOTAGE

As you can see, the conditions that lead to Diversion are powerful. People who allow these conditions find that Diversion is a path they choose over and over, until they are willing to counteract the temptation to give up and give in.

Those who suffer the pain of avoiding the pain of trauma remain trapped inside their own limitations. People who choose the road of strain and setbacks confine themselves to repeating unsatisfactory, illness-provoking behavior.

They live only on the edges of life.

They remain diverted from the fulfillment that is possible when you choose to grow.

14

▲

Pumping
Emotional Iron

Did you know that it is possible for you to condition yourself
to be a survivor, and even a master, in the face of adversity?
It is true. To begin with, if you are willing to adopt three basic
empowering attitudes and do whatever it takes to put each of
them into practice in your everyday life, you will develop an
emotional sturdiness that will see you through tough traumatic
times. Then if you apply the skills you have learned in mastering
trauma to ordinary stress, you will prevent unnecessary daily
strain while reinforcing your capacity to deal with trauma in
the future. Even everyday stress can sometimes equal the impact
of traumatic events if you let it go unresolved. I call this two-
part psychological conditioning program *Pumping Emotional
Iron.*

Through your successful coping with day-to-day stress—
conflicts, traffic jams, deadlines, overscheduling, and minor
disappointments—you build your emotional strength for with-
standing catastrophes. If you practice these empowering attitudes continuously, your behavior in times of crisis will reflect

it. You'll act more quickly and move thoroughly through each stage of adjustment by using the skills you have learned.

▲ HASSLES CAN BE HARMFUL ▲

Recent research findings emphasize how important it is for you to control your reaction to even ordinary annoyances. The work of Allen D. Kanner of Stanford Medical School and Richard S. Lazarus of the University of California at Berkeley shows that the stress of minor hassles can mount and cause damage as severe as that of traumas if it is not managed promptly and effectively.

Effective coping mechanisms for traumatic stress (Chapters Five–Twelve) can be applied to the ordinary hassles of everyday living. The practice you get coping with ordinary stress will help you immeasurably during times of major upheaval.

The following chart lists the hassles most frequently reported by a group of middle-aged adults.

TEN MOST FREQUENT HASSLES

Item	% of Times Checked
1. Concerns about weight (91)	52.4
2. Health of a family member (7)	48.1
3. Rising prices of common goods (70)	43.7
4. Home maintenance (29)	42.8
5. Too many things to do (79)	38.6
6. Misplacing or losing things (1)	38.1
7. Yard work or outside home mainte-nance (112)	38.1
8. Property, investment, or taxes (110)	37.6
9. Crime (115)	37.1
10. Physical appearance (51)	35.9

SOURCE: Allen D. Kanner et al. Comparisons of Two Modes of Stress Measurement: Daily Hassles and Uplifts Versus Major Life Events. *Journal of Behavioral Medicine* 4:1–39 (1981).

Let's examine Part I of your conditioning program.

PART I: ATTITUDE ADJUSTMENTS

The rewards of incorporating these ways of thinking into your everyday existence will be well worth the effort and attention spent. Here are the key attitudes for pumping emotional iron:

1. Observing without argument.
2. Striving to grow—not to be perfect.
3. Trusting yourself to be happy.

A *suggestion:* As you examine each of these attitudes, notice if any seem difficult. Don't be surprised if each one feels a bit strange as you adopt it. All three of these empowering attitudes run slightly counter to how we have been taught by our culture to think about the world.

Empowering Attitude 1: Observing Without Argument

The thrust of this attitude is for you to be willing to look at any situation and *accept* what is happening without complaining that things are not as you would *wish* them to be.

Ryan was fourteen when he lost his right arm in a car accident. No one would have blamed this Little League baseball star for giving up his sport in the face of such a tragic loss. But to everyone's amazement, Ryan learned how to catch, throw, and even bat with one arm. Ryan was able to accomplish this incredible physical feat because he was willing to accept his loss and learn how to compensate for it.

Ryan's objective was to play baseball. He didn't *argue* with reality, he made the best use of what he had to work with. Ryan noted what he had going for him and took advantage of his situation. Try adopting this mental stance the next time you are in a traffic jam, or perhaps when someone lets you down.

You may be one who finds it extremely difficult to stay calm when you observe that circumstances are not going the way you desire or expect them to. Many people suffer untold damage and strain from the internal upheaval they cause themselves by becoming angry and hostile toward the minor stressors that are temporary roadblocks to success. In fact, research by Robert Elliot sheds light on the harmful effects of pent-up anger. His studies show that you can be hard-driving and ambitious, and have a sense of urgency—three prominent characteristics of a Type A personality—without putting health at risk. However, if you get angry when something runs counter to your desires, and if you stay angry about it, your seething hostility will put your health at risk. Elliot calls this tendency to get mad and stay mad the *hot-reactor syndrome*. For many people, helplessness in the face of trauma triggers the hot-reactor syndrome.

I have already pointed out the dangers of unresolved anger in the discussion of viewing trauma as an enemy in Chapter Two. As you recall, if during times of severe crisis you view the traumatic event as an *enemy*, you will react as either a *victim* or an *aggressor*.

The victim and aggressor modes trigger your anger because you set up an adversarial situation between you and your trauma. Then you try to either fight or flee the situation—all to no avail. The fruitless attempt to dominate and to escape escalates your alarm reactions and your hostility.

On a smaller scale, you can recapitulate this dynamic of win-lose with everyday stressful events such as traffic jams and minor disappointments that are not under your direct control. Whenever you complain or argue about what happens, you trigger a strained response in yourself, even if the stressor is a minor annoyance.

What Empowering Attitude 1 suggests is that you learn to *agree* with what happens. To agree with what is your reality means to see it clearly, to accept it, and to problem solve from that vantage point. To agree with your reality does *not* imply that you must be *thrilled* with the annoyance or setback. You can have an accepting attitude toward it, without endorsing it or reveling in it.

Here are some helpful tips to use to *observe without arguing* when something goes wrong. When you follow these steps under the pressure of everyday stressful situations, you will shift from being a *hot reactor* to being a *cool reactor*.

THE MENTAL APPROACH OF THE COOL REACTOR

1. Monitor your first thoughts when you encounter a stressful event such as a traffic jam, missed deadline, or personal disappointment.

2. If your thoughts are argumentative: e.g., "I can't believe this! What did I do to deserve this? I'll show them!"

3. Give yourself a chance to recover by going through a mini-version of shifting from threat to challenge.

Step 1:

Ask yourself, "What is troubling me about this situation?" (Be realistic and specific: e.g., "I want to be on time and now I will not arrive on schedule," or "It was very disappointing that he failed to call because I was counting on a dinner date.")

Step 2:

Then ask yourself, "What are my opportunities and possibilities now?" (Be realistic and specific: e.g., "I can prepare for my meeting while I'm sitting in this traffic and be sure I arrive in a good mood," or "I can call someone else for a night out or find a good book and relax.")

Step 3:

Ask your final question, "What if I were to . . . ?" (Be creative: e.g., ". . . listen to a great audiotape and rehearse my agenda?" or ". . . call Bill—I haven't seen him in ages?")

The approach of the *cool reactor* is to observe without argument. Do you understand how your success in learning to accept situations of minor importance can lead to accepting major disappointments? Sometimes it is difficult to notice that you are not accepting a situation as it is. That was true for Harvey, in the following example.

YOU CAN'T CALL A "DOG" A "FROG"

Harvey was consulting with a bureaucratic organization whose leadership could not bring themselves to announce the cutbacks in staffing for the next year. That lack of communication was causing uncertainty and low morale in the organization. Harvey had an unrealistically positive view of the leadership that was preventing him from helping to solve the organization's problem.

One day, during his three-hour drive to meet his client, Harvey complained to another colleague about the client's hesitancy to act. "Frank," he said, "this director and his top-level managers refuse to confront the real issues with the rest of the organization. I just don't understand it. They seem to be so honest and concerned about people. They've planned this cutback thoroughly. I'm completely puzzled at what has them so reluctant to announce who will be laid off."

Frank listened as Harvey continued to compliment the leadership on their forthrightness and strength of character, and in the next breath express utter amazement at the leaders' inability to act responsibly. Finally, Frank sighed deeply, tapped Harvey on the shoulder, and said, "Harvey, don't you know you can't call a dog a frog?" After a brief pause, Harvey realized what Frank meant by his quip. The quip gave Harvey the insight that he was not viewing his clients objectively. He was, in fact, arguing with reality.

Harvey had completely overlooked the qualities that he *didn't want to see*—the leadership's insecurity and drive for self-protection. He was calling them honest when they were not, and labeling them vitally concerned with employee welfare when they showed cowardly self-concern. It *was* as if Harvey had tried to call a dog a frog. And, as Frank said, you can't do that if you want to deal effectively with what is actually happening.

Harvey's eyes were opened to his distorted image of his client. Even though he didn't like what he saw as their actual shortcomings, at least he had a place to start. That day Harvey discussed his concerns about forthright communication with the director and his staff. He described the situation as it really was, not as he wished it could be.

To his client's credit, the leadership looked in the mirror and took action to correct their self-serving motives and actions. In three days the staff cutbacks were announced to all employees.

Harvey's honest appraisal had far-reaching benefits for his client. Your honest appraisal of troublesome situations can have a wide-ranging positive impact, too.

Empowering Attitude 2: Striving to Grow, Not to Be Perfect

There is a big difference between striving to develop oneself and working solely for perfect results. This was brought home to me recently in a rather unusual setting. I was leading a team of executives in a nerve-racking course of activities that included rappelling and traversing high-tension wires strung between huge trees. The activities were designed by a group called Outward Bound and were intended to challenge one's abilities physically and mentally. For our group, there was no question—they were challenged!

What struck me most about the obstacle course was an incident that occurred to Tom, one of the executive participants. Tom was an *expert* climber with many years of experience walking on tightropes. As we watched him climb to the pinnacle post on the first tree, everyone in the group marveled at his agility and fearlessness. We were spellbound by his grace in moving across the first set of perilous wires.

Then, without warning, he fell. My heart leapt into my mouth as the group yelled for someone to help. The belts and billets held Tom safe, but dangling in midair. As the class gazed up in amazement at Tom, they received a powerful lesson. Tom was scrambling up the ropes and back onto his perch on the high-tension wire faster than his team could visually track him. He performed his recovery with almost the same speed with which he'd fallen.

"What fabulous presence of mind and self-confidence Tom has," one of the participants said. It was true. No sooner had he failed than he recovered. He accomplished his midair reversal with the same confidence he'd had at his starting point.

Tom's behavior indicated to everyone that he treated his failures with the same positive attitude as his successes. In fact, it seemed to matter very little to him whether he was failing or succeeding at the moment. He had been intently concerned with striving. He had given himself a tremendous edge over the long haul of his challenge course by reacting to momentary failure as if it were simply part of what happens in striving for anything important.

Tom's example underlines the value of deciding that it is better to grow through failure than to strive for perfection. Without question he was focusing on striving to learn rather than on achieving perfection. Not only could he tolerate his own imperfections, he used them to reach his goal.

Tom's methods and approaches are antithetical to how we usually address adversity. All too often we get hamstrung by our need to achieve, feeling self-conscious and awkward if we fail. Again, we receive tremendously strong messages from our culture that success equals perfect performance, messages that result in much human misery.

People who do look for success in striving and struggling rather than in results may be out of step, but they are healthy. They work toward self-development and expansion every day. They are motivated by their own need for development and dedicate themselves to personal growth rather than to repairing their deficiencies so they can be *perfect*. It is an attitude that seeks expression rather than gratification, maturation in place of dominance.

When you emphasize self-development and striving, you will improve the quality of your life. If you focus primarily on achievement, you will diminish your chances of happiness.

Charles Garfield has done extensive studies at the University of California Medical Center at San Francisco on what contributes to peak performance among highly successful people. His research shows that successful people are too busy reinventing themselves and finding new goals to be waylaid by traumatic events.

The key to adopting the desire to grow rather than to achieve perfection may be flexibility. The most successful students of my system keep their ultimate goals in mind, but they realize that they won't lose ground if they stumble now and then. The idea is to get right up, keep on going, and try some new approach.

People who are rigid in their methods and even their goals are bound to trip themselves up when life doesn't cooperate with their game plan.

INTERNAL FOCUS

Empowering Attitudes 1 and 2 depend predominantly on your having an internal focus rather than an external one. When you are able to check in with what will make a situation turn out best for you, you put yourself in charge of your life experiences. You don't have to fight with reality, and you don't mind obstacles and failures nearly so much.

There is no question that you must turn inward and be the final judge of what to do in life's small and large matters if you want a rewarding existence resistant to the stress of ups and downs. If you can accomplish this synchrony with yourself, you will be a happy person.

Dr. Bernard Siegel captures this point in his recent book about how to heal major illnesses, *Love, Medicine, and Miracles.*

In a life out of harmony with itself, events seem to conspire to go wrong, but by the same token they mesh wondrously when you start to live your bliss. Don't climb the ladder of success only to find that when you reach the top it is leaning against the wrong wall. As you begin living your life, taking risks to do what you really want to do, you will find things fall into place and you "just happen" to be in the right place at the right time. [p. xii]

This is a powerfully encouraging thought to remember whenever you feel pressured and confused.

Follow your Inner Self and strive to grow, not achieve.

These considerations about an *internal focus* lead us to the final Empowering Attitude I suggest you practice daily to toughen your emotions.

Empowering Attitude 3: Trusting Yourself to be Happy

What is a good definition of happiness? In their most recent book, *Healthy Pleasures,* Robert Ornstein, a research psychologist, and David Sobel, a specialist in preventive medicine, suggest that "happiness lies in narrowing the distance between where you see yourself and where you expect to be." (p. 129) Their thesis is that achieving happiness hinges on our keeping our comparative judgments of the way life is for us and the way we would like it to be as close as possible.

You have, in effect, been practicing this approach. As you have mastered each stage of adjustment, you have brought your expectations in line with what is possible, given your circumstances and skills.

When trauma first strikes, your happiness quotient drops because of the difference between what you expect from life and what it is offering. Then gradually, if you pursue the possibilities and channels of support open to you, you can restore your vitality. Your Empowerment course is a sure path to happiness.

But what *degree* of happiness can you really expect if you find that you must adjust to living the rest of your life without your mate, or without your legs, or without the job that meant everything to you? Could anyone really expect to be happy under circumstances such as those? The answer is yes!

Ornstein and Sobel have compiled the findings from a number of research studies on what contributes to and detracts from happiness. Their report confirms that on a nine-point rating scale of happiness:

$$1\ 2\ 3\ 4\ 5\ 6\ 7\ 8\ 9$$
Not at All   Very

the average rating for people in our society is 6.5.

Their report also confirms that the average rating for people who have won the lottery and for people who have become paraplegics as the result of an automobile accident is almost identical to the national average happiness quotient. One year after their windfall, the average happiness score of lottery winners is 6.8, whereas after adjusting to their trauma, paraplegics give themselves a 6.0 average happiness rating.

The facts are that the extent to which you are happy has very little to do with what happens to you. Happiness depends much more on your frame of reference and your ability to find pleasure in life no matter what your circumstances.

In 1987 journalist and author Nancy Mairs wrote an article on happiness for *The New York Times*. She has given me permission to reprint that article here. I think Ms. Mairs has captured the essence of why we can all trust ourselves to be happy. She helps us to have faith that no matter what happens, the joy of life is there for the taking.

My own graduation, though it took place on a campus just as picturesque, I don't remember as half so lovely. My dress wasn't quite right for one thing. (This is the surviving memory of most of the significant events of my life: that my dress wasn't quite right.) Our dresses were supposed to be white, but mine, made for me by my mother for some other occasion, was embroidered with tiny yellow flowers. The day was overcast and damp, and my spirits were equally gray. College had seemed one long survival test, which I had passed, but without distinction. Although surrounded by a proud and loving family, I was lonely for the one person who made my survival seem worthwhile, my husband, who was sailing in large aimless circles on a radar ship in the North Atlantic.

I knew I would immediately go on to travel to New Mexico for a friend's wedding, and in the fall teach school, and eventually have children. But these ventures all required leaps into unknown territory—the desert, the classroom, the nursery—and I was afraid that they, too, would turn out aimless and undistinguished. These feelings are symptomatic of depression, I know now. But I don't think they're unusual, even for people who aren't clinically depressed, at such radical junctures as leaving college, entering marriage, changing jobs, leaving one house for another. The comfortably familiar past slides away and leaves one gasping at the vertiginous brink of what can seem, to the inexperienced, a void. But in reality, it is only the leading edge of what will become, and surprisingly soon, the comfortably familiar past.

Now, twenty-three years later, I am watching my daughter's commencement exercises from a wheelchair. My multiple sclerosis has gotten much worse in recent months, and I'm safe only if I stay put. A couple of days ago, trying to walk and read a letter at the same time, I fell flat on my face and shattered the edges of three front teeth, which are now painted on temporarily in plastic. Beside me, holding my hand, my husband (the same one) is recovering from the removal of a second melanoma. A few months ago his father died, reminding us that there is nothing that now stands between ourselves and death, and we are trying to help his mother settle into her grief as well as into her new apartment.

At this sweet moment, waiting to hear my daughter's name announced, I am suddenly perfectly happy, in a way I could not have dreamed at my own graduation. If anyone had told me then that by the time I was forty-three, I would be crippled and George would have cancer and my beloved family would have begun to die, I would have cried out (I did a lot of crying out in those days): "Oh no! I could never survive such pain!" But if anyone had told me that, in the presence of these realities, I would find myself, without warning, pierced by joy, I would have been stunned speechless, certain that my informant was either perverse or outright mad.

I wish that I could jump up (a move that would probably result in the loss of the rest of my teeth) and hug my daughter and all her classmates and shout to them: "Listen! No matter how happy you think you are today, you will be happier, I promise you. You can't imagine the women you will grow into, how large your spirits will become, stretching and stretching to encompass the challenges your lives will offer. Take all these challenges as gifts, no matter how dubious their value seems at the time. They'll come in handy one day—you'll see. They'll open you up for joy."

You too can open yourself up for such joy. The joy of being alive and prepared to stay on top whenever your world turns upside down. Trust the process you have learned in this book. It will bring you the joy of striving for the best that life can offer you.

On an everyday basis, and especially when you go through periods that are upsetting to you, why not invite some happiness into your life by concentrating on the small pleasures that are ever-present?

LAUGHING MATTERS

Have you ever wondered why you get that *all is well* feeling after a good hard laugh, even if your humor break is during a disturbing situation? The reasons for this good-all-over feeling has to do with your physical and mental responses to laughter.

Physiologically, when you laugh, your brain secretes the chemical endorphin. This substance is your body's naturally produced morphine, a painkiller that has one hundred times the power of synthetically produced morphine. So, laughter leads to the numbing of pain and a kind of euphoric natural high.

Mentally you have just shifted into a healthier perspective on yourself and the world. When you laugh, it is a sign that the playful, intuitive part of your brain has taken over to give your more serious logical and analytical brain a rest.

Humor usually arises from the sudden perception of incongruity between what we expect and what we get. In a stressful situation we may be able to diffuse the threat by seeing how funny, how unexpectedly, the situation has turned out. Remember, it is impossible to be upset while you are laughing.

For all these good reasons, you may want to invite more

▲ THE HEALING EFFECTS OF HUMOR ▲

There is a growing interest in understanding the relationship between laughter and health. Some researchers believe that laughter triggers the release of endorphins, the brain's naturally produced morphine that is one hundred times more powerful than the synthetically produced opiate. This would account for the pain-relieving effects of laughter.

While recovering from a painful and life-threatening disease, Norman Cousins, past editor of *The Saturday Review*, initiated his own systematic program to induce laughter. This is his account of the positive results, which he relays in his popular book *Anatomy of an Illness:*

It worked: I made the joyous discovery that ten minutes of genuine belly laughter had an anesthetic effect and would give me at least two hours of pain-free sleep. When the pain-killing effect of the laughter wore off, we would switch on the motion-picture projector again, and, not infrequently, it would lead to another pain-free sleep interval. [pp. 39–40] humor into stressful situations. Not only will *you* feel better, so will everyone else. A good laugh is highly contagious.

PART II: SELF-EMPOWERMENT SKILLS IN EVERYDAY LIFE

The foundation and hallmark of health and happiness are a full store of Personal, Productivity, and Partnership resources. As you know, when these three categories of resources are operating well, you are in a state of inner balance. When these categories are depleted, you are not in top shape and are more vulnerable to stress. With this in mind, I recommend that you keep a close watch on your inner balance.

Your degree of Personal, Productivity, and Partnership resources often fluctuates due to changes in circumstances or changes inside of you. For example, if you receive a minor change in your job assignment, this relatively small shift may decrease your sense of purpose and achievement enough that your Productivity resources will need replenishing. Or, perhaps you don't feel as competent as you used to feel socially because you have moved to a new neighborhood. This could lead to a slight depletion of your self-esteem that could disrupt your Partnership resources.

For reasons such as these, you need to review your resource supply in each of the three major categories on a regular basis. That will enable you to decide how to replace them before they drop down too low.

There is no better way I know of being resilient about the stressful ups and downs of living—or about any future traumas that may occur—than keeping your vital resources in great supply.

To do that, fill out the Personal Balance Profile (Chapter Eight) on a monthly basis, to give yourself a systematic look at each of the resource categories. Students tell me that over time the items on this questionnaire become so familiar to them they can do a self-evaluation mentally.

Next, make use of the Reflective Focus skill and lead yourself

---

▲ MUSIC FOR FUN AND FAMILY ▲

Here is a short list of musical pieces filled with good humor and pleasing spirits:

Irish jigs
Scottish reels
Tchaikovsky—Dance of the Sugar Plum Fairy (from *The Nutcracker Suite*)
Victor Borge—*Comedy in Music*
Anna Russell—musical parodies
Haydn—Toy Symphony
Mozart—A Musical Joke
J. S. Bach—Suites for Orchestra
R. Strauss—Till Eulenspiegel's Merry Pranks
Grainger—Handel in the Strand and Others
Gilbert and Sullivan
"I'm Gonna Wash That Man Right Out of My Hair," from *South Pacific*
Beauty and the Beast and *Snow White and the Seven Dwarfs*
Walt Disney recordings for children, especially Bambi, Dumbo, Mary Poppins, Winnie the Pooh
"When You Wish Upon a Star"

Source: Hal A. Lingerman, *The Healing Energies of Music*, p. 85.

---

through the steps of *Curiosity Questioning* (Chapter 8). It will serve the dual purpose of relaxing you and of giving you a more intuitive snapshot of how well you are functioning in each category of vital resources.

After you have completed your Personal, Productivity, and Partnership resource self-assessments, calculate how much time and effort you are spending on each category. It will be easy for you to estimate the amount of daily activity and attention you give to each.

PERCENTAGE OF DAILY ATTENTION	PERCENTAGE OF RESOURCES PRESENT
Personal Resources _____%	_____%
Productivity Resources _____%	_____%
Partnership Resources _____%	_____%
Total ___100%___	___100%___

Now compare your resource supply to the percent of daily attention you give it. Many people find that their resources are most depleted in the categories that receive the smallest amount of their attention.

Many of the people with whom I work find that on an everyday basis they lose Personal resources such as creativity, energy, good mood, and patience the fastest. Correspondingly they've discovered in their comparative assessments that they devote the least time and attention to exercise, recreation, relaxation, and emotional release.

If you are able to monitor your vital resources and do whatever is necessary to keep them in great supply, you definitely will have an edge whenever your world gets slightly out of kilter or turns completely upside down.

STAGES OF ADJUSTMENT TO MINOR HASSLES

The other major self-empowerment skills that you have learned are associated with mastering each stage of adjustment. You will be able to keep these skills sharp if you practice them when confronted by the annoying and frustrating hassles in your life.

Keep the four stages in mind when you encounter anything that causes you to feel stress. Then execute what you have learned in each sequential step until you feel relieved of negative pressure.

Let's work through an example together. Suppose you are faced with a disappointment. Someone lets you down by not doing what they promised they would do. Disappointments like this happen frequently: at the office during complex projects;

at home when dealing with deliveries and such; and in the course of social interaction when people show up late for a dinner party.

You can help yourself deal creatively and effectively with minor disappointments such as these by working through the Empowerment skills stage by stage:

Stage I: Challenge

1. What is troubling me?

2. What are my possibilities and opportunities?

3. What if I were to . . . ?

Stage II: Exploration

1. How have my resources been depleted?

2. How have my resources been increased?

3. What are my channels of support?

Stage III: Invention

1. Given my opportunities in this situation, what are my goals?

2. Given my resources and channels of support, what are my strategies?

3. Which strategies are working and which ones are not?

Stage IV: Transformation

1. What have I accomplished by taking advantage of this situation?

2. How was I able to achieve those accomplishments?

Take a look at the journal notes made by one of my clients as he worked through this process to handle the pressure of losing a big sale to his competitor.

Stage I: Challenge	Notes
What is troubling me?	I have lost a big commission; I'm embarrassed; I'm behind my projected revenue.
What are my opportunities?	To learn what went wrong; to find new customers; to accept failing as part of success.
What if I were to . . .	make five new customer contacts this week; debrief the lost sale; take time to find out what I did right?

Stage II: Exploration	Notes
Depleted resources?	Self-esteem; motivation; financial security; sense of achievement.
Increased resources?	Self-knowledge; energy level; support from my boss.
Channels of support?	Spouse, colleagues, boss; book on how to handle rejection in sales.

Stage III: Invention	Notes
My goals?	To make/sell two new customers; to be comfortable with failing; to restore my self-esteem, motivation, and sense of achievement.
My strategies?	Ask for referrals; ask for help from my boss to close the sale; exercise at least three times per week; read sales books on techniques; make at least five new contacts with customers per week; cut down on family expenses; schedule in recreation.

This client went on to evaluate the success of each strategy over a six-week period. Eventually he was able to catch up on, and even surpass, his projected revenue for the sales year. At the same time he kept himself in top working order mentally and physically. There was no doubt that he had achieved true gains in his sales skills and his ability to stay strong under pressure. Thus he had accomplished true transformations.

I hope that you will take advantage of your minor stresses and strains and keep your empowerment skills sharp by practicing your stage-by-stage process whenever you need it.

A FINAL WORD ABOUT ATTITUDES AND SKILLS

You have seen how important it is to practice self-empowering attitudes and skills in any situation that stresses you, no matter how great or inconsequential it may be. You now understand that sometimes you will have to chisel painstakingly, bit by bit, to fashion new ways of operating in your stressful, upside-down world.

This process is repeated convincingly in the course of every successful adjustment, in response to any trauma, be it a death or birth, divorce, retirement, or illness. As you tackle the requirements of understanding the impact of your trauma, and of integrating success strategies into the very fabric of who you are and how you act, you condition yourself. You stretch your boundaries and remove your blinders and limitations.

When you manage to thrive after adversity, you forge a new person who does not break down when incomprehensible things happen. You build a person who can endure the anxiety of uncertainty, one who thrives on the truth.

When you choose to be challenged by what needs to be accomplished in order to thrive, rather than be threatened by great loss, you add worth to who you are. You increase your capacity to grow in responding to the forces of fate. You enable yourself to capitalize on the blows and the trouble that prevail in life.

Remember, "Rough weather makes strong timber," if you practice the secrets for staying on top when your world turns upside down.

IN SUMMARY

Now that you have completed your self-study course on how to triumph over trauma and adversity, let's briefly review what you have accomplished.

First and foremost, you have come to realize that you must invest yourself, your time, your energy, and your ingenuity to regain the resources you lost as the result of going through your trauma. You have learned that your recovery goals are defined in terms of reinstating your health and happiness by restoring Personal, Productivity, and Partnership resources to the fullest measure possible.

Also, you have gained another insight of great importance. This system of self-empowerment has shown you that when it comes to triumphing over adversity you can expect to work through four stages before you actually achieve your health and happiness goals. Each stage has its own set of objectives, experiences, time frames, and strategies for completion. Each person is unique in the way that he or she grows through the process.

One thing is certain: if you are careful to master the objectives of these four stages,

Stage I: Challenge
Stage II: Exploration
Stage III: Invention
Stage IV: Transformation

you will be able to reinvent your life whenever your world turns upside down, no matter what the cause or circumstances of the trauma might be.

I believe that if you follow the path that my system has laid

314

out for you, you will be tapping into your own inner power as well as the power in the universe that operates for good and that fosters fulfillment. The following passage from Isaiah (60:20) reminds us of the promise that the universe has positive thrust even during traumatic adversity. You now have the knowledge and skills to make this promise come true.

> Thy sun shall no more go down;
> Neither shall thy moon withdraw itself:
> For the Lord shall be thine everlasting light,
> And the days of thy mourning shall be ended.

▲

Appendix

DIAGNOSTIC CRITERIA FOR
POST-TRAUMATIC STRESS DISORDER

A. The person has experienced an event that is outside the range
   of usual human experience and that would be markedly
   distressing to almost anyone, e.g., serious threat to one's life
   or physical integrity; serious threat or harm to one's children,
   spouse, or other close relatives and friends; sudden destruction
   of one's home or community; or seeing another person who
   has recently been, or is being, seriously injured or killed as the
   result of an accident or physical violence.
B. The traumatic event is persistently reexperienced in at least
   one of the following ways:

1. recurrent and intrusive distressing recollections of the event (in young children, repetitive play in which themes or aspects of the trauma are expressed)

2. recurrent distressing dreams of the event

3. sudden acting or feeling as if the traumatic event were recurring (includes a sense of reliving the experience, illusions, hallucinations, and dissociative [flashback] episodes, even those that occur upon awakening or when intoxicated)

4. intense psychological distress at exposure to events that symbolize or resemble an aspect of the traumatic event, including anniversaries of the trauma

C. Persistent avoidance of stimuli associated with the trauma or numbing of general responsiveness (not present before the trauma), as indicated by at least three of the following:

1. efforts to avoid thoughts or feelings associated with the trauma

2. efforts to avoid activities or situations that arouse recollections of the trauma

3. inability to recall an important aspect of the trauma (psychogenic amnesia)

4. markedly diminished interest in significant activities (in young children, loss of recently acquired developmental skills such as toilet training or language skills)

5. feeling of detachment or estrangement from others

6. restricted range of affect, e.g., unable to have loving feelings

7. sense of a foreshortened future, e.g., does not expect to have a career, marriage, or children, or a long life

D. Persistent symptoms of increased arousal (not present before the trauma), as indicated by at least two of the following:

1. difficulty falling or staying asleep

2. irritability or outbursts of anger

3. difficulty concentrating

4. hypervigilance

5. exaggerated startle response

6. physiologic reactivity upon exposure to events that symbolize or resemble an aspect of the traumatic event (e.g., a woman who was raped in an elevator breaks out in a sweat when entering any elevator)

E. Duration of the disturbance (symptoms in B, C, and D) of at least one month.

Specify delayed onset if the onset of symptoms was at least six months after the trauma.

[Source: *Diagnostic Statistical Manual III*. American Psychiatric Association, Washington, D.C.: 1987, 309.89]

▲

Bibliography

Ader, R. Behavioral Conditioning and the Immune System. In *Emotions in Health and Illness*, L. Temoshok, C. Van Dyke, and L. Zegans, eds. New York: Raven Press, pp. 55–69, 1983.

Alloy, L. B., C. Peterson, L. Y. Abramson, and M. E. P. Seligman. Attribution Style and the Generality of Learned Helplessness, *Journal of Personality and Social Psychology* 46:681–687 (1984).

Antonovsky, A. *Health, Stress and Coping*. San Francisco: Jossey-Bass, 1979.

———. *Unravelling the Mystery of Health: How People Manage Stress and Stay Well*. San Francisco: Jossey-Bass, 1987.

Bandura, A. A Human Agency in Social Cognitive Theory. *American Psychologist* 44:1175–1184 (1989).

———. *Social Learning Theory*. Englewood Cliffs, N.J.: Prentice-Hall, 1977.

Barnard, D. Psychosomatic Medicine and the Problem of Meaning. *Bulletin of the Menninger Clinic* 49(1):10–28 (1985).

Bibliography

Baum, A., J. E. Singer, and C. S. Baum. Stress and the Environment. *Journal of Social Issues* 37:4–35 (1981).

Beattie, M. *Codependent No More*. New York: Harper & Row, 1987.

Benard, J. The Eudaemonists. In *Why Man Takes Chances*, S. Z. Klausner, ed. New York: Doubleday, 1968, pp. 6–47.

Benson, H. *The Relaxation Response*. New York: Avon, 1976.

Billings, A. G., and R. H. Moos. The Role of Coping Responses and Social Resources in Attenuating the Stress of Life Events. *Journal of Behavioral Medicine* 4:139–157 (1981).

Birren, F. *Color: A Survey in Words and Pictures*. New Hyde Park, N.Y.: University Books, 1963.

Branden, N. *Honoring the Self: Personal Integrity and the Heroic Potentials of Human Nature*. Boston: Houghton Mifflin, pp. 64–65, 1983.

Breznitz, S., ed. *The Denial of Stress*. New York: International University Press, 1983.

Brimton, C. *Nietzsche*. Cambridge, Mass.: Harvard University Press, 1942.

Bridges, W. *Transitions*. Reading, Mass.: Addison-Wesley, 1980.

Brown, G. W., and B. Andrews. Social Support and Depression. *Dynamics of Stress: Physiological, Psychological, and Social Perspectives*. M. J. Appley and R. Trumbull, eds. New York: Plenum Press, pp. 257–282, 1986.

Bulman, R. J., and C. B. Wortman. Attributions of Blame and Coping in the "Real World": Severe Accident Victims React to Their Lot. *Journal of Personality and Social Psychology* 35:351–363 (1977).

Burns, D. *Feeling Good*. New York: New American Library, 1981.

Campbell, J. *Myths to Live By*. New York: Viking, 1972.

———. *The Power of Myth*. New York: Doubleday, 1988.

———. *Primitive Mythology: The Masks of God*. New York: Penguin Books, 1969.

———, ed. *The Portable Jung*. New York: Viking, 1971.

Bibliography

Cannon, W. B. *The Wisdom of the Body*, 2nd ed. New York: W. W. Norton, 1932.

Carroll, L. *The Annotated Alice*. New York: New American Library, 1974.

Cohen, F., and R. S. Lazarus. Active Coping Processes, Coping Dispositions, and Recovery from Surgery. *Psychosomatic Medicine* 35:375–389 (1973).

Cohen, S., and J. R. Edwards. Personality Characteristics as Moderators of the Relationship Between Stress and Disorder. *Advances in the Investigation of Psychological Stress*, R. W. J. Neufeld, ed. New York: John Wiley, in press.

Cohen, S., and S. L. Syme, eds. *Social Support and Health*. New York: Academic Press, pp. 3–207. 1985.

Colgrove, M., H. Bloomfield, and P. McWilliams. *How to Survive the Loss of a Love*. New York: Bantam, 1979.

Cousins, N. *Anatomy of an Illness*. New York: W. W. Norton, 1979.

———. *Human Options*. New York: Berkeley Books, 1981.

Cramer, K. D. For Emotional Well-being, Work Hard at Reducing Stress. Interview with Hans Selye, *Parameters*. St. Louis, Mo.: St. Louis University Medical Center, 1979.

———. *Individual Profile of Stressors*. Healthline Press. St. Louis, Mo.: St. Louis University Medical Center, 1980.

———. *Stress: A Management Challenge*. Text and 16mm Educational Film. Belleville, Illinois: Geary Whiteaker Associates, 1983.

———. *Stress: A Personal Challenge*. Text and 16mm Educational Film. New York: St. Louis University Medical Center, ABC Video Enterprises, 1981.

Cramer, K. D., R. E. Numerof, and C. P. Rice. Naturally Occurring Coping Strategies Among Hospital Administrators. Academy of Management, Spring Conference, 1985.

Cramer, K. D., S. Shachar, and J. Ferst. Differentiating Cardiac Patients from Normals on Vulnerability to Stress. *Circulation* Supp. 2: 11–114 (1982).

Bibliography

Dement, W., and N. Kleitman. Cyclic Variations in EEG Readings During Sleep and Their Relation to Eye Movements, Body Motility, and Dreaming. *Electroencephalography and Clinical Neurophysiology* 9:673–690 (1957).

Dimsdale, J. E., ed. *Survivors, Victims and Perpetrators: Essays on the Nazi Holocaust.* Washington, D.C.: Hemisphere, 1980.

Dohrenwend, B. S., and B. P. Dohrenwend, *Stressful Life Events: Their Nature and Effects.* New York: John Wiley, 1974.

Dohrenwend, B. S., B. P. Dohrenwend, M. Dodson, and P. E. Shrout. Symptoms, Hassles, Social Support and Life Events: Problem of Confounded Measures. *Journal of Abnormal Psychology* 93:222–230 (1984).

Dohrenwend, B. S., L. Krasnoff, A. R. Askenasy, and B. P. Dohrenwend. Exemplification of a Method for Scaling Life Events: The PERI Life Events Scale. *Journal of Health and Social Behavior* 19: 205–229 (1978).

Donahue, P. *The Human Animal.* New York: Simon & Schuster, 1985.

Dubos, R., *Mirage of Health.* New York: Doubleday, 1959.

Eliot, R. S. *Stress and the Heart: Mechanisms, Measurements, and Management.* New York: Future Publications, 1988.

Elliot, G. R., and C. Eisdorfer. *Stress and Human Health.* New York: Springer, 1982.

Erikson, E. The Problem of Ego Identity, *Journal of the American Psychiatric Association*, 4:56–121 (1958).

———. Identity and the Life Cycle. *Psychological Issues* 1:1–171 (1959).

Flach, F. F. *Choices: Coping Creatively with Personal Change.* New York: J. J. Lippincott, 1977.

Fox, M. *On Becoming a Musical Mystical Bear.* New York: Paulist Press/ Dens Books, 1972.

Frankl, V. E. *The Doctor and the Soul.* New York: Knopf, 1955.

———. *Man's Search for Meaning.* Boston: Beacon Press, 1962.

Freud, S. *The Interpretation of Dreams.* New York: Macmillan, 1900. (English translation by A. A. Brill, 1913)

Bibliography

———. *Beyond the Pleasure Principle*, standard ed., 1920; London: Hogarth Press, 1946.

Fromm, E. *The Anatomy of Human Destructiveness.* New York: Holt, Rinehart & Winston, 1973.

———. *The Heart of Man: Its Genius for Good and Evil.* New York: Harper & Row, 1964.

Frost, Robert. "The Armful." *Complete Poems of Robert Frost.* New York: Holt, 1949, p. 343.

Garfield, C. A. *Peak Performers: The New Heroes of American Business.* New York: Morrow, 1986.

Ghiselin, B., ed. *The Creative Process.* New York: Mentor Books, 1952.

Goldhor Lerner, H. *The Dance of Anger.* New York: Harper & Row, 1985.

Goleman, D. Denial and Hope. *American Health* 3:54–61 (December 1984).

———. To Dream the Impossible Dream. *American Health* 3:60–61 (December 1984).

Hacket, T. P., and N. H. Cassem. Psychological Management of the Myocardial Infarction Patient. *Journal of Human Stress* 1:25–38 (1975).

Hacket, T. P., N. H. Cassem, and H. A. Wishnie. The Coronary Care Unit: An Appraisal of Its Psychological Hazards. *New England Journal of Medicine* 279:1365–1370 (1968).

Hall, S. S. *A Molecular Code Links Emotions, Mind and Health. Smithsonian Magazine* pp. 62–71 (June 1989).

Hobfoll, S. E. Conservation of Resources: A New Attempt at Conceptualizing Stress. *American Psychologist* 44:515–524 (1989).

——— *The Ecology of Stress.* Washington, D.C.: Hemisphere, 1988.
———. Personal and Social Resources and the Ecology of Stress Resistance. *Review of Personality and Social Psychology*, vol. 6, P. Shaver, ed. Beverly Hills, Calif.: Sage, 1985b, pp. 265–290.

———, ed. *Stress, Social Support, and Women.* Washington, D.C.: Hemisphere, 1986.

Hobfoll, S. E., and Y. Leiberman. Personality and Social Resources in Immediate and Continued Stress Resistance Among Women. *Journal of Personality and Social Psychology* 52:18–26 (1987).

Hobfoll, S. E., and M. Lerman. Personal Relationships, Personal Attitudes, and Stress Resistance: Mothers' Reactions to Their Child's Illness. *American Journal of Community Psychology* 16:565–589 (1988).

Hobfoll, S. E., and P. London. The Relationship of Self-Concept and Social Support to Emotional Distress Among Women During War. *Journal of Social and Clinical Psychology* 12:87–100 (1986).

Hobson, J. A. *Dreaming Brain*. New York: Basic Books, 1988.

Holmes, T. H. and R. H. Rahe. The Social Readjustment Rating Scale. *Journal of Psychosomatic Research* 11:213–218 (1967).

Horney, Karen. *Self-Analysis*. New York: W. W. Norton, 1942.

Horowitz, M. J. Psychological Responses to Serious Life Events. *Human Stress and Cognition: An Information-Processing Approach*, V. Hamilton and D. Warburton, eds. Chichester, England: Interscience, 1957.

Iacocca, L., and W. Novak. *Iacocca: An Autobiography*. New York: Bantam Books, 1984.

James, W. *Principles of Psychology*. 2 vols. New York: Holt, 1890.

———. *William James on Exceptional Mental States: The 1896 Lowell Lecture Series*. New York: Charles Scribner's Sons, 1983.

Janis, I. L. *Psychological Stress*. New York: John Wiley, 1958.

Johnson, J. H., and I. G. Sarason. Life Stress, Depression, and Anxiety: Internal-External Control as a Moderator Variable. *Journal of Psychosomatic Research* 22:205–208 (1978).

John-Steiner, V. *Notebooks of the Mind: Explorations of Thinking*. Albuquerque: University of New Mexico Press, 1985.

Jung, Carl. *Memories, Dreams, Reflections*. New York: Vintage Books, 1965.

Bibliography

———. *Mysterium Coniunctionis*, in *The Collected Works of C. G. Jung*, A. Read, M. Fordham, G. Adler, and W. McGuire, eds. Bollingen Series, Princeton University Press, 1962.

———. *Synchronicity*. Princeton, N.J.: Bollingen Series, Princeton University Press, 1973.

———. *Word and Image*, Aniela Jaffe, ed. Princeton, N.J.: Bollingen Series, Princeton University Press, 1979.

Kanner, A. D., J. C. Coyne, C. Schaefer, and R. S. Lazarus. Comparisons of Two Modes of Stress Measurement: Daily Hassles and Uplifts Versus Major Life Events. *Journal of Behavioral Medicine* 4:1–39 (1981).

Kaplan, H. B., ed. Psychological Distress in Sociological Context: Toward a General Theory of Psychosocial Stress. *Psychosocial Stress: Trends in Theory and Research*. New York: Academic Press, 1983, 195–264.

Keen, S. *The Passionate Life: Stages of Loving*. San Francisco: Harper & Row, 1983.

Klausner, S. Z., ed. *The Quest for Self-Control: Classical Philosophies and Scientific Research*. New York: Free Press, 1965.

Kobasa, S. C. How Much Stress Can You Survive? *American Health* 3:64–77 (September 1984).

———. Stressful Life Events, Personality and Health: An Inquiry Into Hardiness. *Journal of Personality and Social Psychology* 37:1–11 (1979).

Kobasa, S. C., S. R. Maddi, and S. Courington. Personality and Constitution as Mediators in the Stress-Illness Relationship. *Journal of Health and Social Behavior* 22:368–378 (1981).

Kobasa, S. C., S. Maddi, and S. Kahn. Hardiness and Health: A Prospective Study. *Journal of Personality and Social Psychology* 42:168–177 (1982).

Kobasa, S. C., S. R. Maddi, and M. C. Puccetti. Personality and Exercise as Buffers in the Stress-Illness Relationship. *Journal of Behavioral Medicine* 4:391–404 (1982).

Bibliography

Kobasa, S. C., and M. C. Puccetti. Personality and Social Resources in Stress Resistance. *Journal of Personality and Social Psychology* 45:839–850 (1983).

Kraus, P., and M. G. Fisher. *Why Me? Coping with Grief, Loss and Change.* New York: Bantam, 1988.

Kübler-Ross, E. *Living with Death and Dying.* New York: Macmillan, 1981.

———. *On Death and Dying.* New York: Macmillan, 1969.

Kushner, H. S. *When Bad Things Happen to Good People.* New York: Avon, 1983.

Langer, E. J. *Mindfulness.* Reading, Mass.: Addison-Wesley, 1989.

Lazarus, R. S. The Costs and Benefits of Denial. In *The Denial of Stress,* Shlomo Breznitz, ed. New York: International University Press, 1983.

———. Little Hassles Can Be Hazardous to Health. *Psychology Today* 15:58–62 (1981).

———. *Psychological Stress and the Coping Process.* New York: McGraw-Hill, 1966.

———. Puzzles in the Study of Daily Hassles. *Journal of Behavioral Medicine* 7:375–89 (1984).

Lazarus, R. S., and S. Folkman. *Stress, Appraisal and Coping.* New York: Springer, 1984.

Lazarus, R. S., and R. Launer. Stress-Related Transactions Between Person and Environment. *Perspectives in Interactional Psychology,* L. A. Pervine and M. Lewis, eds. New York: Plenum, 1978, pp. 287–327.

Lehman, D. R., C. B. Wortman, and A. F. Williams. Long-term Effects of Losing a Spouse or Child in a Motor Vehicle Crash. *Journal of Personality and Social Psychology* 52:218–231 (1987).

Levinson, D. J., et al. *The Seasons of a Man's Life.* New York: Knopf, 1978.

Lingerman, H. A. *The Healing Energies of Music.* Wheaton, Ill.: The Theosophical Publishing House, 1988.

Bibliography

Locke, S., L. Krasu, J. Leserman, M. Hurst, S. Heisel, and R. Williams. Life Change Stress, Psychiatric Symptoms, and Natural Killer-Cell Activity. *Psychosomatic Medicine* 46:441–453 (1984).

McClelland, D. C. Motivational Factors in Health and Disease. *American Psychologist* 44(4):675–683 (1989).

McClelland, D. C., E. Floor, R. J. Davidson, and C. Saron. Stressed Power Motivation, Sympathetic Activation, Immune Function and Illness. *Journal of Human Stress* 6(2):11–19 (1980).

McClelland, D. C., and J. B. Jemmott, III. Power Motivation, Stress, and Physical Illness. *Journal of Human Stress* 6(4):6–15 (1980).

Maddi, S. R., and S. C. Kobasa. *The Hardy Executive: Health Under Stress.* Homewood, Ill.: Dow Jones–Irwin, 1984.

Mairs, N. Essay on Happiness. *The New York Times*; Hers Column, July 23, 1987.

Maslow, A. H. *Toward a Psychology of Being.* New York: Van Nostrand, 1968.

Matlin, M. W., and D. S. Stang. *The Pollyanna Principle: Selectivity in Language, Memory and Thought.* Cambridge, Mass.: Schenkman Publishing, 1978.

Maurois, A. *Prometheus: The Life of Balzac.* New York: Carroll & Graf, 1965.

May, R. *The Courage to Create.* New York: W. W. Norton, 1975.

Meichenbaum, D., and M. E. Jaremko, eds. *Stress Reduction and Prevention.* New York: Plenum, 1983.

Melnechuk, T. Neuroimmunology: Crossroads Between Behavior and Disease. *Advances* 2:54–58 (Summer 1985).

Milburn, T. W., and K. H. Watman. *On the Nature of Threat: A Social Psychological Analysis.* New York: Praeger, 1981.

Milton, J. "Paradise Lost." In *Norton Anthology of English Literature.* 4th ed. Vol. 1, p. 1418, lines 254–255. New York: Norton, 1979.

Ornstein, R., and Sobel, D. *The Healing Brain: Breakthrough Discoveries About How the Brain Keeps Us Healthy.* New York: Simon & Schuster, 1987.

Bibliography

————. *Healthy Pleasures*. Reading, Mass.: Addison-Wesley, 1989.

Paracelsus. *Paracelsus: Selected Writings*, Jolande Jacobi, ed. Princeton, N.J.: Bollingen Series, Princeton University Press, 1979.

Peavey, B. Biofeedback Assisted Relaxation: Effects on Phagocytic Immune Function. Doctoral dissertation, North Texas State University, Denton, Tex.

Peck, M. S. *People of the Lie*. New York: Simon & Schuster, 1983.

————. *The Road Less Traveled*. New York: Simon & Schuster, 1978.

Pennebaker, J. W. Confiding Traumatic Experiences and Health. In S. Fisher and J. Reason, eds., *Handbook of Life Stress, Cognition and Health*. New York: Wiley, 1988.

Pennebaker, J. W., C. F. Hughes, and R. C. O'Heeron. The Psychophysiology of Confession: Linking Inhibitory and Psychosomatic Processes. *Journal of Personality and Social Psychology* 52:781–793 (1987).

Pennebaker, J. W., J. K. Kiecolt-Glaser, and R. Glaser. Disclosures of Traumas and Immune Functions: Health Implications for Psychotherapy. *Journal of Consulting and Clinical Psychology* 56:239–245 (1988).

Peter, L. and B. Dana. *The Laughter Prescription.* New York: Ballantine Books, 1982.

Piaget, J. *The Construction of Reality in the Child*. New York: Basic Books, 1937.

Progoff, I. *At a Journal Workshop*. New York: Dialogue House, 1975.

Rachman, S. J. *Fear and Courage*. San Francisco: W. H. Freeman, 1978.

Reed, G. *The Psychology of Anomalous Experience: A Cognitive Approach*. London: Hutchison, 1972.

Reich, H. *Behavioral Health: Handbook of Health Enhancement and Disease Prevention*. New York: Wiley, 1984.

Rosenblatt, P. C. *Bitter, Bitter Tears: Nineteenth-Century Diarists and Twentieth-Century Grief Theories*. Minneapolis: University of Minnesota Press, 1983.

Bibliography

Rossi, E. L. *The Psychobiology of Mind-Body Healing*. New York: W. W. Norton, 1986.

Rubin, T. I. *Reconciliations: Inner Peace in an Age of Anxiety*. New York: Viking, 1980.

Sarason, I. G. Experimental Approaches to Test Anxiety: Attention and the Uses of Information. *Anxiety: Current Trends in Theory and Research*, vol. 2. C. D. Spielberger, ed. New York: Academic Press, 1972.

————. Test Anxiety, Attention and the General Problem of Anxiety. *Stress and Anxiety*, vol. 1. C. D. Spielberger and I. G. Sarason, eds. Washington, D.C.: Hemisphere, 1975, pp. 165–187.

Sarason, I. G., J. H. Johnson, and J. M. Siegel. Assessing the Impact of Life Changes: Development of the Life Experiences Survey. *Journal of Consulting and Clinical Psychology* 46:932–946 (1978).

Sarason, I. G., H. M. Levine, R. B. Basham, and B. R. Singer. Assessing Social Support: The Social Support Questionnaire. *Journal of Personality and Social Psychology* 44:127–139 (1983).

Sarason, I. G., and B. R. Sarason. Social Support: Insights from Assessment and Experimentation. In *Social Support: Theory, Research and Applications*, I. G. Sarason and B. R. Sarason, eds. The Hague, Netherlands: Martinus Nijhoff, pp. 39–51, 1985.

Scheier, M. F., and C. S. Carver. Dispositional Optimism and Physical Well-being: The Influence of Generalized Outcome Expectancies on Health. *Journal of Personality* 55:169–210 (1987).

————. Optimism, Coping, and Health: Assessment and Implications of Generalized Outcome Expectancies. *Health Psychology* 4:219–247 (1985).

Schneider, J., and S. Witcher. The Relationship of Mental Imagery to White Blood Cell (Neutrophil) Function in Normal Subjects. Paper presented at the 36th Annual Scientific Meeting of the International Society for Clinical and Experimental Hypnosis, San Antonio, Texas, October 25, 1984.

Selye, H. *Guide to Stress Research*. New York: Van Nostrand Reinhold, 1979.

————. *Stress Without Distress*. New York: New American Library, 1979.

Bibliography

Siegel, B. *Love, Medicine, and Miracles*. New York: Harper & Row, p. xii. 1988.

Simonton, D. *Genius, Creativity and Leadership Historiometric Inquiries*. Cambridge, Mass.: Harvard University Press, 1984.

Spencer, D. The Playful Use of Words in Therapy. In *Ericksonian Psychotherapy*. Vol. 2: *Clinical Applications*, Jeffrey Zeig, ed. New York: Brunner/Mazel, pp. 193–209, 1985.

Stress: Can We Cope? *Time* (June 6, 1983), pp. 48–54.

Tennyson, A. "Ulysses." In *Norton Anthology of English Literature*. 4th ed. Vol. 2, p. 1111, lines 56–70. New York: Norton, 1979.

Thoreau, H. D. *The Journal of Henry David Thoreau*, B. Torrey and F. H. Allen, eds. 14 vols. bound as 2. Boston: Houghton Mifflin, 1906.

Trumbull, R., and M. H. Appley, eds. A Conceptual Model for the Examination of Stress Dynamics. *Dynamics of Stress: Physiological, Psychological, and Social Perspectives*. New York: Plenum Press, 1986.

Tyhurst, J. S. The Role of Transition States—Including Disasters—In Mental Illness. *Symposia on Preventive and Social Psychiatry*, 164. Washington, D.C.: Walter Reed Army Institute of Research, 1957.

Valliant, G. *Adaptation to Life*. Boston: Little, Brown, 1977.

Vinokur, A., and M. L. Selzer. Desirable Versus Undesirable Events: Their Relationship to Stress and Mental Distress. *Journal of Personality and Social Psychology* 32:329–337 (1975).

Volkhard, E., ed. *Social Behavior and Personality: Contributions of W. I. Thomas to Theory and Social Research*. New York: Social Science Research Council, 1951.

Volkman, A. G. *Thoreau on Man and Nature*. Mt. Vernon, N.Y.: Peter Pauper Press, 1960.

Von Oech, R. *A Kick in the Seat of the Pants*. New York: Harper & Row, 1986.

———. *A Whack on the Side of the Head*. New York: Warner Books, 1983.

Watzlawick, P. *How Real Is Real*. New York: Random House, 1976.

Bibliography

Weber, M. *The Protestant Ethic and the Spirit of Capitalism*. New York: Charles Scribner's Sons, 1948.

Welwood, J. *Awakening the Heart*. Boulder, Col.: New Science Library, 1983.

Wicklund, R. A., and P. M. Gollwitzer. *Symbolic Self-Completion*. Hillsdale, N.J.: Erlbaum, 1982.

Wolf, C. T., et al. Relationships Between Psychological Defenses and Mean Urinary 17-Hydroxy Corticosteroid Excretion Rates. *Psychosomatic Medicine* I & II, 26:576–609 (1964).

Wurtman, J. J. *Managing Your Mind and Your Mood Through Food*. New York: Rawson Associates, 1987.